ISLAND HEROES

THE MILITARY HISTORY OF
THE HEBRIDES

The Proceedings of a three day conference held in Shawbost,
Isle of Lewis, 11 – 13 August 2008

THE ISLANDS BOOK TRUST
URRAS LEABHRAICHEAN NAN EILEAN

Published in 2010 by The Islands Book Trust

www.theislandsbooktrust.com

© The Islands Book Trust, 2010

ISBN: 978-0-9560764-2-7

Cover photographs © William McGonagle

Typeset and cover design by Two Ravens Press Ltd, Ullapool, Scotland.
www.tworavenspress.com

Printed on Forest Stewardship
Council-accredited paper
by the MPG books group.

Mixed Sources
Product group from well-managed
forests, controlled sources and
recycled wood or fiber
www.fsc.org Cert no. TT-COC-002303
© 1996 Forest Stewardship Council

FSC

The Islands Book Trust
Ravenspoint Centre
Kershader
South Lochs
Isle of Lewis
HS2 9QA
Tel: 01851 820946

THE ISLANDS BOOK TRUST
URRAS LEABHRAICHEAN NAN EILEAN

CONTENTS

List of illustrations

Courtesy of Petra Arge (21-23):

21. British soldier trying out reconnaissance in the Faroes

22. A lot of the soldiers' time in the Faroes went into training. Here some soldiers from the Lovat Scouts train in camouflage in the village of Syðrugøta

23. In addition to military matters, a big part of the soldiers' job was to make sure that the British forces and the Faroese population were on friendly terms. This is just one of many pictures that gives us a sense of how successful they were in doing the latter part of their job

24. The playing of the pipes always attracted much attention from the Faroese, and the pipebands were greatly missed when the war ended. Here a handful of Lovat Scouts play on the harbour in Tórshavn (Courtesy of Alasdair MacEachen)

INTRODUCTION AND CONCLUSIONS

John Randall

This book brings together contributions to our 3-day conference held in Shawbost, Lewis, in August 2008 about 'Island Heroes – The Hebrides and UK Military History'. It was a most enjoyable and instructive occasion, held in the welcoming atmosphere and comfortable surroundings of The Old School, Shawbost – with a memorable visit to see sites of military importance in the Stornoway area followed by dinner at the Royal British Legion.

There were two overlapping themes to the conference: (i) the disproportionate contribution and sacrifice made by islanders to UK military campaigns over at least the last 250 years; and (ii) the role of the Hebrides during World War Two and the memories of those still alive who were based here at that time.

We were pleased to welcome a range of excellent speakers and others who participated in discussion from the audience. These ranged from academic experts and scholars who have undertaken their own research on aspects of this history to local people and visiting veterans stationed here whose memories of the Second World War are still vivid. It was indeed a great occasion, and a real privilege to hear people share their recollections (in English and Gaelic) of traumatic times and personal heroism. No-one could fail to be moved by hearing John Davenport DFC and Ken Watson, both in their 80s, and stationed in the Outer Hebrides during the Second World War, talk of their departed comrades, the hardship and bravery, tragedies and friendships.

As always, it is impossible, and indeed invidious, to attempt to draw out from the three days of intense discussion and emotion any clear conclusions or authoritative summary. Readers are referred to the many detailed contributions in this volume, all of which will repay careful study and consideration. I have simply listed below some points which occurred to me while listening to the talks and exchanges:

1. It is clearly possible, as Frank Thompson and Colin Scott Mackenzie amongst others bring out, to trace the reputation of Hebridean islanders for martial qualities and skills, both on land

and at sea, for many centuries – much longer than the 250 years which formed the time-frame for the conference. Sometimes the references by outsiders were patronising ('Wild Highlanders') or insulting ('No Great Mischief if they Fall'), but one is aware also of a genuine appreciation, not to say fear, of the abilities of island men in battle.

2. There can be no doubt also that the Outer Hebrides in particular has make a disproportionate contribution and sacrifice to UK military and naval endeavours since Culloden. While this has become well-known in relation to the First World War, for example (see Malcolm Macdonald's contribution, and the names on the Stornoway War Memorial), when twice as many Lewismen died in proportion to the population as in the UK as a whole, it was also true in earlier times. In his talk to the conference, Andrew MacKillop of Aberdeen University emphasised the importance of recruitment to the Army and Navy from the Hebrides from the 1750s onwards. Many landlords were determined to demonstrate their loyalty to the British Government and recruited regiments from among their own tenants and sub-tenants, sometimes with considerable financial as well as political benefit to themselves. Some saw this as a way of protecting the old order from the economic changes sweeping the Highlands, but whatever the motive men from the Hebrides were at the centre of the imperial wars in the latter half of the 18th and throughout the 19th centuries in America, Africa, and Asia which created Britain.

3. Why was the contribution of islanders so great then, in the conflicts of the 20th century, and even today? Some competing, but possibly complementary, theories were advanced:

(a) perhaps there was indeed a natural aptitude for bravery, the ability to withstand hardship, and seamanship which reflects the environment and history of the islands. Roddy Mackinnon's chapter on the huge contribution made to the Merchant Navy by men from the islands, particularly Barra, suggests as much.

(b) the remarkable success of the transition from clan loyalty to regimental loyalty, however achieved, was surely also a factor. Of course, there were wider factors at work as within less than a century of Culloden, the kilt, tartan, and bagpipes became icons of the British Army. Nicholas Maclean-Bristol described how the Macleans of Coll followed their chiefs into the Army – they were not coerced. Yet there is clear evidence from other sources that subtle or overt pressure was applied elsewhere, as both Andrew MacKillop and Donald John Macleod emphasise. Economic threats and the press-gang were powerful recruiting agents in the islands. It is of interest to compare and contrast the patterns of recruitment to the armed forces in different areas – landlords recruited mainly for the Army in Lewis and Harris but not in Uist and Barra, possibly reflecting religious differences and the Presbyterian ethos of the Army.

(c) lack of alternative economic opportunities in the islands for young men no doubt played a part in earlier times, as it has certainly more recently. Even today, the names of island soldiers figure prominently in conflicts such as Iraq and Afghanistan.

(d) and once community and family traditions have become established, sons may follow fathers and grandfathers into the same occupation. Colin Scott Mackenzie's researches on the Ross Mountain Battery in Stornoway, the basis for an informative and thought-provoking after-dinner speech at the Royal British Legion, give an insight into this continuity of island character and also changing social conditions.

4. With this enormous contribution inevitably came sacrifice and loss. The scale of that loss is most evident in the incredible scale of island deaths in the First World War, illustrated by an evocative slide-show and commentary on the grave-yards of Flanders by Murdo Beaton and Bill MacGonagle. Pictures of the Menin Gate in Ypres and military cemeteries such as Le Touret provided a chilling reminder of the slaughter at battles such as Festubert, where 26 young men from the Portree area of Skye died in a single day. And then the literally unspeakable horror of the *Iolaire* disaster, whose 90th anniversary has been marked this year (2008), and whose story and statistics are ably chronicled by Malcolm Macdonald. The losses of the First World War cast a long shadow on the Outer Hebrides, resulting in large-scale emigration in the 1920s and 1930s, and social consequences in terms of morale and gender imbalance from which the islands took decades to recover.

5. The Second World War saw further sacrifices by island families on a disproportionate scale, but also a significant influx of armed forces to the Hebrides from other parts of the UK. The latter reflects the strategic importance of the Outer Hebrides in the battle for the North Atlantic, a fact well brought out by Mike Hughes, who with veteran John Davenport produced an attractive new book 'Stornoway in World War Two', with many rare photographs, to coincide with the conference. The experiences of some of the islanders who still survive from the Second World War were graphically recounted in Gaelic in a discussion session ably chaired by Kenny MacIver.

6. We were truly privileged to hear eye-witness accounts of what it was like to be stationed here in the Second World War from John Davenport and Ken Watson, who were based at Stornoway airfield and Rodel radar station, respectively. Both gave valuable accounts of how the Hebrides were regarded by many of their colleagues from the south – the 'back of beyond', quaint, unspoilt, being some of the typical views. Some hated it; some like Ken found his wife here, for all it was a life-changing experience. Clearly, there was a profound difference of culture and outlook between many of the armed forces stationed here and local people. But above and beyond all this, the genuine heroism and remarkable qualities of John and Ken shone through both their addresses. For John it was his first return to Lewis since the 1940s, and being with him when he came across some of the buildings which he had known on Stornoway airfield all those years ago was an incredible occasion.

7. On the final day of the conference, we heard a most interesting account by Erling Isholm of the Faroe Islands during the Second World War, with its occupation by British Forces (including many islanders from the Lovat Scouts) which was welcomed by local people. This demonstrated yet another link between the history of the Faroes and the Outer Hebrides, comparisons we have explored in earlier conferences and which we plan to build on in our week-long visit to the Faroes in summer 2009.

8. The Islands Book Trust would like to thank all those who

contributed to a most successful conference, particularly all the speakers and others who attended, The Old School in Shawbost for the wonderful venue and catering, the Royal British Legion, and our Trustees and staff most involved, particularly our Gaelic student placement Donald Macleod. I hope this volume will be of interest as a permanent memento of an instructive and enjoyable few days.

NO GREAT MISCHIEF...

Frank Thompson

I am only too aware that the subject of this Conference is concerned with the Hebridean contribution to UK military history. However, I have taken it upon myself to extend the time canvas to include a period of time which goes back at least 1,000 years and runs forward to the Second World War, of which some here present may well have memories of personal experiences; if not that then a knowledge of the impact of these events some sixty years ago on their immediate families. I have also placed my own interpretation on the term 'UK military history', simply because, while the United Kingdom is popularly associated with the dates of 1603 and 1707, the military history of the Hebrides has impacted on the gradual development of the British Isles in general, at times to warrant full pages in the history books or else the insertion of significant footnotes on these same pages.

I also make no apology for the title of this talk, which will be more than familiar to many here present, and which highlights a deeply embedded philosophy of those responsible for the military organisation in the British Isles, even up until recent times, that the fighting qualities of these Hebrideans who went into the service of the Army, Navy, Merchant Navy and the Royal Air Force were something to be depended upon in those times when the defence of the British realm and Empire was under severe attack.

Two statements might be of interest. The first, *'The inhabitants of the Western Scottish Isles or Hebrides are all so much accustomed to a seafaring life, and retain so much of the native heroism of ancient Highlanders, that almost everything great and successful may be hoped from their gallantry during the war'.* That statement was to be echoed in its sentiment during the many wartime periods which Great Britain found itself enduring. It dates, in fact, from 1801 and appears in the Naval Chronicle, written at the time when Britain was at war with the Northern Confederacy which included Russia, Sweden and Norway.

The other statement might be more familiar to you. It was expressed by General Wolfe, who advocated the employment of Highlanders in British military service,

*'I should imagine that Highlanders might be of use. They
are hardy, intrepid, accustomed to a rough country, and
no great mischief if they fall. How can you better employ
a secret enemy than by making his end conducive to the
common good? If this sentiment should take wind, what
an execrable and bloody being should I be considered!'*

The Western Isles were used by the Norsemen as a staging
post for their raiding incursions all along the western seaboard
of Scotland and into Ireland, and it is likely, though of course
speculation, that over time some of the native Hebrideans would
have been absorbed into the Norse way of life, not just for the
provision of labour for the farming settlements, by then fairly well
established, but as recruits to follow the military ambitions, if not
lifestyle, of their Scandinavian masters. It is quite conceivable
that there were, for instance, Lewismen embodied in the warring
parties of the Vikings. This is highlighted in a mention in the Irish
Annals of the part Lewismen played in the Battle of Clontarf in
1014. The combined force of Lewismen and Norsemen, led by
the Jarl Sigurd, who ruled over the northern part of the Western
Isles, met the Irish King Brian Boroimhe in a bloody conflict in
which both Sigurd and Brian Boroimhe were killed. The Irish
annalists described the invading force as an assembly *'of ignorant,
barbarous, thoughtless, irreclaimable, unsociable foreigners!'* In
that description we must allow for the biased inclination of the
annalists towards the invaders. Clontarf has been described as
the Irish Bannockburn, a battle in which the immediate effect in
Lewis was the weakening of the grip which Orkney had upon
the island, to be restored, to some degree, by the appointment
of Sigurd's son, Jarl Thorfinn, as the ruler over Lewis. Later, the
northern part of the Western Isles became part of the Kingdom
of Man (the Isle of Man), eventually to be known as the Sudereys.
It might be of interest to mention here that The Western Isles can
even today, lay claim to four seats in the Tynwald, the present day
Manx Parliament. But let that stick to the wall.

In my mention of the Battle of Clontarf, I am indicating that
as far back as 1014, the warring qualities of men from Lewis, if
not the Hebrides, had an impact on part of the British Isles, yet
to become Great Britain.

It is, of course, a matter for speculation how they came to have these qualities; whether they were derived either from their Norse overlords, from seeking to strengthen their military resources or from being pressed into service as and when required.

These very same fighting qualities were maintained through the period of upheaval which followed the defeat of King Haakon of Norway at the Battle of Largs in 1263; that was followed by the Treaty of Perth in 1266, when the Hebrides, notionally at least, came under the control of the Scottish Crown. By that time the warriors of Lewis and the other Hebridean islands had a reputation which was little short of atrocious. The records of the Northern Isles contain many references to 'raiding Lewismen', almost continuing the fierce and bloody characteristics of the Norsemen who had instilled in them the fighting instincts which appealed to the various clan chiefs as they endeavoured to lay claim to lands throughout the Western Highlands.

The Records of Shetland contain references that for some years in the early part of the 16th century, 'the Lewismen' had been in the habit of raiding Shetland every summer. In June 1530, the men of Dunrossness in Shetland were waiting for them and in a great battle the Lewismen were completely routed. At the battlefield, near the Loch of Spiggie, a large mound is still pointed out as being, '*Where the Lewismen are buried*'.

Apart from raiding excursions, it is more than likely that Islesmen from the Hebrides put themselves forward as freelance mercenaries, allying themselves to various branches of the Lords of the Isles in the attempts of the latter to gain new territories or to gain back lands they had lost. It should be remembered that the Lords made alliances with the English Kingdom. A secret Treaty with the English dated 1462 was made public in 1475 and for the 'treason' thus disclosed, the King of Scots confiscated the Earldom of Ross, a territory which the Lords of the Isles had always thought to be in their possession. Thus MacDonalds, MacIntoshes and MacKenzies became involved in a vicious scene of internecine warfare.

It was in this period that the Hebridean Galloglaich, or Gallowglasses, became known as professional and armoured mercenaries, highly prized by both English and the Irish. They were picked men, and had, in addition, more lightly armed helpers as part of their support troops. These men were more often to be found in Ireland, where the pickings were richer than those to be found on the west coast of Scotland. It can be said, with reasonable certainty, that Lewis provided its fair share of these adventurers.

Of the 4,000 Hebrideans who congregated with 180 galleys in Knockfergus in 1545, some 3,000 of them were described by the Irish Privy Council in a letter to the English King Henry, as being *very tall men clothed in the most part in habergeons of mail, armed with long swords and long bows but with few guns; the other thousand being tall mariners who rowed the galleys'*.

These warriors, many of whom became domiciled in Ireland, were described in the following, *'they are very valiant and hardy ...... great endurers of the cold, labour, hunger and all hardness, very active, and strong of their hand, very swift of foot, very vigilant and very circumspect in their enterprises, very present in perils, very great scorners of death. Yes, truly, even in that rude kind of service he beareth himself very courageously, but when he cometh to a piece or pike, he maketh as worthy a soldier as any nation he meeteth with'*.

Moving on a hundred years or so, we come to 1645, some forty years after James VI of Scotland became James I of Great Britain, and entering the period in which we can truly consider the encompass of the title of this Conference: I refer to British or UK history. This was the time of Civil War in Britain and I do not intend to go into the situation in which Covenanters were ranged against Royalists. At that time, George, 2nd Earl of Seaforth was bringing his mind into some kind of focus as to which side he was to support. No doubt intelligence arrived at Seaforth Lodge that the great Marquis of Montrose was achieving victories in Scotland for the Royalist side. This however, did not influence him and he raised and sent a Regiment from Lewis to fight on behalf of the Covenanters. These Lewismen, in 1645, found themselves in the village of Auldearn, near Nairn in Morayshire.

The Covenanting side was thoroughly defeated and the Lewis contingent virtually cut to pieces, with only three men escaping alive. Included amongst the dead was Donald Bayne, the Chamberlain of the Lews and Angus MacAulay, from Brenish in Uig, of the family of the Lewis hero Domhnall Cam. As for the Earl of

Seaforth, he promptly changed sides and declared for the Royalists. That decision might have been premature because only a few months after Auldearn, the Royalist forces, still under Montrose, were defeated at the Battle of Philiphaugh in the Scottish Borders. Seaforth was saved from ignominy because his Lewismen refused to fight for the Royalist side.

We leave Lewis for a moment to go south to the Island of Bernera and meet up with Sir Norman MacLeod, who, along with MacLeod of Dunvegan, declared himself for King Charles II, crowned as King in the old Gaelic capital of Scotland, Scone. Many of the Highland chiefs came out with men in support of Charles, including MacLeod of Berneray, promoted to Lieutenant General. Between the Berneray men and the 700 men raised by MacLeod of Talisker, in Skye, there was a total of 1,000 MacLeods ready to do battle with Cromwell's New Model Army. A description of the Hebrideans runs thus,

'The soldiers make a very uncouth figure, especially the Highlanders; the oddness and barbarity of their garb and arms seemed to have something remarkable in them. They were tall swinging fellows; their swords are extravagantly long and they carry wooden targets. They are in companies all of a name and they scorn to be commanded but by one of their own clan or family. The meanest fellow among them is as tenacious of his honour as the best nobleman in the country and they will fight and cut one another's throats for every trifling affront; but to their own chiefs or lairds are the willingest and most obedient fellows in nature. To give them their due, were their skill and exercises and discipline proportionate to their courage, they would make the best soldiers in the world. They have large bodies and prodigious strength and two qualities above all other nations, viz, hardy to endure fatigue, hunger, cold and hardships and wonderfully swift of foot. The latter is such an advantage on the field that I know none like it, for if they conquer no enemy can escape and if they run even the horse can hardly escape them!'

The King's army, numbering about 14,000, marched its way

south, through Carlisle, Penrith and Kendal and down to the city of Worcester, which they reached on 3 September 1651. Cromwell had a force of 30,000 disciplined troops and thus the Highlanders were seriously outnumbered, but, it is reported, they fought like lions. Norman MacLeod of Berneray was knighted on the field. But the victory was Cromwell's in the end. The MacLeods are said to have lost 1,000 men, and that same loss was said to have granted them excuse from further military service.

MacLeod of Berneray was in fact captured and imprisoned in the Tower of London. He was charged with treason as a Welshman on account of the affinity of his name to the Welsh App Lloyd. He had the charge dropped when his true identity became known. He managed to escape from the Tower in the spring of 1653 and return to Berneray. His memorial slab is in the Church at Rodel in Harris.

Turning over a few more pages in British history, but without going into the historical details which involved the occupants of the British throne, and its claimants, I move to the Jacobite era and the 1715 Rising. That event was well supported by the island of Lewis. The Earl of Seaforth had in fact got himself involved with an ill-fated French expedition with Jacobite connections in 1708, in support of rival Stuart claims to the British throne.

In 1715 there were four captains, four lieutenants and four ensigns named in the Seaforth provision of a force of some 2,500 men from his own estates, including Lewis. The most important battle of 1715 was at Sheriffmuir in the Scottish lowlands. Much blood was shed and lives lost to little purpose. The Earl of Seaforth went back to Lewis, taking survivors with him, but then left for France. But the Jacobite question itself did not go away. In 1719 Earl Seaforth returned to Lewis to become closely involved with plans for yet another Jacobite Rising, the details for which were hatched out in the Earl's island home, Seaforth Lodge, near Stornoway.

Two prominent Scots were involved: George Keith, the Earl Marischal and his brother James Keith, both of whom were to become famous in European military and political spheres. But the proposed Rising was an ill-fated adventure, despite the fact that the Swedish King Charles XII had promised some 10,000 troops. Charles died before this contribution to the Rising came to fruition, and the 1719 plotters, hoping for an invasion of Britain, received a serious setback. Even so, the 1719 companions left Lewis, woefully under strength, with about 100 Lewismen and another 400 from the Lochcarron area. There was also a detachment of Spanish troops. The brave party travelled to Glenshiel to meet up with the Government forces in June 1719. In what was little more than a skirmish, Earl Seaforth was wounded. He fled to France and his estates were forfeit. As for the Keith brothers, George became Prussian Ambassador of the Courts of Paris and Madrid, while James rose to distinction as a Field Marshal of Prussia and one of the most renowned generals of the 18th century, with statues erected to his honour adorning places as far apart as Berlin and Peterhead. As for the Jacobite cause, it was kept simmering until it eventually came back to the boil in 1745.

The details of the 'Forty-five' are too well known even to be outlined to an audience here. Suffice to say that it marked a social and economic watershed in the Highlands in general which, some might argue, still haunts us today. What is important, and relevant to the subject of this Conference, is an awareness of the various powers that existed in the 18th century and of the existence of the Highlanders as an almost unique military asset.

As far as Lewismen were concerned, at the outbreak of the Seven Years War, 1756-63, 140 men from the island were on active service in America with the 77th Regiment of Montgomerie's Highlanders, which was one of the newly raised Highland Regiments. Only 34 of these men returned home, with 18 of them classed as Chelsea Pensioners. The annual income from this recognition might seem to be of real benefit to them and their families. The only problem was that they had to go personally to Inverness to collect their pension. As it can be imagined, this was extremely difficult for them as they had to pay their own way to get to Inverness and then return to their homes. I have in my possession a letter written to London by a Uist Minister on behalf of Chelsea Pensioners in that island to plead for their money to be sent to a collecting point much nearer home. Whether the Minister's solicitations were accepted I do not know. The point here is that Chelsea Pensioners could be found in the Hebrides in the early years of the 19th century.

We now come to the year 1778. In that year, Kenneth MacKenzie, in gratitude for his elevation to the Peerage of Ireland, raised the 78th Regiment of Highlanders, which was 1,130 strong and included 200 men from Lewis. This force was destined for duty in India. On the way, the Earl died and by the time the soldiers reached Madras, some 250 men had perished from scurvy. The Regiment was then taken over by the cousin of the Earl of Seaforth, Frederick MacKenzie Humberstone, who at the time had a commission in the 100th Regiment of Foot. This Regiment, along with the 78th Seaforth Highlanders, saw service against the Dutch East India Company at the Cape of Good Hope, in which 24 Lewismen served with conspicuous merit. The two Regiments were then combined to become the 72nd Seaforths and, a century later, the 1st Battalion the Seaforth Highlanders.

The Regiment saw active service in India, Ceylon, Mauritius, Afghanistan, the West Indies and in the Crimea. It was named 'The Saviour of India', for its heroism during the Indian Mutiny.

In 1793 the new Earl of Seaforth, known as Mac Coinneach Bodhar, the Deaf MacKenzie, was given a Letter of Service to raise 1,000 men. His efforts to recruit were met with some opposition, and the potential soldiers had to be persuaded by rhetoric to take up a military life. Seaforth also had recourse to press-gang techniques to achieve his requirement of 1,000 men, who were paraded at Fort George. The battalion, known as the 78th Seaforth Highlanders, were also known in Lewis as Saighdearan Mhic Coinnich Bhodhair, Deaf MacKenzie's soldiers.

There were further efforts at recruitment for the armed forces, but it was a source of concern that what was termed 'over-cropping' was to the detriment of the economic and social fabric of the island. In the 1795 Statistical Account, the Parish Minister of Stornoway was occasioned to write, *'By reason of the multitudes levied for the Army and Navy, the great number of sub-tenants, and the many hands wanted for the fishing boats, labourers and farm-servants are become very scarce and difficult to be found'.* Bear in mind, also, that this period saw large emigration from the islands, which had the effect of reducing the recruitment potential of the Hebrides.

In 1797, problems arose in respect of the amount of men raised for the British Army. One quote, in response to a request from the British Home Secretary for further recruiting in the Highlands and

Islands was, 'Your Grace must be very sensible that this country has been much drained by different levies, so much so that if the number now proposed are taken out of it there would be great danger of a total stop of the operations of husbandry'. Yet another quote, 'It appears from the great drain the country has sustained it will be almost impossible to raise the body of men proposed'.

The Seaforth and Cromarty estates on the Ross-shire mainland and in the Isle of Lewis were estimated to have contributed over 11,000 men in forty years; this was in addition to men enlisting in two Ross-shire Fencible Corps and in other Regiments. Skye, according to the Historical Record of the 42nd Regiment, had supplied the Army with nearly 700 officers and 10,000 men over thirty years.

In this same period, one might mention Colonel Colin MacKenzie, born in Stornoway, who went into service with the East India Company. He was not only an engineer but took part in many military operations. In time, he was promoted to the post of India's first Surveyor-General. He died in 1821, before he was able to get back to the town of his birth.

During the Napoleonic Wars the loss of manpower to Lewis was immense, especially during the years 1795-1796. According to research, in less than two years some 500 men were claimed by the Army and 80 by the Navy, in addition to those press-ganged.

It was about this time that the term 'Militia' appeared, or rather re-appeared, as it had come into use in 1663 for levies raised by local Commissioners under the supervision of the Privy Council in London. They recruited men able to serve; that is all able-bodied free men aged between 16 and 60 years. This, as can be imagined, was not popular and some of those balloted to serve were able to pay others to act as their substitutes. Deserters from the ballot fled to Harris for refuge. Even so, the Militia provided a good recruiting ground for the regular Highland battalions, with 400 men being drafted in the year 1800 alone. Many islanders were to see service with the Seaforths in the Crimea and were involved in the suppression of the Indian Mutiny. The Seaforths in fact earned national acclaim for their conduct at the Relief of Lucknow.

There were also existing in the quasi-military firmament, the units called 'Volunteers', a kind of force intended for Home Defence. In Lewis there were, seemingly, two such companies of

Volunteers, one with 160 men. Another Volunteer Company in Harris had 346 men. Most of these units had eventually disappeared by 1808, though in the middle years of the 19th century similar units tended to crop up.

It was not until 1859 that the Royal Navy decided to follow the example of the Army to have a reserve of men who could be called up in a National Emergency. This resulted in the passing of the Royal Navy Reserve (Volunteer) Act. Before this date, fishermen, regarded by law as sea-faring men, were always under the threat of being impressed for the Navy. But in 1807, the British Admiralty decided to exempt those who worked off the west coast of Scotland on condition that one man out of every six enlisted for the service.

Many seamen, attracted because of the financial retainer involved, went into the RNR whose training only involved short periods away from home and this did not interfere too much with their means of livelihood. In 1874 the Navy established its own local RNR HQ in Stornoway on the site already being used by the Stornoway Volunteers, known locally as The Battery. Each year between 4,000 and 5,000 reservists would gather at Battery Point for training. In its day it was the largest RNR Station in the United Kingdom. For a few weeks in November, December and January, between 250 and 650 men came to drill at Stornoway, including some from Wester Ross, across the Minch.

In 1900, the Navy decided that the training at the Battery was too restricted, if not divorced, from the prevailing conditions in the Royal Naval Service and, due to a lack of ready response to the requirement that they go elsewhere to a British Naval port for up-to-date training, HMS 'Camperdown' was sent to Lewis, on which ship many Reservists completed a month's training in the new naval techniques. The Base was eventually closed and Reservists had to go for training to Chatham and Portsmouth. In fact, many of the lads, after their training period, proceeded to London where they began a career in the Merchant Navy, thus establishing the link between the Hebrides and the Seven Seas which was to be so important, particularly in the years of the Second World War.

On the 4th August, 1914, buff-coloured envelopes were delivered to the homes of the Militia and Reservists, the latter including fishermen working off Scotland's east coast who reported directly for duty without taking the time to return home.

Islesmen from all over the world volunteered, coming from the USA, Canada, Australia and New Zealand, South Africa, Alaska and Punta Arenas. One man in Africa, Stornoway born, was known as The Elephant Hunter: his name was James Sutherland. His father was a fishcurer in the town. James went to South Africa and was engaged in various occupations until he became famous as an elephant hunter in Portuguese East Africa. At the outbreak of World War I, he happened to be in German East Africa and escaped being captured by the Germans. He made it to Nyasaland where he was engaged as an Intelligence Officer for the British because of his extensive knowledge of Central and Eastern Africa.

When it was decided to attack German East Africa, Sutherland was further promoted to Chief Intelligence Officer and Provost Marshall with the rank of Lieutenant, later Captain. He was mentioned in Despatches several times and was awarded the Croix de Guerre. He died in 1925 and his death made headlines in British, American and African newspapers.

We now come to the fateful years of the First World War, which I still have a habit of calling the Kaiser War, which perhaps somewhat betrays my age. I will not dwell too much here on the contribution which Lewis made to the demands of 1914 to 1918. Suffice to bring to your attention a book with the appropriate title 'Loyal Lewis Roll of Honour'. It is worth reading if only to bring home the contribution and, indeed, sacrifice made by Lewis men from all parts of the island. As for the contributions made by men from the other parts of the Hebrides, you need only look at the names inscribed on the tablets fixed to the war memorials in their respective localities. The number of names on the Lewis War Memorial is 1151.

The burden of the call for more men in the First World War, tended to fall on the sparsely-populated areas of the Highlands. The County of Ross-shire, for instance, had a total population of about 65,000, including women and children. It seems incredible that, in addition to the men already in the Regular Forces, to which Lewis in particular, made a large contribution, the Royal Naval Reserve should number, from the island of Lewis, its men in thousands rather than hundreds. And that Lewis, in particular, should, in addition, raise practically the whole of the 3rd Special Reserve Battalion of the Seaforth Highlanders, and also contribute some hundreds to the 3rd Gordons and the 3rd Camerons.

Lewis lost 1,151 men out of 6,712 serving (a little more than 17 per cent). It must be remembered that practically every fit man was early in the forces, or 6,712 out of a total population of 29,603 men, women and children. If the ratio of the killed to the total population is considered, the island paid twice as much as the rest of the United Kingdom in sacrifice. The ex-Servicemen came home after the War expecting the Government to stick to its promise that they would be coming home to a land 'fit for heroes'. But the promised homes were not to be in their native islands, but over seas. To swell the loss of 1,151 dead, some 3,000 Lewismen, mostly young ex-servicemen, left the island for Canada in the three years following the termination of hostilities.

Commenting on the exodus of young men from the Western Isles, and the statement in a contemporary Journal that they presented a splendid appearance, the standard of physique being exceptionally high and *'that they are sure to be an acquisition to the land of their adoption'*, a Scottish Regimental magazine (that of the Seaforth Highlanders) said,

> *'...what is Canada's gain is unfortunately our loss ... Millions upon millions are sunk for the development of the Empire in all parts of the earth, but here at home we look in vain for even a small share of those monies which, if properly spent, would transform the Highlands and Islands and provide suitable occupations for the population'.*

You may be surprised to know that Stornoway itself has four War Memorials. The main structure is that overlooking the town, situated so that all the Parishes of Lewis can be seen, on a reasonable day. One is located in front of the Drill Hall on Church Street, erected to commemorate the contribution of the Ross Mountain Battery at Gallipoli. The other is in the building of Museum nan Eilean on Francis Street to remember the senior pupils of the Nicolson Institute who made the supreme sacrifice in the Kaiser War. Another school plaque commemorates pupils who lost their lives in the 2nd World War.

There are many stories of heroism from the Kaiser War. One of these concerns Major Angus MacMillan, of Lemreway. He enlisted in the 2nd Battalion Seaforth Highlanders in 1904. By 1911 he had reached the rank of Sergeant, when he purchased his discharge to enter into the Army Reserve. He rejoined the regular service on the outbreak of war in 1914 to take up the post of Quarter Master Sergeant with the 7th Battalion of the Seaforths and took part in the Battle of Loos a year later. He was commissioned on the field as Acting Captain. He was awarded the Military Cross 'for conspicuous Gallantry in action'. In 1917 he was mentioned in Despatches for services at the Battle of Arras. In the summer of 1918 he distinguished himself at Buzancy where he was awarded the Distinguished Service Order, the Legion of Honour and the Croix de Guerre. The French declared him the 'Hero of Buzancy'. After the war he went back to the substantive rank of Lieutenant to serve out his time at Fort George.

Because the sinking of the *Iolaire* is being highlighted at this Conference by another contributor, I will only mention that the loss of so many in that disaster created a situation in Lewis which left the island starved of men who would have made a significant social and economic contribution to the future welfare of the island. Many others took passage in the ships of the Canadian Pacific Railway, the *Metagama*, the *Canada* and the *Marloch*, in 1923 and 1924. That is a story in itself.

Within two decades of the ending of the Kaiser War, Britain was once again placed on the defensive, this time not to protect the shores and lands of the Empire, but to face the threats from Nazi Germany. It has been estimated that some 4,000 men from Lewis saw active service, this time accompanied by island women who rendered great service in many spheres for the war effort, including the WRNS, ATS, WAAF, NAAFI, the Land Army and in munitions factories. More than 500 men were in the Merchant Navy. Inevitably, more names were to be added to the tablets of the war memorials throughout the Western Isles.

I am only too well aware that I have stretched the time frame of this Conference back to those times when the British Isles were a geographical reality but not a unit in political terms. I have done this to increase the awareness of the fighting qualities of the men from the Hebrides, which were to be plundered so much

13

by the so-called powers that be in the years from the mid-18th century. From General Wolfe's observations about the Highlander there was always an underlying recognition that in the north of Scotland there was a human resource which could be rendered of significant service in the creation of the future British Empire. The contribution of the Highlander and Islander to the spread of those red coloured parts of the map of the World, so familiar to me in my schooldays in the Nicolson Institute, was something that was never made known to us. Then in the classroom, history was 1066 and all that. Only much later did my generation come to realise that the creation of the British Empire was due in no small part to the efforts and sacrifices of men from these islands and others from within the Gaidhealtachd.

I am also aware that this talk has a higher Lewis content than I would have liked. But that is because it was extremely difficult to get relevant and specific details of the contribution from men from the Southern Isles to U.K. military history. I also express the hope that some speakers at this Conference will do justice to those who were involved, in particular, in the Second World War, who served in Services other than in the Army. I refer to the Services such as the Navy, the RAF and the Merchant Navy, which, after all these years has only recently been recognised nationally for its contribution in the dark days of the Hitler War.

I finish with a thought, one which might be echoed in the contributions to this Conference by others over the next day or two. Inevitably, in the course of much reading for my subject, I have been conscious that I was dealing with facts and figures, descriptions of conflicts, mass destruction and stories of individual heroisms. All these came from the cold print in books. Only gradually came the realisation that there was a sub-text, written in the pain and anguish which each participant in any theatre of war must have undergone. That is something of which we should never lose sight. I leave you with a poem by Wilfred Owen, from his 'Anthem for Doomed Youth',

> What passing bells for those who die as cattle?
> Only the monstrous anger of the guns,
> Only the stuttering rifles' rapid rattle
> Can patter out their hasty orisons.

No mockeries now for them; no prayers nor bells,
Nor any voice of mourning save the choirs,
The shrill, demented choirs of wailing shells;
And bugles calling for them from sad shires.

Select Bibliography

The Last Warrior Band, C. S. MacKenzie, Stornoway
Scotland's War Losses, Duncan Duff, Glasgow, 1947
Lewis – An Island History, Donald MacDonald, Edinburgh, 1978
A MacDonald for the Prince, Alasdair MacLean, Stornoway, 1982
The Flowers of the Forest, Trevor Royle, Edinburgh, 2006
Celtic Warfare, J. M. Hill, Edinburgh, 1986
The Book of the Lews, W. C. MacKenzie, Glasgow, 1919
Loyal Lewis Roll of Honour, Stornoway, 1919
The Kingdom of the Isles, R. A. MacDonald, Edinburgh, 1997
Lewis and Harris Seamen, J. & A. Morrison, Stornoway, N.D.
Highland Regiments, Iain C. Taylor, Inverness, 1971
Short History of the Highlands, W. C. MacKenzie, Glasgow
The Seaforth Highlanders, F. W. Walker, London, N.D.
Scots of the Line, John MacLennan, Edinburgh, N.D.
An Cogadh Mor, Stornoway, 1982
Stornoway and District Roll of Honour (1939–45), Malcolm MacDonald, Stornoway, 2004
Surprise Island, James Shaw Grant, Edinburgh, 1983

THE OUTER HEBRIDES DURING THE WARS OF EMPIRE AND REVOLUTION, 1750–1815

Andrew MacKillop

On 21 July 1781, a British naval force with troop transports heading for India captured five large Dutch East India Company ships in the harbour of Saldanha Bay, along the North coast from the Cape of Good Hope. The battle was not just a much-needed victory for Britain at a time when the country's six year war against her North American colonists was slowly but surely being lost, it was also an extremely lucrative event for the army and naval personnel involved. Once the Dutch ships and their expensive cargoes had been sold, the Navy's share of the prize money came to £68,000 – a vast sum for the time.[1] Given that the Royal Navy at Saldanha Bay was led by Commodore George Johnstone, who hailed from Westerhall near Dumfries, and the British Army regiments commanded by General William Medows from Surrey, it could well be asked what this now largely forgotten incident has to do with the military history of the Outer Hebrides?

Also present at the battle was the 100th Lincolnshire regiment, commanded by Lieutenant-colonel commandant Thomas Frederick Humberston-MacKenzie, a close kinsman of the recently deceased Kenneth MacKenzie of Seaforth. As the new head of the Seaforth family, Humberston-MacKenzie had used his formidable economic, social and cultural influence to recruit a 100 strong company of men from across his vast Ross-shire estates. These lands encompassed Fortrose, Brahan and Urray, Glensheal, Kintail and Lochalsh and, of course, Lewis.[2] Estate records show that at least one ensign (the equivalent of a junior lieutenant), George MacKenzie from Stornoway and 23 other men in the 100th regiment hailed from the island. They included the sons of cottars from Crowlista in Uig and Upper Holm in Point, to four men from the farm of Habost in Lochs. As one of the expedition's senior army officers, Seaforth's share of the Saldanha prize money amounted to £1,500 – equivalent to the total combined rents of the parishes of Uig and Lochs. Each of the 23 Lewis soldiers present also got a small share of the spoils.[3]

Although occurring many thousands of miles away in the southern hemisphere, this incident reveals a number of important, if neglected, aspects of Hebridean military history. It directly challenges some basic assumptions about the geographic and chronological scope of the region's history, the processes by which Hebrideans became involved in Britain's armed forces, and the profound social and economic consequences arising from military service. For good and understandable reasons the written and oral histories of the Western Isles associate service in Britain's armed forces with the two great conflicts of the twentieth century. The carnage of the Great War, the dreadful loss of the *Iolaire*, and the heavy sacrifices of the Second World War dominate perceptions of the islands' disproportionate contribution to Britain's military forces. There is also the hugely important fact that these wars are still close to us in historical time; until relatively recently there were men and women throughout the Outer Hebrides who lived through the Great War. The Second World War is in this sense still a living conflict; there are individuals in the Western Isles whose direct experiences and memories give it a much greater immediacy and hold on the community's understanding of which wars are important and why.

The wars undertaken by Britain in the eighteenth and early nineteenth centuries seem, by comparison, to be dim and distant affairs, fought for reasons that are obscure at best and aggressively imperialist at worst. These battles for empire lack the attractive, humanitarian principles that underpinned the nation's effort against Nazi Germany, and they were fought by a pre-democratic British society that bears little political, economic or social resemblance to our own. It is hardly surprising that events such as the Spanish War of Succession (1702-1713); Austrian War of Succession (1739-48); Seven Years War (1756-63); the American War of Independence (1775-1783); the French Revolutionary War (1793-1801) and the Napoleonic War (1803-1814) are now largely forgotten and unknown in the Western Isles. But these conflicts are hugely important in their own right and their substantial legacies need to be incorporated into any assessment of Hebridean history. This chapter explores how the Western Isles participated in these wars and assesses what such involvement tells us about the place of the islands in the age of Britain's emergence as a global imperial power.

For all of the eighteenth century Britain was locked in a process of attrition against the great powers of France and Spain, as each sought to dominate the emerging world economy created by the acquisition of colonies in the Americas, Africa, Asia and the Antipodes. The wars for empire were complicated by the development of other ideological factors. In the last third of the eighteenth century there arose new political and social ideas that resulted in revolution in North America and on the European Continent.[4] The competing forces of imperial expansion and revolution sparked a new phase of warfare that would not be matched in scale and intensity until 1914. The wars of empire and revolution were truly global in scope, fought out across Europe, Russia, Arctic North America, the coast of South America, South Africa, India, the Philippines and the China Seas.[5] The significance of these conflicts cannot be exaggerated; they not only necessitated a massive build up in Britain's military and naval capacity, but also helped to shape the country itself by providing a common enemy around which Scotland, England and Wales could genuinely unite. International hostilities were central to the emergence of Britain and a British national identity in this period. [6]

The empire acquired during these wars had an immense economic and social impact, offering social elites as well as ordinary populations from all parts of Britain and Ireland – including the Hebrides – the opportunity for financial gain and upward social mobility. While the Western Isles tend to be pigeonholed as part of the political, economic, social and cultural margins of Britain, the extent of their participation in these wars suggests that the opposite was in fact the case: through disproportionate involvement in military service the Hebrides and its people lay at the centre of processes which were reshaping eighteenth-century Britain and its empire. Examining these old wars resituates the Hebrides in surprising ways by showing how individuals and communities from the islands often engaged confidently with the wider world rather than meekly accepting their fate as passive victims of processes beyond their control.

It is worth noting that this high profile in the British military was far from inevitable. Prior to the 1750's the islands were not especially militarised. The mass deployment of Hebridean redshanks in seasonal military emigration to Ireland began to die out during the early decades of the seventeenth century. The MacDonalds and MacLeods committed large numbers of men to the Scottish and English civil wars of the 1640's and 1650's and suffered accordingly. It has been estimated that of the 1,000 men raised in Glenelg, western Skye and Harris who fought at the Battle of Worcester in 1651, approximately 600 never returned. The later decades of the seventeenth century were characterised in the Hebrides – and indeed the whole of the Western Highlands – by the slow decay of militarised clanship.[7]

For all the prominence of the Jacobites in popular history, island manpower did not play a large part in the risings on mainland Scotland in 1715, 1719 or 1745-6, partly because of severe political divisions among the MacKenzies, MacDonalds and MacLeods as well the RN's ability to prevent the movement of men across the Minch. After the failure of the '15, the largest and most threatening of the Jacobite risings, the government's official disarming policy in the north of Scotland concentrated on the MacKenzies. In a confidential government memorandum of January 1726, the means by which the clan could be demilitarised was discussed, and included preserving MacKenzie honour by allowing them to surrender their arms to regular British regiments rather than army units manned by traditional regional opponents like the Munros and Frasers.[8] Several hundred Lewis, Harris and North Uistmen did serve in independent companies in 1745-6, although these 100-strong units were more akin to a local police force than a field army. The third independent company given by the crown to the MacKenzies was raised in Lewis, and in March 1746 it joined the bulk of the government's northern forces, then garrisoned in Skye.[9] But the reality is that Hebridean manpower did not play a significant role in the '45, a fact which ensured that the outer islands escaped the worse excesses of the British army in the aftermath of Culloden.

It was during the 1750s that a new military economy emerged in the region as more and more isles men enlisted in the British Army. The Seven Years War of 1756-63 marked a major turning point in the islands' relationship with the British military. Most of the landed families in the area were desperate to wipe away any residual taint of Jacobitism, and so made conspicuous efforts to supply men to the army. The conflict consolidated the place of Highland regiments as a distinctive aspect of Britain's armed forces. Other than the Black Watch, which had been formed in 1739, the relatively short period from 1757 to 1799 witnessed all the British Army's well known Highland regiments – the Argylls, Sutherlands, Seaforths, Gordons and Camerons – come into existence. Many more units existed temporarily before being disbanded during the mass demobilisations of 1763, 1783, 1801 and 1815.[10]

These regiments were recruited in a distinctive way and are best understood as public-private partnerships between landlords and the state. Prominent landed families like the Seaforths, the MacDonalds of Sleat, who held North Uist, or the MacLeods of Dunvegan and Harris were contracted by the crown to raise manpower; these landlords in turn subcontracted the job of gathering men to their kinsmen and other neighbouring gentry. In return, the state awarded army commissions, rank and status to those involved. Technically all recruits were volunteers, but landlords had a number of influential levers they could deploy to coerce their tenants and dependents into the army. There was the lure of land and secure leases at a time when landlords had begun to abandon clannish paternalism for a more commercialised attitude towards their estates and their tenants. Military service was one way in which communities could attempt to prevent the onset of the sort of social and economic processes that ultimately resulted in the Clearances of the 1820s to 1850s.[11]

The idea of land in return for military service was central to the new links between the Highlands and the British Army. But this exchange was not the only means by which men could be drawn into the military. Contrary to the myth that the British army was composed exclusively of volunteers, the Seven Years War and American Revolutionary War witnessed the use of 'Impressment Acts' that conscripted men while also designed to prompt individuals into volunteering before being forced. The affect on the Highlands and Islands was profound. Conscription seems to have been dreaded and taken as evidence of an individual's social disgrace and alienation from their community. Across the

Highlands, hundreds of men volunteered rather than face the ignominy of conscription. Land, the threat of conscription and other positive factors such as the honourable place of military activity in Highland society and, of course, pay proved a powerful combination.[12]

In early 1757, the crown raised two new Highland regiments for service in North America. One of these units was given to the brother of the Earl of Eglinton and the other to Simon Fraser, the son of the executed Jacobite, Simon Fraser of Lovat. The officers of these regiments made a herculean effort to raise men all across the west Highlands and Islands. They combined a number of tactics, encouraging individuals to enlist as volunteers while also relying on a fear of the conscription acts to drive men into the army. The letters of Alexander MacLeod of Ullinish in Skye, a sheriff-substitute for Inverness-shire during the Seven Years War, show how this intensive recruiting drive affected the Outer Hebrides. With the press act having come into operation in the autumn of 1756, Ullinish reported on 21 February 1757 that he had gathered 24 conscripts in Skye and expected more men from the outer islands. This levy was followed by a second round of conscription in the autumn of the same year. By 9 November, men from the Inverness-shire part of the Long Island (namely Harris) had been transported over the Minch, followed in March of the next year by six men from Barra and South Uist, and a similar number from North Uist and Harris.[13]

These totals do not seem especially impressive, but the social dislocation and anxiety caused by the process of conscription should not be underestimated. One group that was especially badly affected were the local constables authorised to select men under the terms of the act. In close knit communities this must have had a terribly divisive affect on social and personal relationships. Ullinish noted that parts of the isles had become 'drained' of men and the farms held by the constables were 'ill attended' as they spent more and more time scouring their localities for suitable candidates for enlistment.[14]

Historians are fortunate to have a contemporary record of the consequences of army recruitment during the Seven Years War. In 1764, just a year after the conflict came to an end, the Reverend Dr John Walker, a Kirk of Scotland minister, travelled to the Western Isles on behalf of the General Assembly. Walker's mission was to assess educational provision, religious attainment and the potential for moral and social improvement in the area. It is a measure of the war's impact that in every island he noted the number of men who had been drawn into the army. Table 1 summarises his findings and reveals the intensity of military levying during the 1750's.

TABLE 1: THE OUTER HEBRIDES AND THE SEVEN YEARS WAR, 1756-1763 [15]

ISLAND	POPULATION	RECRUITED	RETURNED	CHELSEA PENSIONERS
LEWIS	1331*	170	34	18
HARRIS	430*	118	14	8
NORTH UIST	2465	60	?	?
BENBECULA	?	28	?	?
SOUTH UIST	1580	72	?	?
BARRA	1285	31	6	?

[* = ELIGIBLE MALE POPULATION BETWEEN 16-60. OTHER FIGURES SHOW TOTAL POPULATION]

Walker's figures are striking for a number of reasons. As a minister he had contact with his colleagues in each of the island parishes, and so his estimates can be taken as fairly accurate. They reveal an extraordinary rate of recruitment, which ensured that the outer islands supplied nearly 500 souls for the army, although these men would have been dispersed among a number of different regiments. The drain of manpower was profound, and was compounded by very poor rates of men returning home after the peace. It was understood at the time that these losses were not the result of battle casualties, but largely a voluntary decision on the part of ex-soldiers to establish lives for themselves elsewhere. Many chose to take up the government's offer of free land in North America.[16] One of the crucial effects of military service, then as now, was an increase in social and geographic mobility; indeed the British Army was one of the key institutions which first created the transatlantic links and migratory connections that were to become such an important feature of the islands' history for the next two hundred years.

The same pattern occurred again during Britain's war against the Americans from 1775 to 1783. In the first year of the war Norman MacLeod of Dunvegan and Harris raised 100 men for the Black Watch, obtaining the rank of captain in return. He drew recruits from across Skye and Harris, although it is not clear if he had to resort to taking men from St Kilda, as had been the case with his grandfather's levying effort in 1760.[17] In late 1777 and early 1778, both Sir Alexander MacDonald of Sleat and Kenneth MacKenzie of Seaforth received appointments as lieutenant colonels of new Highland regiments.[18] The result was a sustained round of recruitment that spread across the Uists, Harris and Lewis. The intensity of levying, combined with persistent press gang activity for the Royal Navy, began to seriously deplete the Outer Hebrides of landless labourers. In order to protect income generated from their farms and sustain the labour intensive kelp industry, landlords targeted young single men from the lowest rungs of society while seeking to avoid tenants responsible for rent and married men with families who might become a burden on the community if deprived of the main bread winner. This social profiling could be brutal and uncompromising. As early as 1777, Seaforth's agent in Edinburgh had written to George Gillanders, the factor in Lewis, recommending he assist the process of recruitment. Levying was to focus on those guilty or simply suspected of petty theft, with the agent adding that in this way military recruitment '...*will be doing much good to the country in getting clear of such vermin.*' [19]

With Seaforth himself committed to raising men from the early months of 1778, the drive to enlist became ever more comprehensive. The way in which men were raised in Lewis for the 78th Highland Regiment is a classic example of how the recruitment economy worked across the whole of the Highlands during the later eighteenth century. On 1 April 1778, Gillanders was told that, '*A list will be made out of such as is able to serve and that can be spared without material loss. I am afraid there must be some rough wash to persuade some of the West side wet feet to leave the Island of Lewis*'. [20] Coercion, in other words, would be deployed from the start. The consequences for the island come across clearly in the appeal by the Presbytery of Lewis to Seaforth in August 1779. They noted *'that this district [Lewis], consisting of four parishes has within the last two years furnished upwards of 300 men for the army and navy and can spare few more without laying lands waste'.*[21]

Contrary to the idea that all Hebridean men saw military service as an attractive option, the surviving evidence shows that there was genuine fear at the prospect of entering a regiment destined for service in the empire, especially if it looked like the unit would be sent to India. When the news reached Lewis that the Earl had been awarded a new regiment, Kenneth MacLeod, the ground officer at Seaforth Lodge noted that *'there is a great clamour through the country about this affair'.* [22] Faced with the policy of social profiling that targeted landless labourers, the Leòdhasaich did what any sensible Leòdasach ought to do, they attempted to cross into Harris. John MacIver, one of Seaforth's estate officers, suggested placing patrols on the roads and byways leading south into Harris in order to pick up the usual suspects. Recruitment thus became a tool of social and economic control.[23] With so many men draining into the army, wages spiralled and landless labourers and cottars refused to enter into contracts with tenants, preferring to keep a flexible approach to the job market in order to maximise their income. On 29 July 1778, Seaforth responded by ordering that any men guilty of minor misdemeanours, such as illicit peat cutting or theft, and, above all, those seeking to negotiate higher wages were to be targeted for enlistment.[24]

Recruitment in many ways mirrored the agricultural economy. The male population was envisaged as a crop, to be harvested at regular intervals before a period of 'fallow' enabled manpower levels to recover. As men and boys considered too young in the first phase of enlistment came of age, landlords looked to supplement regiments with further rounds of levying. In February 1780, two years after the first intensive recruitment drive for the 78th Highland Regiment, Seaforth again returned to Lewis in search of men. He noted that *'I must have men, and many boys that two years ago we thought unfit for service will now be stout fellows, at any rate you* [Gillanders] *must strain every nerve as we are now near 100 short.'*[25]

War came again to the islands in the spring of 1793, when Britain entered into hostilities against Revolutionary France. Almost immediately Francis Humberston-MacKenzie was offered another regiment.[26] Recruitment for the second 78th regiment [the Seaforth Highlanders] began on 31 March with the drawing up of lists from every township in Lewis. In five weeks 220 men were levied from across the island.[27] It is important to stress the intensity of enlistment. Set against a total population of approximately 6,300, 220 men might not seem particularly significant. But the effect on individual townships could be immense, and reached a level that was not matched until the Great War. Swordale in Point sent 15 men into the regiment in a matter of days, prompting George Gillanders to note that land in the *Rubha* was already lying waste. He went on to describe how enlistment impacted on families and communities, adding that '*the wives of those who went with you have thrown their lands away*'.[28]

In 1799, recruitment began in North Uist for the 'Fencible' Regiment of the Isles – a unit designed only for service within Britain. The process was to have a profound influence on patterns of landholding in the townships. One reason for this was that Lord MacDonald relied heavily on local tacksmen – the leading tenants – to supply recruits. This policy had paid dividends in early 1778, when MacDonald had raised the 76th Highland Regiment and granted lieutenancies to the sons of Colin MacDonald of Boisdale (then serving as factor for Clanranald's estate in South Uist), and North Uist tacksmen such as the MacDonalds of Vallay, Baleshare and Milton.[29] In return these prominent local families were expected to levy their own tenants and subtenants. A similar reliance on estate manpower occurred in 1799. A detailed list in the MacDonald of Sleat papers reveals the complex process of awarding land to those who gave their sons and brothers to the regiment. Less well appreciated is that this exchange necessitated the removal of established tenants and their families; practically every township in North Uist was affected in some way or another.[30]

The fate of women left saddled with farms that required intensive labour, but who now had to do without husbands, brothers, sons or cousins to help them, points to the wider consequences of the recruitment economy. Too much military history focuses on the soldiers or sailors doing the actual fighting, without noting how the rapid and mass departure of men left women vulnerable to a host of social and economic problems. If the deserved reputation of isles men for service in the army and navy forms the basis of much of Hebridean military history, so too should the experience of women left to pick up the pieces. As estate economies in the Hebrides cracked under the strain, women could be left exposed to the landlords' efforts to increase the pool of available labour. In this context women were liable to face eviction. What is to be made of the fact that in June 1793 the widow of 'John MacVurrich Oig' in Shawbost refused to give up to the army the only male servant she had left to tend to her run rigs.[31] The surviving record does not record the factor or landlord's reaction, but the odds are that she faced eviction and downward social mobility into the ranks of the landless labouring classes. Whatever happened to the widow in Shawbost, her story is as much part of the military history of the Hebrides as that of any soldier.

All these examples seem to point to the conclusion that the islands existed in a hostile and sometimes deeply negative relationship with Britain's armed forces. There were of course very good reasons for men and their families to consider a military career. This was especially the case for the landlords. Norman MacLeod of Dunvegan and Harris in the 1770's and 1780's and the MacKenzies of Seaforth throughout the 1770's to early 1800's used military service to augment their income and reduce the high levels of debt which threatened their ancestral estates. As was the case in the twentieth century, military and naval wages and pensions provided crucial financial support for struggling Hebridean communities. In 1759, John Beaton, a private in the 77th Highland Regiment serving in North America, sent home the sum of £5, 8 shillings to his family.[32] This was an extremely large sum of money for the time and represented a major injection of cash into Beaton's home community. His family lived in Trotternish in Skye, but their experience could stand for numerous other families in the outer islands with men in the army or navy. To the Saldanha Bay prize money mentioned at the beginning of this chapter could be added the annual 'Chatham' pensions given to sailors discharged from the RN. Treasury accounts from 1815, the year that Britain finally prevailed over its arch enemy France, reveal six Chatham pensioners living in Stornoway and receiving a combined income of £55 per annum, again a substantial sum for the time.[33] These amounts may seem trivial, but they provided one of the real benefits that offset the personal and social distress caused by the loss of so many men abroad for years at a time.

Not all forms of British service were automatically disruptive of local work patterns and community life. Regiments such as the Seaforth Highlanders are taken to exemplify the martial traditions that linked the Hebrides to the British military. The problem was that these regular regiments operated abroad in the empire for years at a time, drawing men away from their homes, often for good. Yet the eighteenth century was also a time when multiple forms of military service were possible. A wide variety of units were established during the course of a conflict and would disappear immediately upon the outbreak of the peace. The Navy was another important factor at play. The Royal Navy, particularly the Royal Naval Reserve (RNR), is closely associated with the islands' role during the two world wars. Attitudes towards the RN were radically different during the eighteenth century, when forcible impressment was the primary means of levying men. In July 1782, 20 men were taken by the Navy from Lewis and further eight from Harris and the Uists. Each year, during the war against the Americans, the arrival of the navy's sloop sparked panic among fishing families the length and breadth of the Western Isles.[34] In 1779, it was noted of the population in Lewis that '*our people are in terror about the Orkney tender, expected every day with these north easterly winds. It may be well, if matters can be made right with him* [Captain Napier, the officer in charge of the press gang], *for a certain number which might yet be spared, were it possible to get hold of the proper chaps*'. [35] The process repeated itself during the war against France in the 1790's. On 15 October 1793, two RN warships entered Stornoway harbour and immediately press-ganged 14 men.[36]

In contrast to the fear and dislike of the Navy's activities among the general population, Hebridean landlords often sought the presence of naval forces in an effort to deter enemy raiding. During the American Revolutionary War, privateering became a real problem along the west coast of Scotland as the Americans sought to counter Britain's naval supremacy with what was in effect a naval guerrilla campaign. With most of the RN stationed in the southern approaches to Britain, the eastern seaboard of

North America or the West Indies, there was little real protection available for the Outer Hebrides. By 1781, American privateers operating in the Atlantic had driven freighting costs to and from the islands to prohibitive levels. The situation was compounded in the autumn of the same year when an American ship captured a local vessel carrying 29 tons of processed Lewis kelp; reluctantly, the Seaforth estate authorities agreed to ransom the ship and its contents for the huge sum of 200 guineas. This incident prompted the observation from Gillanders that, *'the times are really very bad and these repeated captures will discourage people to carry on trade, the losses are so great'.* [37]

For obvious reasons merchants and landlords lobbied for naval protection, sometimes successfully, as in August 1793, when a frigate and a sloop were stationed at Stornoway for the purpose of monitoring shipping and the fishing fleet in the Minch.[38] Similar problems affected the southern islands; during the 1775-83 war a French privateer entered Lochboisdale and destroyed a number of fishing vessels. One consequence of this disaster was that a small battery was built at the end of the loch and garrisoned by local men.[39]

These South Uist men represent one of the most important but neglected aspects of Hebridean military history in the eighteenth and early nineteenth centuries. In contrast to the usual emphasis upon the regular British Army or Royal Navy, all the historical evidence shows that the really popular forms of military activity were those which kept men in their communities and enabled part time soldiering. This is clearly the case with the reaction of Hebridean communities to the creation of local 'Volunteer Companies' during the invasion scares of the 1790's and 1800's. Designed purely for parish defence or, at a push, the county, volunteering was a form of part-time soldiering that integrated well with the other economic requirements of island communities. Men mustered twice a week (normally at the parish church) for two to three hours drill. In return they received either 1 shilling or 2 shillings, depending on the particular conditions granted by the crown when the unit was first raised. It is difficult to exaggerate the popularity of volunteering in later eighteenth-century Scotland: by 1804 the country had raised 52,000 men in 228 volunteer corps. Indeed by 1797, with around 15% of Britain's population, Scotland supplied 36% of the United Kingdom's entire volunteer force.[40]

Nowhere was volunteering more popular than in the Outer Hebrides. Men got a steady income while remaining within their townships. It was the perfect accommodation between the need for national defence and local concerns, and unlike the regular army and navy, social and economic disruption was kept to a minimum. In marked contrast to the reluctance that often characterised attitudes to the regular army, volunteering was genuinely popular. When in November 1795, MacNeil of Barra called for the formation of a 63 man strong volunteer company, 392 men offered to enlist.[41] Table 2 shows the volunteer companies raised in the Inverness-shire districts of the Outer Hebrides during the French Revolutionary War.

TABLE 2: VOLUNTEERING IN THE OUTER HEBRIDES, 1794-1799 [42]

COMPANY	CAPTAIN	FORMATION	MEN	ANNUAL PAY
BARRA	JAMES MACDONALD	19 NOV 1795	63	£327
SOUTH UIST	JOHN BUTTER	11 SEPT 1794	63	£327
BOISDALE	RANALD MACDONALD	6 OCT 1795	63	£327
3RD SOUTH UIST	JOHN MACDONALD OF BORNISH	27 NOV 1798	63	£163
NORTH UIST	ARCHIBALD MACDONALD OF VALLAY	11 SEPT 1794	63	£327
2ND NORTH UIST	EWEN MACDONALD OF GRIMINISH	13 DEC 1796	63	£327

HARRIS	ANGUS CAMPBELL OF STROND	16 MAY 1795	63	£327
2ND HARRIS	WILLIAM MACLEOD OF LUSKENTYRE	6 FEB 1799	63	£163
TOTALS			504	£2,288

Not only was the total number of men substantial – equivalent in fact to a whole army battalion – but there were real benefits in the fact that regular and reliable state income was distributed throughout all of the southern islands and Harris by means of part time military service. While lacking the status of the regular forces, this sort of military activity guaranteed revenue, as well as the social and cultural prestige associated with soldiering, for communities that seemed far removed from the centres of conflict on the Continent and in the Empire.

There is no contradiction between highlighting the activities of Lewismen at the Cape of Good Hope in 1781 or the seemingly far less glamorous version of soldiering undertaken by men in the Harris, Uist or Barra volunteers. These radically different examples are all part of a crucially important process of engagement with Britain's military that swept across the Outer Hebrides over the course of the eighteenth century. Although never 'total' wars in the manner of the 1914-18 or 1939-45 hostilities, these earlier wars of empire and revolution did have a major impact on men, women, tenancy arrangements and patterns of social mobility in the Hebrides. The intensity of levying for the army could remove hundreds of men from island communities that had much smaller populations than would be the case during the world wars. Large numbers of isles men found themselves in India, North America, the West Indies and Europe, a process of mobility that radically altered pre-existing patterns of emigration from the Hebrides. It was not the Clearances of the nineteenth century that first scattered people from the islands across the globe – that process was already underway by the second half of the eighteenth century. Through the medium of military service the islands participated fully in what is now recognised to be an early and crucial phase of globalisation.[43] Far from being marginal, or a political, economic, social and cultural backwater, the Outer Hebrides played a full and sometimes disproportionate part in the wars that helped to shape the emergence of the modern world.

Endnotes

1. National Archive of Scotland, Edinburgh [thereafter NAS], Seaforth Muniments, GD46/6/104/1.
2. H. M. Chichester, 'Humberston, Thomas Frederick Macken-zie (1753–1783)', G. J. Bryant, *Oxford Dictionary of National Biography*, Oxford University Press, 2004 [http://www.oxforddnb.com/view/article/14127, accessed 8 November 2008].
3. NAS, Seaforth Muniments, GD46/17/4, p. 258; GD46/17/11: Miscellaneous Correspondence, 'List of soldiers now alive and the representatives of those dead belonging to the late 100th regiment of foot, who were at the capture of the Dutch ships at Saldanah Bay in the year 1781 and residing in the Island of Lewis.' For the rental of Lewis in 1780 see, NAS, Gillanders of Highfield Papers, GD427/13/14, 'Lewis Crop, 1780.'; GD427/49.
4. P.J. Marshall, *The Making and Unmaking of Empires: Britain, India, and America, c.1750-1783* (Oxford, 2005), pp. 1-11.
5. C.A. Bayly, *Imperial Meridian: the British Empire and the World, 1780-1830* (London, 1989), pp. 1-4, 75-191.
6. John Brewer, *The Sinews of Power: War, money and the English State, 1688-1783* (London, 1989), pp. 29-45. For an excellent summary of the impact upon Britain of warfare against her continental enemies, see Linda Colley, *Britons: Forging the Nation, 1707-1837* (London, 1992), pp. 56-71.
7. A.I. Macinnes, *Clanship, Commerce and the House of Stuart, 1603-1788* (East Linton, 1996), pp. 57-9, 109.
8. National Library of Scotland, Edinburgh [thereafter NLS], Yester Papers, MS14503, fos. 15-16.
9. Peter Simpson, *The Independent Highland Companies, 1603-1760* (Edinburgh, 1996), pp. 127-31.
10. Andrew Mackillop, *'More fruitful than the soil': army, empire and the Scottish Highlands, 1715-1815* (East Linton, 2000).
11. Eric Richard, *The Highland Clearances: People, Landlords*

and Rural Turmoil ((Edinburgh, 2002), pp. 47-49.

12. The National Archive, Kew, London [thereafter TNA], War Office, General Correspondence (Out), WO. 4/53, p. 30; Andrew Mackillop, 'Continuity, Coercion and Myth: the recruitment of the Highland Regiments in the Later Eighteenth Century', *Scottish Tradition*, 26, (2001), pp. 30-55.

13. NAS, Scrymgeour-Wedderburn Muniments, GD137/3383, 3387-88.

14. NAS, Scrymgeour-Wedderburn Muniments, GD137/3390.

15. M.M. Mackay (ed.), *The Reverend Dr John Walker's Report on the Hebrides, 1764 & 1771* (Edinburgh, 1980), pp. 39-85.

16. Allan I. Macinnes, Majory-Ann D. Harper & Linda G. Fryer (eds.), *Scotland and the Americas, c.1650-1939: A Documentary Source Book* (Edinburgh, 2002), pp. 106-111.

17. Dunvegan Castle Muniments [thereafter DCM], 3/68/4, p. 20; 3/68/238-40; 3/307/1.

18. TNA, War Office, General Correspondence (Out), November 1777-February 1778, WO 4/101, 189, 396; NAS, Methven Collection, 'Letter book of William Macdonald', 22 December 1777.

19. NAS, Gillanders of Highfield Papers, GD427/302/2; GD427/217/6, 15, 17.

20. NAS, Gillanders of Highfield Papers, GD427/304/2; GD427/303/4, 6.

21. NAS, Gillanders of Highfield Papers, GD427/217/25.

22. NAS, Gillanders of Highfield Papers, GD427/303/1.

23. NAS, Gillanders of Highfield Papers, GD427/302/11.

24. NAS, Gillanders of Highfield Papers, GD427/217/6; GD427/306/4; GD427/296/1.

25. NAS, Gillanders of Highfield Papers, GD427/305/5 (2).

26. NAS, Seaforth Muniments, GD46/6/25/6 & 8.

27. NAS, Gillanders of Highfield Papers, GD427/307/2, 4.

28. NAS, Seaforth Muniments, GD46/17/3, Stornoway, 17 June 1793.

29. NAS, Methven Collection, GD1/8, 'Letter Book of William Macdonald', Edinburgh, 21 January 1778; GD 1/8/17, 'Letter Book of William Macdonald, 1776-1784', pp. 4-130.

30. Clan Donald Trust Library, Clan Donald Centre, Armadale, Skye, Lord Macdonald Papers, GD221/4388.

31. NAS, Gillanders of Highfield Papers, GD427/224/12.

32. University of Glasgow Business Records Centre, J.A. & J.L. Campbell and Lomond, UGD 37/2/2, p. 148.

33. TNA, T47/21, 'Receipts of Naval pensions paid by Scottish Commissioners of Customs, 1815.'

34. NAS, Gillanders of Highfield Papers, GD427/135/4.

35. NAS, Gillanders of Highfield Papers, GD427/217/23.

36. NAS, Gillanders of Highfield Papers, GD427/212/15.

37. NAS, Gillanders of Highfield Papers, GD427/210/19; GD427/134/9-10

38. NAS, Seaforth Muniments, GD46/17/3, Stornoway, 13 August 1793.

39. NAS, Seafield Muniments, GD248/1526, 'Letter Book of Sir James Grant, Lord Lieutenant of Inverness-shire, June 1794-June 1796.'

40. J.E. Cookson, *The British Armed Nation, 1793-1815* (Oxford, 1997), pp. 128, 140-1.

41. NAS, Seafield Muniments, GD248/1526, 'Letter Book of Sir James Grant, Lord Lieutenant of Inverness-shire, June 1794-June 1796: 26 November 1794.

42. The figures in Table 2 are drawn from NAS, Seafield Muniments, GD248/1529, 'Letter Book of Sir James Grant, Lord Lieutenant of Inverness-shire, 1798-1801', pp. 3 & 42-5.

43. C.A. Bayly, *The Birth of the Modern World, 1780-1914* (London, 2004), pp. 62-4, 88-96, 474-5.

FROM CLAN TO REGIMENT – THE CASE OF THE MACLEANS OF COLL

Nicholas Maclean-Bristol

In his book 'Clanship, Commerce and the House of Stuart, 1603-1788',[1] my old acquaintance Professor Allan Macinnes of Aberdeen University states that, *'The military ethos of the clan … should not be overstressed.'*

I hold the opposite view and believe that even as late as the Napoleonic Wars the ethos of at least one clan was thoroughly military. I base my argument upon the clan Maclean of Coll, which I have studied for 50 years. I do not know if this is typical of other clans: that is for other historians to research.

The Macleans of Coll emerge as an important element in the wider Maclean federation in the late 14th Century. It was then that Lachlan, a younger son of Lachlan Lubanach of Duart invaded Coll [Table 1]. He killed Macaulay, who had previously possessed the island. Willie Matheson argues that those Macaulays who survived fled to North Uist.[2]

In addition to most of the island of Coll, the first Macleans also owned Quinish in Mull, Drimnin in Morvern and the Isle of Rum. They later obtained Lochiel in Lochaber, and the Isle of Muck. In my latest publication, 'From Clan to Regiment',[3] I use the example of the whole estate to make my point. In this paper I will concentrate on the island of Coll.

There can be little doubt that for the first 250 years of its existence clan Maclean of Coll needed to be organised along military lines. Lachlan, the first Maclean of Coll won his estate by the sword and later died by it.[4] His son John Garbh had to win back his inheritance by defeating and killing his step-father,

---

[1] Allan I Macinnes *Clanship, Commerce and the House of Stuart, 1603-1788* (1996), 30.m

[2] William Matheson 'Notes on North Uist Families' *TGSI* Vol. LII (1980-82), 337.

[3] Nicholas Maclean-Bristol *From Clan to Regiment: 600 Years in the Hebrides* (2007).

[4] Nicholas Maclean-Bristol 'Lachlan Maclean 1st of Coll' *WHN&Q*. Series 3, No. 96-7.

MacNeil of Barra. His son, known as John Abrach from his living in Lochaber, was killed at the battle of Blarnicara, near Corpach, by the captain of Clan Cameron.

John Abrach's son John Cam fought unsuccessfully for his lost lands in Lochaber, not with the sword but in the law courts in Edinburgh. His sons however, had to resort to both court and sword to defend their inheritance against their cousins the Macleans of Duart, who in the sixteenth century were attempting to turn the Macleans into a unitary clan.[5] Duart's attempts to take over Coll were put on hold after the defeat of his men at the battle of *Sruthan nan Ceann* in Coll by Neil Mòr,[6] Coll's younger brother, and finally lost in 1596 when Lachlan of Coll (1583 -1631) won his case in the courts.

The Macleans of Coll continued to need fighting men in the seventeenth and eighteenth centuries. In the early seventeenth century they took part in the government's campaign against the Macdonalds of Islay and in hunting down the Maciains of Ardnamuchan. In the Civil Wars they fought for the King. They distinguished themselves at Kilsyth and were slaughtered at Inverkeithing. They fought at Killiekrankie, Dunkeld, Sheriffmuir and at Culloden, where they appear to have fought on both sides.[7]

Stories of their exploits in these campaigns continued to be told in Coll late into the twentieth century. And one of the reasons why I think that Professor Macinnes is wrong about a military ethos is the evidence of the many stories about the military that have survived.

Stories of the military exploits of the ancestors of several men in Coll in my own day are still told. For example Big Archie Maclean only died a few years ago. Archie's ancestors were all big powerful men. His great-great grandfather Donald Bàn was at the Battle of Culloden in 1746. John Johnston (1830-1926), the Coll seanachie, says of him that, *'he was famous for his strength and was said to have cut the barrel of a musket in two belonging to a Hanoverian soldier with one blow of his sword'*.[8]

---

[5] *Records of the Privy Council of Scotland* I, 31-33.

[6] *From Clan to Regiment*, 8-9.

[7] Details of the history of the Macleans of Coll are to be found in *From Clan to Regiment*.

[8] Breacachadh Castle Papers (hereafter BCP) Johnston Box File 1.

In the retreat after Culloden, Donald Bàn and three companions were pursued by a horseman. Donald alone stood his ground and the soldier levelled a blow at him with his sword, which Donald parried. The trooper's sword, however, cut him on the temple, at which Donald '*got in such a rage that he gave a terrible stroke in return, which nearly cut the trooper in two*'. He then took to his heels and fled. He was one of the few men from Coll who returned home after the battle.

I am at present collecting stories about Coll to enable my grandchildren and others at the primary school to learn something of their heritage. This is not an easy task when they are more interested in dinosaurs and when I have been asked not to tell too many stories of battles.

As we shall see, battles are exactly what many traditional stories are about. It is these stories that have been remembered and it is easy to imagine how young boys were inspired to follow their ancestors' exploits and become heroes themselves by listening to old men's tales of *Fionn Mac Cumhaill*, Niall Mòr or of the battle of Inverkeithing.

It was the primary duty of a chief to protect his clan and provide them with land; a duty symbolised by his receiving his father's sword when he was inaugurated as chief. In exchange, a clansman was obliged to obey him, to defend his person and property, and make his house open to him. In return the chief was bound to listen to his 'man's advice'. In addition a clansman paid his 'calp'. This was a gift from the clansman's family made to his chief at the time of the clansman's death. This gift was often the tenant's best beast and could be looked on as a payment for a lifetime's protection.

The actual protection of clansmen was the duty of the chief's professional fighting men. It is necessary to identify these men in order to understand the structure of the clan. Obviously they did not at first consist of men of the same surname. In the fifteenth century there were not enough Macleans to go round, and the first Macleans of Coll had to compete with other Maclean chiefs, who were carving out their own empires at the same time.

We have no idea who the first Maclean of Coll's followers were. But in the following generation at least one is remembered. He was a servant of Coll's named *An Gille Riabhach*. His leap is still remembered in Coll: during the fight at Grishipol he is said to have leapt backwards across the burn and killed MacNeil. Afterwards Coll gave him a farm in Mull as a reward.

The normal method of building up a following was by bonds of manrent. These bonds admitted men who were not of his blood to the same obligations as those that were. They came from an exclusive social group and were considered to be 'gentlemen'. It was rare for anyone below the rank of laird to issue bonds of manrent, and many of those who gave their bond to a chief were men of wealth and position. The point was that it was a chief seeking to attract men to his affinity, rather than the other way round.

The only Coll bond of manrent known to me that has survived is that of 'Jone bain Mcdonelour' and his nephews, given to Hector of Coll and dated 25 February 1568-9. In it they oblige themselves and their posterity to be true and faithful servitors to Hector of Coll. They also agreed to give him their *'calpes ... that is to say ane hors of us efter our deces in tokin and sign that he is our maister and chife'.*[9]

The terms by which a chief built up his following of fighting men are stated in a report to Sir Robert Cecil in 1596 by the Dean of Limerick.[10] It was then proposed that a force from the Hebrides, including Macleans, should go to Ireland to fight for Queen Elizabeth. It states how they should be clad and armed. The description resembles the effigies of men in armour found in St Clement's Church in Rodel, and other graveyards in the Hebrides. It also says that,

> *'na labourers of the ground are permittit to steir furth of the countrie quatevir their maister have ado, except gentlemen quhilk labouris not, that the labour belonging to the telling of the ground and wynning of their corns may not be left undone.'*

The dean goes on to say that,

---

[9] Jenny Wormald *Lords and Men in Scotland: Bonds of Manrent 1442-1603* (1985), 328.

[10] Nicholas Maclean-Bristol *Murder Under Trust: The Crimes and Death of Sir Lachlan Mor Maclean of Duart 1558-1598* (1999), 138-141.

> *'Ilk merk land sustain daylie and yeirlie ane gentleman in
> meit and claith, quilk dois na labour, but is haldin as ane
> of their maisters household men, and man be sustenit and
> furneisit in all necessaries be the tennent, and he man be
> reddie to his maisters service and advis.'*

This assessment would suggest that each merkland produced
two men. One presumably being the gentlemen clad in armour,
whilst the other was probably more lightly armed and was perhaps
his servant. The dean says that Coll had 30 merklands. Another
source says that the island could raise 140 men.

Professional fighting men in the Hebrides were trained from
their youth in seamanship and the use of weapons. Professor
Macinnes suggests that they received this training in their chief's
household. He is probably correct, for such training would require
central control. They also had a great deal to learn; how to handle
broadswords and targets, bows and arrows and later, firearms.

Mòr Nic Phàidein was perhaps thinking of the training of the
young men at Coll's castle, Breacachadh in her 'Lament for her
sweetheart Niall Og' [Table 3], for she sings,

> *'I am attending the parade ground, with men in order
> Going past: I see none like you among them.
> A noble, brave, courageous man, handsome and confident,
> Is the generous one they call Niall Og.'*

Perhaps Niall Og, a son of the Neil Mor who defeated the
Duart men at *Sruthan nan Ceann*, had been responsible for training young men in archery for she continues,

> *'And at the approach of evening, when I see no target hit,
> The playing of the youths has increased my tears.'*[11]

Professor Macinnes goes on to say that at the end of their
training the ablest students graduated into the *luchd-tighe* or
household men.

---

[11] Colm Ò Baoill 'Lament for Niall Og *West Highland Notes & Queries* (hereafter *WHN&Q*)Series 1, No. XXVI (April 1985), 4-13; No. XXVII (August
1985), 3-17.

It would appear that membership of this retinue became hereditary in certain families in Coll. They continued to produce soldiers into the twentieth century. It is possible to work out who some of these families were from two lists of the garrison at Breacachadh Castle, made when it surrendered to the Earl of Argyll in 1679 [Annex A]. Foremost among them are three Maclean brothers descended from Neil Mòr, whose father commanded the Coll men at Inverkeithing. Captain Lachlan and his two eldest sons were killed there [Table 3]. At least one of these surviving brothers accompanied Lachlan Maclean of Coll to Holland in 1681 when Coll commanded a company of Collachs in the Dutch army. The youngest of these brothers was another Neil Og. He had a son who fought at Sheriffmuir. We know this from a list of the men from the Inner Isles, Morvern and Ardnamurchan, who handed in their arms in 1716.[12]

Membership of the *luchd-tighe* was not limited to cadet branches of the family of Coll but included incoming families who probably made a bond of manrent to Maclean of Coll. Often these men were the descendants of families who had lost their own land and wished to maintain their status as 'gentlemen' by becoming professional soldiers. For example, the old Campbells of Barbreck lost their property when an heiress married back into the Argyll family. Representatives of the family are to be found in both the 1679 and 1716 lists. Another family to join Coll's *luchd-tighe* were the MacFadyens. They probably descend from the family who once owned Lochbuie in Mull. They too are to be found in both lists.

It is probably significant that the 1679 garrison lived in farms within an easy distance of Breacachadh Castle. Several of them probably lived at Feall, the most populous farm on the island. Among the tenants there in 1776, when the catechist made the first complete list of the population of Coll to survive, are several tenants who are probably either descended from cadets of the family of Coll or from families such as the Mackinnons, who came to Coll in the early sixteenth century. One at least, a Donald *Mugach*, fought at *Sruthan nan Ceann*. These Mackinnons too were probably members of the *luchd-tighe*.

---

[12] Nicholas Maclean-Bristol (ed) *Inhabitants of the Inner Isles, Morvern & Ardnamurchan 1716* (Scottish Record Society, 1998), 163.

When did the *luchd-tighe* cease to exist? There is evidence that Maclean of Kingerloch still had his as late as 1788. Coll's, from the evidence of the 1716 list would appear to have to have survived until at least that date.

The lack of surviving muster rolls for Coll's company in the Argyll Militia in the '45 prevents us from knowing whether it was in existence at that time. I suspect that it was. Hugh Maclean of Coll (c.1720-1786) wrote a memorandum to King George III in which he argues that the Lochiel estate should be given back to him for his family's loyalty during the '45. He states that he and his elder brother Hector, who was laird of Coll at the time, were ordered to raise a hundred men in their islands and send them to Inveraray, *'under proper officers to join Major General John Campbell to assist in quelling the unnatural rebellion'*. [13]

Hugh Maclean goes on to say that, *'these men joined his Majesty's Forces and went to Culloden and few of them ever returned'*. This statement is contradicted by James Boswell, who says that when the men from Coll arrived at Inveraray, the Argyll Militia already had sufficient men, and the Coll contingent was sent home.[14] It would, however, seem almost impossible that Hugh could make such a statement if it were not true.

Members of Coll's *luchd-tighe* were not equal. The senior decendant of Neil Mòr is listed immediately after Coll's brother in both 1679 lists and was probably his lieutenant. His younger brother Neil Og was given the farm of Crossapol by Lachlan of Coll before the latter's death in 1687. His grandson held the farm in 1773 and with his eldest son helped entertain Johnson and Boswell on their famous visit to Coll.

Crossapol had the highest rented farm in Coll in 1773 [15] and it is clear that by then the old *luchd-tighe* were no longer getting their farms rent free for service. Some were, however, still in their traditional holdings. In 1776 the MacFadyens were in Ardnish and the Mackinnons and several Macleans were in Feall. The Campbells were in a single tenancy farm at Toraston. [16] It is not

---

[13] BCP. Box File. Maclean of Coll. NRAS 1074. 2/1-20.

[14] Frederick A Pottle & Charles H Bennett (eds) *Boswell's Journal of A Tour to the Hebrides* (1936),279.

[15] *Ibid*, 283.

[16] National Archives of Scotland. CH 2, 70.1. 29-48.

41

clear when the old *luchd-tighe* became farmers or when the *nativi* were no longer tied to the soil – possibly during the Civil Wars when every able-bodied man of the islands needed to be mobilised.

Certainly fighting men who were not settled on traditional *luchd-tighe* farms also went to war in 1715. It is easier to identify incomers with surnames that were new to Coll rather than native Collachs in the 1716 list. For example, the Mathesons or Mackenzies (the names appear to be interchangeable), came to Coll when Florence, a daughter of Macdonald of Morar, married a younger son of Maclean of Coll and brought her foster brother Murdoch Matheson with her to Coll. When her husband died, '*knowing the fidelity and sagacity of her foster brother Murdoch, she kept him as guardian of her young son Allan*'. Murdoch was so devoted to his charge that he was thereafter known as Murdoch Allan. Allan (1695-1716), who became tacksman of Grishipol, repaid this devotion at his guardian's death with a tribute at his funeral, '*Och is mi gun Mhurachadh agam*' (Alas I am now without a Murdoch).[17]

Murdoch Allan lived as a sub-tenant at Grishipol. He had three sons, and many of their descendants became soldiers. The eldest of these sons, *Maoldomnaigh* or Ludovic (1698-1807), was out in the '15 and was at the battle of Sheriffmuir.

Another family of late military incomers were the MacKays in Cornaig. They are not mentioned in the catechist's list of 1776, so they probably moved to the island after that date. On 3 July 1785 Hugh MacKay and his wife Ann MacDonald's daughter Catherine was baptised in Coll. Hugh is said to be a native of Sutherland. He served in 79th Foot with his four sons, '*until after Waterloo when they were discharged with pensions. The father settled in Mull and died about 1840*'.[18]

Why did the MacKays come to the island? The date they are first mentioned in Coll is perhaps significant. The War of American Independence began in 1775 and ended in 1783. Perhaps Hugh MacKay served in the army during the war; if his eldest child was born in 1774 and the second in 1784, it suggests that Hugh could have been away in America. It could also explain how

---

[17] BCP. Coll Families Box File. Mackenzie/Matheson.
[18] BCP. Australia Box File. Private letter of The Rev. RJ Willson dated 20 August 1971.

Hugh MacKay came to settle in Coll. Perhaps he served with one of Donald Maclean of Cornaig's sons. Both served as officers in the war. It would not be the only time when an officer from Coll brought one of his soldiers home with him at the end of a war.

It is unlikely that members of these incoming families were any less imbued with the military ethos than those they joined in Coll.

No muster rolls appear to have survived to provide clues as to the identities of the hundred men whom Hugh Coll claimed he sent to serve in Fraser's Highlanders during the Seven Years War (1756-63). Thereafter, military records are far better preserved and it is possible to make a detailed assessment of Coll's contribution to the British Army.

Hugh of Coll's sons were too young to have served in the Seven Years War. [Table 2] They were, however, to play their part in the American War of Independence. Even before the war began, Highland tacksmen, seduced by the New World, had begun to emigrate, sometimes with all their tenants. It was therefore believed that there could be a shortage of Highland recruits in a new war.

Hugh Coll's eldest surviving son, Alexander, was determined that his brother should obtain a commission in a new regiment that Simon Fraser of Lovat was raising. On 16 December 1775, he wrote to Lovat on his brother's behalf to say that if he had not chosen all his officers,

'You cannot name one that can with so much ease & expedition raise whatever number of men the commission he gets shall require, for this reason, that my father has not yet by raising his rents or other harsh usages forced his tenants to leave their country, as too many other proprietors have done. The fact is there are actually at present too many people upon the estate, & more of the ancient attachment subsists between him and his tenants than most Highlanders can now boast of, this consequently gives him a command of men.'[19]

However, Alexander failed to get his brother a commission in Fraser's. Instead he became a captain in 2/73rd Foot and served in

---

[19] Edinburgh University Library. La ii, 300.

the siege of Gibraltar.[20] Donald Bàn's son Allan was also serving there, as a seaman in the Royal Navy.

Alexander's next eldest brother Hector joined the Honourable East India Company's service. He sailed for India in 1775 and joined the 5th Native Infantry. He was soon in action against the rajahs of North Arcott. In 1778, he took part in the siege of Pondicherry and was action against Hyder Ali.[21] Hector was following in the footsteps of his cousin Captain Lachlan Maclean who served twenty years in India and was lame from a wound from a cannon ball. He returned home to Coll in 1766. Dr Johnson remarked cynically of him that *'having dethroned no Nabob he was not too rich to settle in his own country'*.[22]

Roderick, the fifth son, was commissioned on 30 December 1775 into the 81st or Aberdeen Highland Regiment. He was sixteen. His father was at the time Provost of Old Aberdeen and the Merchant and Trade Society, *'out of respect to the son of their Provost offered a bounty of one guinea over and above all bounties to every recruit that shall enlist ... with Lieutenant Maclean son of Hugh Maclean Esq. of Coll.'*[23] Roderick served in Captain Ferguson's company. Of a total of 82 men, 31 had surnames which suggest they came from Coll's estate.[24] The regiment spent the whole war in Ireland. Two of Hugh's other sons received commissions in the war that followed.

Alexander himself served in His Majesty's 1st or Western Fencibles. In 1779, his company was stationed at Dundee, therefore they were not one of the five companies that mutinied in Edinburgh.[25] After the mutiny was suppressed the mutineers received a flogging.

If Alexander Maclean Sinclair is to be believed, Alexander was not prepared to allow any of his men to be flogged. One of them, John Macdonald from Hough in Tiree, neglected to perform some duty entrusted to him on a bridge. The acting command-

---

[20] *From Clan to Regiment,* 170

[21] A Seanachie *An Historical & Gewnealogical Account of The Clan Maclean* (1838), 316.

[22] Samuel Johnson LLD *A Journey to the Western Islands of Scotland* (1817), 185.

[23] *Records of Old Aberdeen* Vol. 1, 324.

[24] TNA. WO12. 8520.

[25] The National Archives (hereafter TNA) WO1.1003., 589.

ing officer Major Hugh Montgomery decided that he should be flogged. Alexander, who had known Macdonald since he was a boy, pleaded for mercy. Montgomery, however, was adamant.

When the flogging was about to begin, Alexander drew his sword and cut Macdonald free from the whipping post. Montgomery challenged him to a duel with swords. As Montgomery was a well known swordsman, some of the 'jocks' let him know that if he killed Alexander, Montgomery himself would be shot, and although Coll turned up for the duel at the appointed time, Montgomery stayed away.[26]

Other officers from Coll took part in the war. Both of Donald of Cornaig's sons did so. The eldest, Lachlan, served in the 84th Foot or Royal Highland Emigrants in North America.[27] He was later tacksman of Grishipol. His brother John initially served in Alexander's company in the Western Fencibles. On 25 December 1778, he transferred to the 2nd Battalion the Royal Scots. They were to relieve the 2/73rd Foot in Gibraltar.[28] The following day he was replaced by Allan Maclean the younger of Crossapol. He in turn was also transferred to the Royal Scots, serving with the 1st Battalion in England.[29]

Another Allan Maclean from Coll was the former minister's son who had trained as a doctor in Glasgow. He was then commissioned into the Black Watch and served in America.[30] He saw plenty of action but became sick and died at sea on his way home.

The number of officers Coll contributed to the wars in the American War of Independence is particularly impressive, considering that the total population of the island in 1776 was only 930.

Although one can make an educated guess as to the identities of the men who served in the American War of Independence, it is not until the next war that it is possible to identify them with certainty. This is because enlisting records had improved to the extent that they give details of the men's age, height, colour of hair and eyes and their occupation. These details were presumably given in case they deserted.

---

[26] Alexander Maclean Sinclair *Clan Gillean* (1899), 380-1.
[27] *From Clan to Regiment,* 165.
[28] TNA. WO12. 1949.
[29] TNA. WO13. 3962. 28182.
[30] TNA. WO12. 5478.

In 1786, Alexander succeeded his father as Maclean of Coll. In 1793, he obtained a company in the 1st Battalion, Breadalbane's Fencibles. He raised 120 men, 40 of whom came from Coll. Andrew Mackillop comments in '*More Fruitful than the Soil*', that Coll's recruits 'belonged to the labouring class' … and suggests that '*recruitment relied heavily on upon cottars and agricultural day labourers*'.[31]

That this is too simplistic a judgement is clear from what follows. Most of Alexander's 40 recruits from Coll are aged about 20. They mainly enlisted on 6 April 1793. Many can therefore confidently be identified in the Coll catechist's list of 2 December 1776. Most were then under age (i.e. under 7 years old). Several were descendants of the old Coll *luchd-tighe*. For instance Hugh Maclean, aged 20, was a son of Lachlan Maclean in Fiosgaradh [Tables 3 & 6], who was a younger brother of Neil Maclean of Crossapol, the representative of Neil Mòr and an elder of the kirk. Hugh is described as a 'Labourer'. He later became a sergeant, as did two of his brothers. The son of one of them was killed at Waterloo.

The sons of both Coll and Lachlan of Grishipol's pipers are also described as 'labourers'. Coll's piper was tacksman of Cliad and also an elder. His son,Coundullie,[32] was to become a Major in the 104th Foot and High Sheriff of Prince Edward Island. Alexander Rankin, the son of Grishipol's piper, became a corporal. He was court-martialled for allowing a prisoner to escape and was reduced to the ranks.

Murdoch Maclean also enlisted on 6 April 1793. He is described as a tailor in Arnabost. He was a member of a family with a long military tradition and was descended from Neil Buidh [Table 1], a famous archer and the subject of many tales. He also became a sergeant in the Argyll Volunteers [Table 6]. I could quote many other examples, but the point I am trying to make is that these were not penniless cottars. They were the sons of men who had a stake in the community.

There is not time here to tell all the stories about the Breadalbane Fencibles; for that you will have to read '*From Clan to Regi-*

---

[31] Andrew Mackillop '*More Fruitful than the Soil*' (2000), 143; *From Clan to Regiment*, 200-201.
[32] *TGSI*. Vol. XXXVII (1934-6), 75.

ment'. It was, however, very much a Maclean of Coll battalion. Alexander of Coll later became commanding officer. His cousin Lachlan of Grishipol was the second-in-command and Alexander's eventual successor as commanding officer. The adjutant, Hector Maclean, came from Tiree, but his grandmother was a member of the Maclean of Coll family, as was the Sergeant Major [Table 4]. Several sergeants [Table 6] were related. It was a situation that led to problems with the men from Breadalbane.

In addition to his company in the Breadalbane Fencibles, Coll raised three companies of volunteers. Whereas the Fencibles could serve anywhere in Scotland, volunteers were only for home defence. In all, 200 men were raised on the Coll estate for the Argyll Volunteers.[33] The Coll Company was commanded by Allan Maclean, tacksman of Crossapol, [34] who had formerly served in the Western Fencibles. His subalterns were his Maclean brothers-in-law.

The Isle of Rum Company was commanded by Crossapol's elder brother, Mr Donald Maclean, Minister of the Small Isles.[35] His subalterns were not only Macleans, but his own cousins, descended from a younger son of Neil Og of Crossapol, a member of the garrison at Breacachadh in1679, who had settled on Rum. One of them was the factor.[36]

It is more difficult to work out which of the soldiers in the regular battalions came from Coll than it is for the Fencibles and Volunteers, except when the muster rolls, in fading red ink, state, 'Labourer from Coll or Mull'.[37] Several served in the 79th Foot.

Old soldiers sometimes came home to Coll. Two such settled in Grimsary. Just below *Carn a'Bharraich* [Grid Reference NM 176557] in Grimsary are two ruined houses that are known as the Barracks. In the second half of the nineteenth century, these houses were inhabited by two old soldiers and their wives. Their names were John Maclean and Donald Macinnes. Neither was born on Coll, but probably on Coll's estate of Quinish in Mull.

---

[33] NAS. GD112. 52. 69. 6.
[34] TNA. WO13. 4169. Part 3.
[35] NAS. GD248. 661.1.1.
[36] *From Clan to Regiment,* 259.
[37] TNA. WO12. 8383.

John was certainly born in Kilninian in Mull in about 1780.[38] He probably joined 79th Regiment of Foot and is said to have served at the taking of Copenhagen and in the Peninsula. During one engagement he rushed over to the French lines, seized the regimental colours and returned, bringing them back in triumph amidst of a hail of bullets, yet he was unharmed. He attributed his safe return to having in his youth learned the Charm against death in war.[39]

John was living in Coll by 1851, when he is described as a Dublin Pensioner in Grimsary, aged 70, with a wife Margaret aged 60 and having both a house servant and a farm servant. He was still there at the time of the 1871 Census when he is described as a widower and a Chelsea Pensioner. On Coll, John Maclean was known as the *Pensioner Mor* and he was noted for his powerful build and good nature. As a result of his bearing and his military training, he was often chosen to officiate as 'caller out' at funerals.[40]

Two other pensioners lived in the same area as the *Pensioner Mor*, though not in the barracks. One was Hector Maclean, who lived at *Cnocleathan* (Broadhills, NM 172552] from 1820-1865. It is almost certainly Hector who is described by Gregorson Campbell as having a problem with an old woman who stole the laird's milk and could turn herself into a sheep or a hare.[41]

The other pensioner in the area was William MacKay (1784-1856). When he was a child, an old woman predicted that one day his golden curls would be entangled with the seaweed. He too joined the Cameron Highlanders, serving at the sieges of Copenhagen, Flushing, Cadiz and Burgos; in the campaigns in Portugal and Spain from 1808 until 1814; in Flanders and France from 1815-1818, and also at Corunna, Busaco, Fuentes de Oñoro, Salamanca, Pyrenees, Nivelle, Nieve, Toulouse and Waterloo.

John MacFadyen, the last of the Coll seanachies, told me that,

'After being discharged from the army MacKay came home with his wife and family and settled in a little thatched cot-

[38] From Clan to Regiment, 339.
[39] Ronald Black (ed) The Gaelic Otherworld (2005), 212.
[40] Betty MacDougall Folklore from Coll (no date), 35.
[41] The Gaelic Otherworld, 187.

*tage by the roadside on Ballard farm, where he intended
to spend the rest of his life quietly, and prove that Mor
Abradh's prophecy concerning him was all nonsense, he
would never again cross the oceans or leave the island.*

*He was fond of fishing off the rocks and his favourite
place was Grianaig Arileod. One afternoon he went and
didn't return when expected. A party went to look for him,
but darkness fell and the search had to be given up till the
following day, when his corpse and his fishing rod were
found entangled in the seaweed where the high tide had
left him on the beach.'*[42]

William MacKay's death certificate dated 7 February 1856,
states that he died by *'drowning – fell off a rock while fishing'*.[43]
What is one to make of these pensioners? Firstly I think it is
worth noting that they were remembered well into the late 20th
Century when so many others who lived in Coll at the same time
were forgotten. Secondly none of these pensioners were evicted
when John Lorne Stewart purchased the island. They were among
the few natives allowed to end their days in Coll. I suspect this
was because the old soldiers were respected, both by their peers
and by the new landowner. But why should they be the subjects
of such a number of superstitious stories? Perhaps a reader can
make a suggestion.

Following the end of the Napoleonic Wars and the beginning
of large scale emigration in 1819, the military ethos of the island
probably did decline. It was kept alive by the Waterloo veterans
coming home and telling their stories and certainly on Coll's
estate at Dervaig in Mull, it is said that *'the young men would be
delighted to be in one of the Highland Regiments'*.[44]

Superstitions concerning soldiers in Coll continued into the
twentieth century. In the First World War there was a family of
four Macinnes boys from Coll who joined the 51st (Highland)
Division. Hector MacDougall writes,

---

[42] BCP. John Hyne's book, 83-4.

[43] General Register Office. Register of Deaths. 551/2; *From Clan to Regiment,* 645.

[44] *Royal Commission(Highlands & Islands, 1892),* 870-881.

*'It was in the Spring of 1918 and we may recall those anx-
ious 'backs to the wall' days, and we may imagine how the
exhortation must have affected the parents and relatives
of those facing the final attack of the German hordes. The
mother of those four sons retained the full hope that her
sons would return safe and well, however, and I will now
explain the reason why.*

*On a certain morning when anxiety was at its height,
she and another woman had gone along to the machair to
procure some potatoes and convey them home from the
potato pit. Their conversation, naturally, was on the great
events now pending and the danger their absent relatives
were in. As they approached the potato pit four rabbits,
very much alive, scampered out of the pit and made off
over the machair. Kate [the mother] gave an exclamation of
delight. 'My four sons will come back to me safe and well',
she said and from then on till the Armistice was declared
in the following November she retained these undimmed
hopes, be the cause what it may, in which she was fully
justified, for her four sons came back safe and well.'*[45]

A sister of these Macinnes boys married James Mackinnon, a
fisherman in the East End of Coll. His ancestor, Hugh Mackinnon,
was originally from Feall and his wife Margaret Maclean was
descended from the Macleans of Coll. Two of their sons fought in
the Second World War. Hugh the elder, who died recently, was in
the 8th Argylls. He was captured at St Valery and for some reason
pretended to be Polish, speaking nothing but Gaelic to fox the
Germans. His brother Allan served in the 60th and was killed in
Tunisia in 1943.

Their nephew was one of my 'jocks' when we re-established
the T&AVR in Coll in 1972. It was a detachment of D (A&SH)
Company 51 Highland, which I commanded for two years after
leaving the regular army. In doing so I did not then realise that I
was following in the footsteps of my great-great-great grandfather
who had commanded the Rum Company of Argyll Volunteers
in the 1790s.

The detachment in Coll and others in North Argyll were

---

[45] BCP. Betty MacDougall Papers.

destroyed by the second sight. Big Archie Maclean, whose ancestor cut the trooper in half at Culloden, had second sight, as did
most of his family, including his cousin Neillie John, who ran the
ferry boat in Arinagour. One day, I was to run an exercise for the
Company in Islay and had gone ahead to organise it. The 'jocks'
were to follow later. One of them was Neil Galbraith, whose father
farmed Cliad in Coll. On his way to the pier he was stopped by
Neillie John, who said that if he went on the exercise, something
bad would happen. Neil went anyway.

In Oban he joined up with another soldier from Dunbeg and
they started drinking. By the time they got to Dumbarton they
were very drunk and my Sergeant-Major sent them home. They
went up to the station and fell asleep on the platform. In the early
hours of the morning a railwayman woke Neil and said, 'Have
you got a mate with you?' Neil said, 'Yes'. 'Well he's dead' said
the railwayman. Apparently Neil's companion had fallen asleep
too close to the track and when a freight train roared past, it had
sucked him under its wheels. All that were left were his boots.
This incident killed off the TA in North Argyll.

Why did the men from Coll join the army? In the First and
Second World Wars they had little choice. It is fashionable today
to say that in the eighteenth century men were forced out by
wicked lairds. Some may have been, but certainly not all.

I will leave the last word to a minister of the Free Church, Dr
Macintosh Mackay who had no love for lairds. He writes of the
year 1844 and says,

*'Though nearly the whole population of the island had
joined the Free Church, the chief [Hugh Maclean of Coll
(1782-1861)] believed that if proper arguments were addressed to them, and if personal influence were brought to
bear, they would return to the Establishment. He engaged
a minister he had confidence in to accompany him to Coll;
sent word fixing a particular Sabbath, and invited his clansmen and dependants ... to come and meet him.*

*Duly at the appointed time the chief was on the spot
with his champion. The people whom he had called were
seen gathering along the roads, but instead of meeting him
at the Established Church, they kept streaming past, on*

their way to the Free Church service in the open air. It was in vain that the chief addressed them, placing himself on the road along which they had to go, reasoning and remonstrating with groups and with individuals, urging them to come and at least give his friend a hearing. Their reply was respectful but firm refusal. 'Ask us anything but this', they said, 'and we are ready to comply; we will serve you – we will follow you as our fathers have followed your fathers in days of old – we will stand by you to the last – but our consciences are our own, and our religious convictions we cannot surrender.'

Dr Mackay went on to say that despite this incident *'there is still a very strong feeling of attachment to Mr Maclean and his family'*, and they were *'universally beloved by the people'*.[46]

I rest my case.

---

[46][46] Thomas Brown *Annals of the Disruption* (1893), 422-3.

THE ROLE OF THE MERCHANT SERVICE DURING BOTH WORLD CONFLICTS – WITH PARTICULAR EMPHASIS ON THE ISLE OF BARRA

Captain Roderick MacKinnon

To me, this succinct verse by Omar Khayyam portrays the futility of war more than any other expression of words I know, *'The worldly hope men set their Hearts upon, Turns Ashes – or it prospers, and anon Like Snow upon the Desert's dusty Face, Lighting a little Hour or two – is gone.'* I am of the opinion that if more men appreciated these words, there would be fewer wars!

I am glad that now the contribution made by men and women from the Highlands and Islands to both World Wars is becoming more widely known than it was in the years following both wars. This I put down to more prominence being given to the rest of the United Kingdom, due to an abundance of war correspondents, historians, journalists, writers and of course the media, and a dearth of the same, particularly in the Western Isles. Per capita, the contribution in terms of human resources made by the Western Isles to both wars is staggering. Percentages are more than twice as high when compared with other parts of the United Kingdom. During World War I, the tiny Isle of Barra alone – the southern most island in the Hebridean chain – provided over a thousand men and women in support of the war effort. The women went to the ammunition factories; the men to the Royal Navy, the Army and the Merchant Service. Seventy of the foregoing men lost their lives whilst serving, mostly in the Merchant Navy. There were decorations given out to some of those who died, and also to some of those who survived.

In 1939 came the Second World War, and once again, the male members of virtually every family on the island aged between sixteen and sixty five joined the forces; the Army, the RAF, the Royal Navy and the Merchant Service. Around 80% of these joined the Merchant Navy. In some instances three and four from the same family served. For instance my own father served in the *Athenia,* my eldest brother was torpedoed off Freetown, my second brother was bombed off Spitsbergen, and much against my mother's wishes, I signed up and served in the Atlantic for the last six months of the War. Eight seamen from the island, although fortunate enough to survive the sinking of their ships, were taken prisoners in Germany and Japan. Fifteen medals were awarded for various acts of courage and dedication to duty. Fifty-eight became casualties; they were either blown up, drowned, or died of thirst and starvation in open boats. It's worth noting that there were a number of other decorations and commendations awarded, but my information in respect of these is somewhat sketchy so I decided not to include them here. As most people are aware, the Merchant Navy was crucial to the survival of our beleaguered nation during the Second World War. In this respect, our debt to the men of the Merchant Service can never be repaid.

In 1939, at the beginning of the War, Admiral Donitz put fifty-seven U-Boats into the Atlantic. With these, he said he would blockade Britain and starve her into submission, and he nearly succeeded. In the dark days of 1942, he launched another three hundred and thirty-six U-Boats into the Atlantic, making a total of three hundred and ninety Boats, all hunting ships of the British Merchant fleet in the North and South Atlantic and Indian Ocean. Whilst the staff of the highly secret Naval Station, Bletchley Park, or Station X, as it was known to the British Admiralty, met with a large measure of success in breaking the German Enigma Code, we were somewhat cavalier about the security of our own codes. Thousands of signals were being sent out to Allied ships. The Germans were intercepting and decoding some 80% of these in 1942 and the beginning of 1943. This cost us dearly in both men and ships. In 1942, eleven hundred ships were sunk and 30,000 British seamen were forced to take to lifeboats. Far too many of these brave men were blown to pieces along with their ships, or died before they reached land or were picked up by rescue ships. In that year, 10,000 British seamen lost their lives. I clearly remember the arrival of some of the crew of a vessel called the *Oakcrest*. This ship, belonging to Crest Shipping, had a crew of forty four and was bound from Liverpool to New York when it was torpedoed by U-123, commanded by Karl-Heinz Moehle, 250 miles west of Fastnet and 500 miles west of Barra Head. One lifeboat with twenty four men aboard managed to escape the doomed vessel before she plummeted to the bottom. Twenty of the crew perished immediately following the attack by the U-Boat. Of the twenty four crewmen who escaped with their lives, ten were to die of hunger, thirst and exposure in dreadful weather conditions before they reached land, some 14 days later. Among the ten was a twenty two year old Barra man, one John MacKinnon of Glen. John died of exposure on the fifth day following the sinking, having been flung into the water after the torpedo struck. He was pulled into the lifeboat by his shipmates. The death of the young Barra man is reported by both the Registrar of Shipping in Cardiff, and the Tower Hill Memorial (Panel 75) as having taken place on the 22nd of November, 1940.

Fourteen days after the sinking, the lifeboat made landfall, driven ashore on the west coast of Barra island at 4 am on Sunday December 1st, during a particularly violent storm. There were fourteen crew members; one dead, one dying, and another four who were to die before daylight. Three died whilst trying to crawl ashore, a wave literally lifted the boat, which was broadside on to the beach, and crushed the three to death. The boat was driven ashore on a tiny shingle beach known as Bagh Heige. Long after the incident, people were still trying to figure out why the boat was not smashed to matchwood on the dangerous reef which stretches across the bay estuary which leads to the beach. Two of the more able crewmen scrambled ashore in order to summon help. On their way they came across a fresh water stream. Having run out of water several days before the landing, one literally drank himself to death. The other survived to reach a house one and a half miles away. Help was then organised.

All in all, thirty six of the forty four crew of the *Oakcrest* perished. The eight who survived were shipped to the mainland following a rest period on the island. Five bodies were interred on the Isle of Barra, and one was claimed by relatives and removed for burial on the mainland.

Another epic story, truly worthy of mention, is a tale of bravery and high endeavour. In 1942, the island of Malta was being constantly bombed by both German and Italian Air Forces. The besieged island was on the point of submission in August of that year. Britain wished to maintain control of Malta at all costs, it being of strategic importance. Churchill and his War Cabinet, well aware of the pummelling being dealt to Malta, decided to take desperate measures. Knowing that the island was close to giving in, they decided to come to the rescue with as much help as they could muster. Thus 'Operation Pedestal' was mounted. A convoy of fourteen ships set offloaded with food, ammunition, aircraft, aircraft spare parts, aviation fuel and other supplies for the beleaguered island, and escorted by fifty four men-of-war, i.e. two battleships, four aircraft carriers, twelve cruisers, and forty destroyers – it was the most guarded flotilla of ships ever to leave British waters. Churchill considered the island of Malta to be of such strategic value he was known to say, *'Even if half of the warships were destroyed, and only one merchant ship got through, the operation would be considered a success.'* Nine merchant ships, together with two carriers, four heavy cruisers and eight destroyers, were either sunk or badly damaged by German and Italian forces. Eventually four merchant vessels and the 10,000 ton oil carrier *Ohio* got through. The *Ohio* arrived two and a half days after the other four merchantmen. She was hit four times by German and Italian bombs. After each hit the fires were extinguished, and she limped into Valletta harbour escorted by three destroyers, one on each side and the third ahead, towing. Hundreds of cheering Maltese people lined the harbour to welcome the stricken tanker. She delivered all of her much needed aviation fuel. On board the *Ohio* was one Hector MacNeil from the Isle of Barra. The entire crew were commended for bravery and dedication to duty.

The merchant ships taking part were as follows, *Dorset, Rochester Castle, Port Chalmers, Santa Elisa, Almeria Lykes, Wairangi, Waimarama, Melbourne Star, Empire Hope, Clan Ferguson, Deucalion, Brisbane Star, Glen Orchy* and *Ohio.* The ships which got through the blockade were, *Rochester Castle, Port Chalmers, Brisbane Star, Melbourne Star* and of course the *Ohio,* an epic story in itself.

The loss of three hundred and fifty officers and men, and so many fine ships of the Merchant Navy and escorting fleet of the Royal Navy was grievous. The story of the ships of the Malta Convoy has a special place in the pages of maritime history. People are still stirred by the tales of high endeavour and supreme sacrifice.

This journal would not be complete without mentioning two brothers from the west side of Barra, Neil and Calum MacNeil. The younger of the two, Calum, was serving aboard the tanker *San Demetrio*, which, as we will see below, made maritime history, and several books and publications were written about her, including a book by Calum himself, simply named 'San Demetrio, London'.

The ordeal of the *San Demetrio* began at 4.30pm on November 6th 1940. Convoy HX 84, escorted by the armed Merchantman *Jervis Bay*, under the command of Captain Edward Fegan, was en route to the U.K. from Halifax, Nova Scotia. They were in mid Atlantic when over the horizon appeared the German Pocket Battleship *Admiral Scheer*. Captain Fegan, who immediately appreciated the danger the convoy was facing, ordered all ships to scatter, turned his own ship towards the pocket battleship and as soon as his guns were within range, opened fire. Captain Fegan was fully aware that his six inch guns were no match for the eleven inch guns of the *Admiral Scheer*. This action however, bought enough time for some of the remaining ships in the convoy to escape. A brave action indeed! Captain Fegan also knew that his ship faced certain destruction when he turned to engage the *Admiral Scheer*, yet he chose this path in order to give the other ships in the convoy a fighting chance. The *Jervis Bay* was reduced to a blazing hulk of twisted metal by the time the *Admiral Scheer* was finished with her. One hundred and ninety of her crew lost their lives, and only sixty five survived. They were picked up by the neutral Swedish ship *Stuneholm*. Captain Fegan, who was killed on the bridge of his ship, was later awarded a posthumous V.C.

The *San Demetrio* was also targeted by the German raider, by reason of her precious cargo. Tankers were always a prime target because of their valuable cargo. She was badly hit, and the order was given to abandon ship. As the lifeboats dropped astern, the crew could see that their ship was now ablaze from stem to stern. The raider kept firing at her, seemingly determined to sink her.

That night they saw four burning ships, one of them being the *Jervis Bay*. Every now and again star shells burst high in the sky as the raider continued to hunt for other prey. Huddled in one of the *San Demetrio's* lifeboats were sixteen officers and men, among them one Calum MacNeil from Barra. The weather had been fine, but by midnight a full gale was blowing. A sea anchor was launched in order to keep the boat head to wind. The Barra islander had been at the tiller ever since they left the blazing tanker. He was assigned this task by the Second Officer who later said, *'He knew more about small boats than anyone else on board.'* When dawn broke, they could see just exactly how high the sea was running. They also sighted the Swedish ship that had picked up the survivors from the *Jervis Bay* as well as survivors from some of the other ships that were sent to the bottom by the *Admiral Scheer*. These were not spotted by the Swede, which is not surprising, considering the height of the waves.

Around midday they sighted a tanker. Some five hours later they managed to pull up alongside. It turned out to be their own ship, the *San Demetrio*. She was still on fire, with a film of gasoline on the sea all around her. In mid Atlantic in November, dusk comes early, usually between five and six. As it was almost dark, they decided not to board the burning tanker that night. They dropped off astern, determined to keep her in sight, not an easy task with a full gale blowing. At daybreak she was nowhere in sight. Disappointed in the extreme, they decided to hoist a sail, the weather having moderated slightly. Then, by an extraordinary stroke of luck, they once again sighted the blazing tanker. Blow high or blow low, this time they decided to board her. I believe the words Calum used were, *'Better to fry than to freeze.'* She was burning in several places so they set about extinguishing the fires with buckets of water and fire extinguishers. Down below, the engineers set about getting up steam, in order to activate the pumps, so that the crew on deck could more actively tackle the fires. The sea water was up to the plates in the engine room, and pumps were needed to get rid of this hazard if they were to get the engines going.

By dawn the following morning, the Chief Engineer had enough steam pressure to operate the fire hoses. Before light came the following day, all the fires had been put out and the fractures, splits and cracks caused by the shelling were plugged. Practically all the food in the ship had been destroyed by the fire, but enough was found to sustain life. Shortly after the fires were put out, the engineers started the main engines. As soon as the vessel got under way, they headed East, guided only by the sun by day and the stars at night, the compass having been badly damaged when a shell nearly destroyed the entire bridge.

Eight days after the raider struck, the *San Demetrio* made landfall. There was great jubilation as it turned out to be Malin Head. The ship was then navigated to the Clyde under her own steam, with the assistance of a tug. Only a small quantity of the ship's cargo was lost; the remainder, some eight thousand tons, was discharged with the ship's own pumps.

Calum's brother Neil Macneil's story was somewhat different. Whilst serving as 2nd Officer aboard Lyle Shipping Company's *S.S. Cape of Good Hope*, his ship was torpedoed in the South Atlantic.

At 2.40pm on the 11th of May 1942, the *Cape of Good Hope* was shaken by a deafening explosion. All on board realised immediately that they had been torpedoed. Shortly thereafter, the order was given by the Master to abandon ship, it being clear that she was sinking fast. Everyone took up their respective stations on the boat deck and two lifeboats were launched without anyone displaying the least sign of panic. As the last boat pulled away from the sinking ship, the long grey hull of U-502 submarine was observed to surface approximately 2,000 yards distant. By now the ship was well down by the head and sinking fast, although apparently not fast enough for the sub commander (Jurgen von Rosenstiel), who opened fire with his 4.7 inch gun on the ship's superstructure, until finally the inevitable happened – a tremendous explosion, followed by a huge cloud of thick black smoke. Minutes later the *Cape of Good Hope* was swallowed up by the Atlantic forever.

The submarine then steamed slowly towards the two lifeboats, with her twin machine guns trained on each one. Everyone expected it to rake both lifeboats with machine gun fire. The suspense was both overwhelming and crushing. As the seconds ticked by and nothing happened, no one dared to relax. They knew only too well that they were far from being out of danger. U-boats had been known, before now, to machinegun survivors in lifeboats launched by sinking ships. However, when the U-boat stopped beside the lifeboats, the tension seemed to break. The commander addressed both lifeboat crews in excellent English, and asked if there was anyone injured. Fortunately there were no casualties so his services were not required in that respect. On learning that there were no injuries, he wished both boat crews a safe landfall and made off at high speed, leaving both boats and their crews at the mercy of the wind, sea and scorching sun, some seven hundred miles from the nearest land. The crew of the *Cape of Good Hope,* thirty-seven men in total, was divided between the two boats.

Before hoisting their sails and heading west, it was agreed that both boats were to keep within sight of each other for as long as possible. Thus they began a voyage to an unknown destination. The first night passed without incident. Spirits were high as everyone was certain they had a good chance of being sighted by a plane or rescue ship, which may have been dispatched in response to the distress message sent out before the ship was abandoned. Second Officer MacNeil, who was in charge of food and water, calculated that they had enough food for seven days. However, fresh water was their greatest problem. Soon they settled down to their daily routine and meals of corned beef, hard biscuits and condensed milk. A light North Easterly breeze prevailed throughout the night and the next day, enough to give the boat steerage-way with full sail set. Under the hot and copper sky, the sea was almost flat calm, with a long peaceful swell. At about 10.30am on the third day, Bowyer, the ship's gunner, was sitting in the bow. Suddenly he cried, '*I can see a plane right ahead!*' All eyes immediately turned in that direction. Sure enough, it was a plane and heading straight for them. The aircraft circled round the boats for some ten minutes then, diving close to them, they dropped two containers stocked with emergency rations and an encouraging message, assuring them that assistance was en route, and would arrive that night or the following morning. Sadly the promised assistance never materialised. During the days that followed, the wind, which had previously been in their favour, shifted round, coming in from the South West with much greater force. This made it necessary to tack in order to make a little headway in the right direction, or even hold their own. Dark clouds were gathering all around them and by noon it was deemed necessary to heave to, as it was now blowing a moderate gale. To stop drifting in the wrong direction and to keep the boat's head to wind, a sea anchor was put over the bow with an oil bag attached to it. This helped smooth the heaving seas which were now breaking all around them. As time passed, things didn't get any better. Heavy squalls and even rougher seas developed, which at times threatened to swamp the boat. During the night they lost their rudder, presumably due to the constant pitching and pounding of the boat. Immediately the situation became more serious. The boat could not be manoeuvred under sail except with the assistance of a steering oar, on which they could not altogether rely. They were now at the complete mercy of the wind. When it blew from an easterly direction, their spirits rose because they knew that it would eventually blow them to safety. On the other hand, when it shifted round to the South West, their spirits sank, because they were well aware that they were heading for disaster and probably death.

For two whole days they were hove to and still there was no sign of any assistance forthcoming. Finally the weather moderated slightly, so it was decided to set the sail once again, although the wind direction was not as favourable as they would have liked. In view of the fact that they were all growing weaker with every day that passed, they decided to ship four oars in an attempt to cover as much distance towards the West as possible while they had some strength left. That evening, to add to their misery, the boats lost sight of one another. On about the eighth day, the lack of water was beginning to take its toll. Their throats were parched and they could swallow only with the greatest of difficulty. The wind was now a little more favourable, and it was blowing them in a westerly direction at a fairly fast clip. They were all hoping for rain to ease their thirst and their dried up salivary glands. All that morning they watched showers approaching, only to fade away before any of them reached them. The elements, which had thrown everything else at them, seemed to deny them what would have been a luxury. Hour after hour, day after day, under a hot and azure sky, they sat in the torrid and blistering heat. They soaked their clothes in salt water every few minutes in an attempt to keep cool. To add to their apprehension, the sea around them was alive with sharks. All that morning they waited and waited for rain, but rain never came their way. They knew that if it did not rain before long, it was only a matter of time before death from thirst overtook them. They also knew that dying of thirst was a most terrible form of death. On the morning of the ninth day, someone suggested that they should pray for help. That afternoon, as if in answer to their prayers, the wind shifted abruptly to the North East and a tremendous black cloud appeared overhead. Soon, to their great joy and relief, down from the heavens poured the rain in great sheets. The deluge lasted for about half an hour, during which they all drank their fill, and filled every receptacle they could lay their hands on. The euphoria soon wore off however, as the sun appeared and began to beat down on them just as fiercely as ever. Relief came only when the sun set and darkness came. On the eleventh day, joy of joys, land was spotted. Indescribable elation took over every member of the boat crew. They did not know which country it was, but whether friendly or hostile, they were determined to land there.

When daylight came the next day, they saw a sailing sloop on the horizon, heading towards them. The sloop turned out to be the *Sparrow* of Virgin Gorda, commanded by Captain Robinson O' Neil. They were more than delighted when O'Neil informed them that the island on which they were about to land constituted a part of the British Empire. They were landed on Tortola in the Virgin Islands.

In the mid 1990s, three crew members from the Isle of Barra who survived the sinking of the *Cape of Good Hope* revisited the island of Tortola, where they received a tumultuous welcome. They were Captain Neil MacNeil, Roddy MacNeil A.B., then Second Officer and Malcolm Galbraith O.S.

As a footnote to the saga, we return to Commander Jurgen von Risenstiel of the U-502, one the top twenty U-boat commanders. On the 5th of July, whilst returning from the successful patrol in the Caribbean which saw the sinking of the *Cape of Good Hope*, U-502 was sunk in the Bay of Biscay by depth charges dropped from a British Wellington bomber from 172 Squadron. The entire crew of fifty-two went down with the boat, and the U-502 became the first submarine to be sunk by a Wellington bomber (http://uboat.net/).

Whilst remembering those who served, we also remember those who suffered, namely, the families left behind. It is difficult to imagine anything as sorrowful as the dreaded telegram sent to the relatives of war casualties, which always read the same, '*We regret to inform you, that your husband/son is missing in action, and is presumed lost.*'

The Isle of Barra was constantly reminded that a war was raging all around them. Its western shores, which are washed by the Atlantic, were the recipients of scores of bodies; from sunken Merchant ships, warships and downed aircraft, and sometimes of lifeboats with their dead, and half dead, tenaciously hanging on to life, but slowly dying of thirst, starvation, and hypothermia.

Apart from the devastation at sea and the considerable evidence continually being washed up on the island, Barra experienced other reminders of the war. On the night of May 12th 1942, Catalina JX 273 was flying a night operational exercise out of 302 FTU Base at Oban. Due to a slight navigational error, in which the light beacon at Castlebay harbour was mistaken for the Barra Head light, the aircraft dropped altitude to around three hundred feet. This would have been a perfectly safe manoeuvre, had they been where they thought they were as they would have been over the sea. Instead, they were heading straight for Heishival Mhor, a 619 foot high peak on the North side of Vatersay. On discovering their mistake, the pilot attempted to gain enough altitude to clear the peak. It wasn't to be. The Catalina crashed into the hillside, one hundred feet below the summit. Out of the crew of nine, three were killed outright and the other six escaped with varying injuries. Most of what remained of the aircraft's equipment was later shipped to the mainland.

There were services on and around Barra which also did their bit to help the war effort. For example, the RNLI lifeboat, manned by a crew from the island, was constantly called upon to answer distress calls from ships of every description. On the 5th of September 1943, such a call came from the steamship *Irlanda* which had run ashore off Idrigill Point during a S.S.E. gale. Following a daring feat of seamanship, her crew of fifteen were rescued from the stricken vessel by the lifeboat *Duke of Connaught*, coxswained by ex merchant navy man Murdo Sinclair. After sheltering for several hours ten miles away at Carbost, Isle of Skye, the lifeboat took five hours to journey the forty miles back across the Minch to Barra. For the foregoing rescue Coxswain Sinclair was awarded the coveted RNLI silver medal.

A proud Memorial now stands on a hill overlooking both the Minch and the Western Approaches, dedicated in 1993 to the one hundred and twenty eight brave men who made the ultimate sacrifice in the cause of freedom, during both World Wars.

Courage under the threat of death, as displayed by so many of the young men who fought in both World Wars in order to preserve their way of life, is I think very aptly depicted by a log entry written by the Master of the sailing ship *Curlew,* wrecked under the iron cliffs of Tierra Del Fuego, in the year 1853. It reads as follows, '*New fashions dispossess the old, and the world moves on, but eternally unchanging are men and the sea, each to the other bosom friend, yet mortal enemy. Our shipmates endured, then perished, with God their only witness.*'

WALKING IN THE FOOTSTEPS OF HEROES

M. N. Beaton and W. McGonagle

'I could see that our leading waves had got caught by their kilts.
They were killed hanging on the wire, riddled with bullets, like
crows shot on a dyke'

Pte. J S Reid, 2nd Seaforths

'I did see poor Aggy Fife (one of our pipers). He was riddled with
bullets, writhing and screaming. Another lad was just kneeling,
his head thrown right back. Bullets were just slapping into him,
knocking great bloody chunks off his body.'

Pte J Elliot.

"I vividly remember Colonel Ritson standing in the British front
line, tears streaming down his face, saying over and over "My
God! My boys, my boys!""'

L/Cpl S Henderson.

In July 2008, Urras an Eilean, a Skye based Gaelic charity, orga-
nized a visit to the great battlefields of Flanders and Normandy,
particularly those that involved the 51st Highland Division. It
hardly seems credible today that these men, many of them just
teenagers, could advance into the mad slaughter of these battles
as machine gun bullets whistled round their ears, shells exploded
in front of them and comrades fell all round them. Small wonder
then that the imposing memorial to the Highlanders at Beaumont
Hammel bears the Gaelic inscription 'Là a bhlàir 's math na càir-
dean' (In the day of battle it is good to have comrades) and that
the famous pipe tunes 'The Taking of Beaumont Hammel' and
'The Battle of the Somme' seem to have a very special resonance.

Today these battlefields hide their terrible secrets well and
it is difficult to imagine the horror and the hellish carnage that
took place there. It is best described in the words of the men who
were there:

'Lice, rats, barbed wire, fleas, shells, bombs, bodies, blood,

65

alcohol, artillery, filth, bullets, death – that's war. It's the devil's work.'

'Amid the explosions, with bullets raining down on us, we saw those who had been killed in the earlier fighting and buried in the ground being blown out of their graves by shells.'

'At the medical posts the limbs were piled up as the surgeons amputated them. Some of the men had gangrene that made even the kindliest orderlies go outside to vomit because the smell was so vile.'

'I walked by a soldier who was choking on mud that reached up to his knees. We could not get him out so we left him there. After two days the poor man was still there but we could only see his head and he had gone mad.'

The Battle of Festubert

In early May 1915, the commander of the British Expeditionary Force, Field Marshall Sir John French, came under severe pressure to support a major French offensive at Artois, so he ordered his First Army under General Sir Douglas Haig to attack Festubert. The British attack took place, for the first time in the war, under cover of darkness and the onslaught was preceded by an artillery bombardment of the German trench line lasting 60 hours.

On the evening of Monday 17th May 1915, the 4th Camerons, a territorial battalion formed at Inverness, which contained a large number of Gaelic speaking islanders, received orders to take 500 yards of German trench line at the end of which were ruined houses which the Germans had converted into machine gun posts. Despite the appalling conditions, they succeeded in taking the German trench, but they found the fortified houses too strongly held and when the Germans counter attacked the Camerons came under intense fire. To make matters worse, the neighbouring battalion which was to have advanced in line with them had been held up and they realised that their position had become untenable.

They suffered heavy losses that day, including their commanding officer Colonel Fraser, Captain D.F. MacKenzie (Dunvegan), who was secretary of the Gaelic Society of Inverness, Captain Ronald MacDonald (Portree), CSM William Ross (Portree) and many others. It is reported that when the news of the day's events finally reached Skye, the ministers in the village of Portree alone had 26 death messages to deliver. Dugald MacEchern gives a vivid description of the burial of Captain MacKenzie in his book 'The Sword of the North,'

> *'He fell at Festubert, where the 4th Camerons with desperate bravery had taken German trenches, from which however they had to withdraw, no adequate support being at hand. Captain Roderick McErlich having discovered where Captain MacKenzie's body was lying, he and Lt Col. Murdoch Beaton determined to bury it although it was not far from the German trench.*

> *Three men volunteered to help – Lt (Then Sgt) Donald MacDonald, Sgt Major Duncan MacMillan and Sgt Malcolm MacLean – all three from the island of Raasay. The body was lying in the open just beyond a ditch along which the Camerons had passed in that terrible battle. Beaton, McErlich and their three companions tied their kilts around their waists and moved along the ditch which contained water, dead bodies, mud and green slime with rank grass on its lip. When they arrived opposite the body McErlich and MacDonald, being the best shots, lay on guard with their rifles over the lip of the ditch, MacMillan and MacLean took the spades and Colonel Beaton directed. Cpt. MacKenzie lay curled up as if asleep and as they dug upwards towards the body it gently rolled down towards them. Then they dug a grave in the bank, removed his New Testament from his tunic pocket and interred the body, raising over it a little cross. The distance between this spot and the German trench has since been measured – it was exactly 64 yards.'*

It is interesting to note that the body of Capt. MacKenzie was subsequently lost and he is now commemorated on the Le Touret memorial near Festubert and on the Dunvegan War Memorial.

When the British attack at Festubert ended on May 27th, Col. Harry Walker of the Black Watch addressed his men with the words '*Well lads, you may have been boys yesterday; but you're men today – yes men.*' They had won territory a mile in depth across a 3000 yard front, but at a high price – British casualties numbered 16,000, while German losses totalled 5000 men, and it would seem quite probable, given these statistics, that more Highlanders were killed at Festubert than at Culloden where total casualties on both sides came to around 2000 men.

The 2008 Pilgrimage

> '*Yours is a pilgrimage in memory of those who passed this way. You will tread reverently, for it is holy ground. It is the shrine of those who won the right for us all to have a country of our own.*'
>
> Battlefield Guidebook

1. Ypres and the Menin Gate

The group took a leading part in the Last Post ceremony at the Menin Gate in Ypres watched by a crowd estimated at over one thousand visitors. This imposing memorial bears the names of over 56,000 soldiers whose bodies were never found. It was an awesome setting and there was not a dry eye in the house as it echoed to the sound of the great highland bagpipes playing 'Amazing Grace', while a wreath was being laid by Farquar MacBeath from Glenelg and Norman Stoddart from Skye. It is believed that this was only the second time this sober, daily ritual was performed in Gaelic. The following is a list of the Skye men who died in the Ypres salient and whose bodies were never found – it is not difficult to imagine how long that list would be if it included the whole of the Highlands and Islands.

Menin Gate and Tyne Cot – Ypres

Sgt John Robertson, Portree, Canadian Infantry
Pte Charles MacLean, Broadford, Canadian Infantry
Pte William Mackinnon, Milovaig, Camerons
Gdsmn John Smith, Milovaig, Scots Guards
Pte Roderick MacKenzie, Waternish, Gordons
Lt Godfrey MacDonald, Sleat, Scots Guards *(Son of Lord
& Lady MacDonald – he had two brothers also killed in action
and his son was killed in North Africa in 1942)*
Pte John Campbell, Struan, Camerons
L/Cpl Ian MacLeod, Broadford, Camerons
Pte Kenneth MacNeill, Glenmore, Camerons
Pte Charles Martin, Raasay, Camerons
Pte Alexander Robertson, Ferrindonald, Sleat, Camerons
Pte Archie MacKenzie, Sligachan, Camerons
Cpl Kenneth MacKay, Vatten Bridge, South African Infantry
Pte Murdo Graham, Isleornsay, Canadian Infantry
Pte James MacPherson, Calligarry, Sleat, Australian Infantry
Pte John MacLeod, Mill Place, Raasay, Camerons
Pte Peter MacInnes, Aird Bernisdale, Seaforths
Pte Malcolm MacDonald, Staffin, Black Watch
Pte Ewen MacKinnon, 1 Bayfield, Portree, Seaforths
Pte Ronald Lamont, Uig, Argylls
Pte Donald Martin, Raasay, Argylls
Pte Neil Chisholm, Kildonan, Camerons
Pte John MacLean, Borreraig, Glendale, Camerons
Sgt. John Rankin, Waternish, Seaforths
Pte Forbes Nicolson, Teangue, Sleat, Camerons
Sgt George MacLeod, 1 Mill Road, Portree,
Northumberland Fusiliers
Cpt. Malcolm Graham, Uig, Gordons
Pte John Stewart, Portree, Camerons
Pte Roderick MacNeill, Bridge Cottage, Struan, Camerons
Pte Donald MacKenzie, Carbost, Camerons.
Pte Angus Ross, Idrigill, Machine Gun Corps
Lt. John Angus MacKinnon, Stenscholl, Staffin, Royal
Berkshire Regt.

'WHO WILL REMEMBER PASSING THROUGH THIS GATE THE UNHEROIC DEAD WHO FED THE GUNS'

These rather bitter lines were written at the Menin Gate by Siegfried Sassoon, the great war poet – he is answered once a day, every day of the year.

2. The Somme and Festubert

The group visited the battlefields and memorials of the Somme and in the late afternoon again held a short service of remembrance in the cemetery in Festubert. The small, immaculately maintained cemetery in this rural French village has just over 1000 burials including two brothers, Duncan and Neil MacInnes, the sons of William and Maria MacInnes who lived at Mill Bridge in Broadford. They were with the Cameron Highlanders near Festubert on 22nd July 1915 when a shell landed among the men of "B" Company. Eight men, all from the Islands, were killed, five of whom came from Skye – along with the MacInnes brothers were Private Murdo MacSwan, aged 21 from Duirinish, Private James Mackinnon, aged 19, from Torrin and Private Donald MacRae from Scullamus. Private MacRae's brother Neil, also in the 5th Camerons, was killed at Loos on 25th September 1915, some two months later. Who can even begin to imagine the agonies of grief that the families of these young men endured.

At the conclusion of the service the pipers played a new tune composed by Blair Douglas 'Laoich Festubert' (The Heroes of Festubert) and, taking place as it did beside the gravestones of so many of our young men, this was a most poignant and moving experience.

The event was much appreciated by the local population, who came out of their houses and were waving and cheering. One farmer who happened to be passing on his tractor at the time immediately pulled over onto the verge, switched off the engine, jumped off and stood to attention until the ceremony was over. The following is a list of the Skye men who perished at Festubert and who have no known grave and again we can only imagine how long it would be if it included the whole of the Highlands and Islands.

Le Touret Memorial

'We could not believe that we were expected to attack in such appalling conditions. I never prayed so hard in all my life. I got down on my knees in the mud and I prayed to God to get me through'

Pte Norman MacAskill, Geary, Seaforths
L/Cpl Duncan MacRae, Portree, Seaforths
L/Cpl Alasdair MacDonald, Coillore, Struan, Seaforths
Pte Neil MacMillan, Edinbane, Camerons
Pte John Grant, Portree, Camerons
Cpl Kenneth MacDonald, Raasay, Camerons
Pte John MacFarlane, Beaumont Cres., Portree, Camerons. *(His father built the war memorial in Portree)*
Pte Ian MacKinnon, Elgol, Camerons
L/Sgt Donald MacLeod, 1 Mill Road, Portree, Camerons
Pte John Nicolson, 3 Bayfield, Portree, Camerons
CSM William Ross, Portree, Camerons
Cpl Charles Sinclair, Marine House, Portree, Camerons
L/Cpl James MacGregor, Portree, Camerons
Cpt. David H MacKenzie, Dunvegan, Camerons
L/Cpl William Turnbull, Portree, Camerons *(Son of Thomas Turnbull, Registrar and involved in the business of Thomas Turnbull & Son)*
L/Cpl William MacDonald, Portree, Camerons
Pte John MacDougall, Portree, Camerons
Pte John Robertson, Medical student at Broadford Hospital, Camerons
Pte Donald MacLean, 9 Roag, Camerons
Gdsmn William MacInnes, 7 Scullamus, Scots Guards

'THOSE TO WHOM THE FORTUNE OF WAR DENIED THE KNOWN AND HONOURED BURIAL GIVEN TO THEIR COMRADES IN DEATH'

3. St Valery-en-Caux

The group visited St Valery en Caux, where acts of remembrance in which the local people also took part were held in the military cemetery in the town and at the memorial to the 51st Highland Division (a large pillar of granite taken from Rubislaw quarry in Aberdeen and placed on the clifftop overlooking the town). Afterwards the group were taken to the Town Hall for a civic reception during which the Mayor presented special medals to Johnnie Matheson and Willie MacKenzie, two Seaforth Highlanders who had been captured at St Valery in 1940 and who had endured the infamous long walk into captivity. The day was rounded off with the pipers playing on the steps of the Town Hall, a recital which was much appreciated and cheered to the echo by the people of St Valery who could not do enough to show their gratitude for what the Highland regiments had done both in 1940 – and in 1944 when the 51st Division were the liberators of the town following the D-day landings.

Perhaps the feelings of the population of this small, picturesque French town who made us feel so welcome can best be summed up by quoting from an e-mail received after our return home,

> 'We were very pleased to meet your group and I want you to tell them that I think of them every day. Maybe you will be back on June 14th, the anniversary of the Battle of St Valery-en-Caux. St Valery-en-Caux remain sacred land of the Highlanders and we will never forget THAT OUR HIGHLANDERS gave their lives for us.
> All my best wishes
> Raphael Distante'

HEBRIDEAN SERVICE WITH THE ROYAL NAVY

Donald John Macleod

Hebridean Service with the Royal Navy is a vast subject, but I will try to do some justice to this important part of our maritime history. I am not a scholar but I hope that the information that I have put together relating to the naval saga of our progenitors may be of interest to you.

Those who are unacquainted with the interesting history of the Western Isles of Scotland are surprised when they learn of the large quota of sailors, soldiers and, in World War II, airmen, from the islands who have served in the forces of the Crown.

Having been, metaphorically, 'born on the sea' it is natural that the islanders would enrol in the Royal Navy or voyage on the oceans with the Merchant Navy. There is little doubt that some of the seafaring qualities and roving instincts of the Western Islanders have been inherited from their Norse progenitors. Barbara E. Crawford in her book, 'Scandinavian Scotland' states, *'The sea culture of the Western Isles has been pinpointed as a significant legacy of the Viking Age in the West.'*

It is likely that the first time our islanders sallied forth as a coherent naval force was in 1263, when the Viking longships from the Western Isles joined King Haakon's fleet to fight the Scots at the Battle of Largs. But it is not until islanders began joining the Royal Navy that we begin to get an understanding of just how competent they were as seamen. For instance, even as early as 1801, the Naval Chronicle stated, *'The inhabitants of the Western Isles of Scotland or Hebrides are all so accustomed to a seafaring life, and retain so much of the native heroism of ancient Highlanders, that almost everything great and successful may be hoped from their gallantry during the war.'* This was obviously the opinion of a very senior naval officer.

We find this type of account, praising Hebridean seamen, in books, newspapers and journals right through the centuries. More recently for instance, in 1940, during the dark days of the war, naval officers were commenting on the islanders' prowess at sea,

'*Of course, no ship has its real complement of seamen without men from Stornoway in the Hebrides.*' ('Terriers of the Fleet')

Researching the history of the islanders at sea has its own difficulties and unlike the Army, where local regimental records are an excellent source of information, it is much more difficult to research the services of islanders in the Navy. Naval records are mostly held in archives and repositories in the South of England, making it an expensive and time consuming task for anyone from Scotland engaged in the research of naval history. However, we are lucky in one respect, and that is the ability to identify men of Hebridean extraction by their names. Any Donald John MacLeod that you come across is almost certainly of Hebridean extraction, and not from the Rhonda Valley (although sometimes you can never tell).

But research also leads us in other strange directions, from which we can draw some conclusions. Witness the advertisement that appeared in 1708 in the 'Edinburgh Courant'. The advertisement asked for a person who could play the bagpipes, and who was willing to engage on board a British man-of-war. Presumably there were plenty of Scots on board including islanders. This was only one year after the Treaty of Union was signed. A similar request came much later, when the captain of a naval patrol boat in 1940 asked the Scottish Piping Society of London to send him a set of bagpipes, as fully 90% of his crew were from the Hebrides.

Information I have come across relating to the Royal Navy in the 18th century shows a number of seamen with island surnames. In 1785, for instance, the South Sea Company chartered a vessel called the *King George* for a voyage of trade and discovery around the world. The chief mate on this ship was a MacLeod, who died on board ship and was buried on French Island in the China Seas. We cannot ascertain if MacLeod was an islander, but the way his surname is spelt it is likely that he had kinship with the Hebrides. This information proves that in the 18th century, a man bearing an island surname was considered to be such a capable officer that he was selected for this important voyage (Life and Adventures 1776-1808 by John Nicol, Mariner).

Two others who may have had roots in the Islands are William Morrison, who in 1796 was one of ten seamen hanged for mutiny at Sheerness, and it's possible that Morrison was one of the many men who had been impressed by the Navy. Also there is Peter MacKinnon, a ship's gunner who in 1797 was one of the witnesses at the trial of the mutineers from *HMS Monmouth*.

The work of James Shaw Grant shows that James Morison from Stornoway was one of the mutineers on the *Bounty* in 1789 and was sentenced to death. Later Morison was reprieved and served with distinction until he was drowned on *HMS Blenheim* in 1807. Morison may have had delusions of grandeur, as on his left leg he had a garter tattooed with the motto of the Order of the Garter, '*Honi soit qui mal y pense*,' (Evil be to him who thinks evil).

We know, of course, regarding recruitment (if you can call it that), that the Royal Navy was manned by impressed men, criminals supplied by courts and men escaping from incarceration in the Debtor's prison. In the 17th and early 18th centuries, the reputation of the Navy was of a harsh and oppressive life. Floggings were common-place, food was insufficient, and being eaten by lice and ravaged by disease were customary. Life on board ship was truly horrendous; sailors had to eat salt junk, drink stinking water and try and rest in the distressing darkness of the cockpit. In action, conditions were so bad that the men perspired profusely and often vomited in the roaring hell of the gun deck. It is no surprise then that the relationship between our islanders and the Navy was not always harmonious, especially when the press gangs prowled both land and sea to hunt down able-bodied men.

Service with '*na balaich-ghorma*' (the boys in blue) was not popular and islanders hid from the press gangs in caves on the moor, under upturned boats on the seashore, in fanks, barn lofts and any other hideaway they could find. They also lived with the knowledge that their houses could be raided at any time, and the men taken away by the Navy, never to return to their homes.

Believe it or not, I owe my existence to the press gang. My great, great grandfather, Murdo MacDonald (Murchaidh Mac Ian, 1788-1876) from Enaclete, Uig, as a teenage lad, was taken by his father over the mountains to Ardhasaig, Harris. There he was left with a friend of the family, who was entrusted to keep Murdo safe from the press gang. Murdo was concealed from the press gang but not, it seems, from the fair maidens of Harris, and later he was pressed into another service, (and I hope a more pleasant one), that of marriage to my great, great grandmother, Isabella MacLeod (1787-1861) in Ardhasaig.

The seriousness of the problem and the lengths to which the Navy would go to impress men is illustrated well by an incident in Lochs in 1808, where the Minister in the Parish Church of Lochs summoned the parishioners to attend the church on a religious pretext. Once the congregation was seated, the church doors were locked from outside. Then the press gang entered and dragged away all the able-bodied men. I do not know if any of these men ever returned home.

At Knockaird, Ness, all the males in the village between 16 and 60 years of age were marched away by the press gang. The women folk tried to free them but their attempts were foiled by the soldiers prodding the women's breasts with the point of their bare bayonets. Years later a sole survivor, John MacDonald, returned home, only to find that his old father had been evicted from his croft.

Norman MacLeod, Mangersta, along with many others from the parish of Uig, was impressed into the army. They fought in the ill-fated expedition against the Turks in Egypt and the few who survived returned home blind. Norman though blind, became a noted preacher in Uig.

For many islanders, the press gang was just the start of their problems, as Gaelic speakers were frequently flogged for not understanding orders given by officers with English public school accents. Some islanders were saved from this abuse and pain, due to the fact that they learned English from East Coast fishermen, or from East Coasters who worked at many curing stations in the islands. My uncle, Donald MacLeod (Timsgarry, in Uig), for instance, spent a large part of his life working on East Coast fishing boats, and was as fluent in Doric as in Gaelic. Those who spoke the two languages were referred to as having the '*two spokes*', as an island wit once described a person fluent in Gaelic and English.

For the researcher, the stated place of birth of some seamen bearing island surnames can be very deceptive. I suspect that in some instances the place of birth shown is actually where the man enlisted, or where he was seized by the press gang. The Navy did not keep accurate records of their sailors; here are some examples

I have come across,

Donald MacLeod, place of birth, *'Believed Greenock.'*
Murdo MacLean, shown as having been born in Tipperary, Ireland.
Donald McLoud, address shown as Shadwell, (London docklands).
Mordock Morrison , address shown as Ratcliffe Highway, (London docklands).
Angus McDonald, shown as born in New York.

I suspect that all these seamen were Hebrideans, if not by birth, at least by descent.

In military records the birth-place of islanders is frequently shown as Ross-shire or Inverness-shire, the counties that administered the Western Isles before Comhairle nan Eilean Siar was established.

The most famous battle in British naval history, the Battle of Trafalgar in 1805, saw seamen from the Hebrides serving on a number of the ships. There were at least fifteen seamen who bore the Lewis surname of MacLeod, the surname being spelt in a number of ways; for instance, McLeod, McLoud and McCloud. Often the place of birth is not listed:

Quarter Master's Mate Murdh Mc Leod, *HMS Spartiate,* is shown as born on *'Loose Island'*, definitely Lewis. Obviously he gave his name in Gaelic, 'Murchadh' (Murdo) and it was written down as 'Murdh.' He was possibly impressed into the service.
Carpenter's Mate James McLeod, born Scotland. Being employed in this capacity indicates that he was probably from a boat-building family, possibly in the Hebrides.
Lieutenant Roderick McLeod, *HMS Minotaur,* no birthplace shown.
Marine William McLeod, *HMS Revenge,* no birthplace shown.
There are two John McClouds shown as born in Whitehaven, Cumbria. This was a major seaport at the time and I wonder if they were seized by the press gang from a

merchant ship berthed in this seaport.

William McLeod, *HMS Orion*, no birthplace shown.

Able Seaman Thomas McCloud, born America.

In addition I have identified some other islanders at Trafalgar:

Master's Mate James Robertson, Stornoway, served on *HMS Victory* with Lord Nelson, and may have assisted in hoisting the signal '*England expects*.......'

Able Seaman Angus Campbell, *HMS Agamemnon*, Isle of Harris.

Lieutenant Donald Campbell, Royal Marines, also served on this ship, and I wonder if they were related.

Able Seaman John MacIver, age 34, *HMS Ajax*, born Lewis.

Ordinary Seaman Malcolm MacDonald, age 23, *HMS Bellerophon*, born Lewis.

Able Seaman John Morrison, age 24, *HMS Leviathan*, born Stornoway.

Able Seaman William Campbell, age 26, *HMS Revenge*, born 'Lowesh.' He obviously gave his birthplace in Gaelic, 'Leodhas' (Lewis.)

Ordinary Seaman Malcolm McNeil, *HMS Prince*, born Scotland. Judging by the surname he may be from Barra.

Able Seaman Angus MacDonald, *HMS Ajax*, no birthplace shown.

Alexander MacKenzie, *HMS Orion*, birthplace not shown.

Buried in the chapel at Eye Cemetery is Lieutenant John Morison, from Aignish, who was held in such high regard by Lord Nelson that the latter presented his walking stick to him. His tomb has been neglected and has fallen into ruin. We seem adept at ignoring our local history.

When a ship returned to a naval depot in the south of England after a long tour, the crew were not allowed ashore in case they deserted. The shore, however, came to them and naval ships were soon surrounded by small boats filled with drink, women, goods and swindlers. With the women came drink, and very soon there was bedlam on the lower deck. The living quarters on a ship in port became filthy and fights were commonplace. After the ship sailed, many seamen learned that 'Lovely Nan' was not as lovely as she first appeared.

As well as the disgusting living conditions, more often than not the true danger to the men was not the enemy at all, as witnessed by a naval report from 1810, which gives the following break-down of the death rates of ratings; 56% of the men died as a result of disease, 31% died as a result of accident on board ship and only 5% were killed by the enemy.

I remember in my youth hearing the story of Seoltair (Sailor) MacAulay from Uig, who had a leg blown off below the knee in a naval battle. To quench the flow of blood he stuck the stump in a barrel of tar. How he made it back to Lewis is unknown. However, even more amazing is the fact that he then bought a boat and with one leg managed to fish the stormy seas west of Uig under sail for many years. He died at a ripe old age and the ruins of his house can still be seen beside the first house at Cliff, on the left hand side of the road to Valtos.

Once the wars had ended or ships had returned from foreign stations, the seamen were often dumped on the dockside, usually in naval ports in the south of England. They had little money and no sooner were they ashore than they were often easy prey for prostitutes, criminals and publicans, all well versed in the art of swindling sailors. Impressed men from the Hebrides would have been amongst the many destitute sailors who died as emaciated starving vagrants in the alleyways and passages of London, Portsmouth, Chatham and Plymouth.

With the expansion of the British Empire and the phenomenal growth of our merchant fleet during the 19th century, the Royal Navy had to be strengthened to protect our trade routes. Given the islanders' reputation as capable seamen, it is no surprise then that the Admiralty established a base in Stornoway in 1874 to train naval reservists.

At one period this station was the largest in the UK and according to naval reports, the physique and efficiency of these Reserve-men were surpassed by none.

I now wish to mention some islanders whose acumen and expertise contributed to the operational functions and training schedules of the British and American Navies:

Captain John Robertson from Stornoway was one of the most capable skippers in the China tea trade. On his voyages to the Far East he charted the China Seas. The Admiralty asked for his charts which they copied. This enabled Royal Navy ships to navigate in these eastern waters.

In the First World War a Lewisman, William A. Martin, was one of the most influential men in Britain involved with the war at sea. He was responsible for planning and organising the convoy system. Surprisingly he was not a seaman, but an officer in the London Scottish regiment. Appointed chief assistant to Sir Norman Leslie at the Ministry of Shipping, Martin was given the crucial task of operating and directing the convoy system.

Lieutenant Commander Alexander MacKenzie, from Shader in Point, served with the U.S. Navy during WW1 and wrote a text-book on navigation that was, and probably still is, used by the US Navy.

During WWI, Captain Alexander MacDougall from Islay conceived the idea of prefabricating ships in foundries to make good the heavy ship losses. Between 1917 and 1918, thirty-seven ships were built in his MacDougall-Duluth shipyards, USA.

Captain Donald MacLean, from Stornoway, was seconded to the Royal Navy College at Greenwich in WWII. He invented the MacLean Pilotage Teacher and the MacLean Rule of the Road Teacher, and both were adopted by the Admiralty for instruction in the Royal Navy. After the war he became Commodore of the Cunard Line and commanded the *Queen Mary* and the *Queen Elizabeth*.

Lieut. Commander Donald MacLennan, from Tong, was the first British naval officer to enter the notorious Japanese prisoner of war camp at Changi, Singapore in 1945.

And, finally, let us not forget Thomas MacLeod from

Stornoway, who has created for himself a niche in maritime history, by being the only seaman who sailed with both Scott and Shackleton on their voyages of exploration to the Antarctic.

Of course in 1914, recruitment became conscription and thousands of islanders were mobilised into the Navy and the Army on the outbreak of war. Hundreds of island fishermen who were fishing on the East Coast were called up, and not one was allowed back to the Hebrides to visit relations. Many of them were lost in the war without ever being allowed home on leave.

The price was often high. In Fraserburgh, a young herring girl from North Tolsta waved goodbye to six of her brothers who were mobilised from fishing boats in the harbour. Along with another brother, these seven Campbells served with the Royal Navy Reserve, possibly a British record for the number from one family serving as naval reservists. King George V sent a personal letter of congratulation to their widowed mother. Three of the Campbell brothers made the supreme sacrifice, but there was no letter of sympathy from the King after the war.

Being well-trained in gunnery at the base in Stornoway, many island reservists were drafted on to merchant ships, where they earned the reputation of being fearless and intrepid gunners.

The seafaring capability of the Western islanders even made the *Sydney Sun* in 1915 after *HMS Orama* docked in that seaport. I quote a couple of sentences from the article, '*There is a big grey ship in the harbour just now, which holds things more terrible than even her grim exterior suggests. She numbers amongst her crew 70 sailors who speak nothing but Gaelic, and 25 of them are MacLeods. No wonder the German ship Navarra tried hard, though in vain to escape.*' The gunnery instructor on *HMS Orama* was Chief Petty Officer Roderick MacLeod, from Back, who served in and survived six wars between 1886 and 1945.

Further publicity enhancing the islanders' seafaring reputation occurred in 1916 when naval reservists from Lewis, serving on *HMS Emperor of India,* won the Fleet Rowing Race and were presented with the Admiral's Cup. They defeated all the regular Royal Navy rowing teams and this caused consternation amongst senior naval officers who, in the main, despised reservists.

The senior officers were astonished when a team of supposedly amateurish RNR rowers beat the semi-professional regular navy rowing teams of the Grand Fleet.

Well, it's no surprise really, as the champion rowers were all ex-fishermen who, since boyhood, were accustomed to rowing in the seas around the coast of Lewis. Eight cutters took part in the final, seven regular navy teams and one from the Royal Naval Reserve. In the preliminary rounds, some of the other crews said there was no use in them taking part in the final if the big High-land fellows from the *Emperor of India* were going to compete. On the day of the race a stiff head wind was blowing and there was a choppy sea running. The distance to be covered was around three miles and for two of those miles the naval team that had won the cup on several occasions kept a good lead. The Coxswain, Andrew Coull from Montrose started shouting, '*Na Gaidheal air guaillibh a cheile, remember you are Highlanders. Now my lads, come on, let us show them all what we can do.*' The Lewismen responded, and, with a powerful spurt, slashed through the surg-ing waves with such speed that it appeared as if the other boats had dropped anchor. When the victors returned to the *Emperor of India*, the officers mustered the whole crew on deck and the islanders stepped on board amidst the deafening cheers of their shipmates.

To these island reservists who were born and bred to the sea, rowing a naval cutter with light oars was like a day's holiday. They could handle small boats with a dexterity all of their own. Donald Nicolson, North Tolsta, was the stroke oarsman, making him a very important member of the crew. For the remainder of WWI, the Royal Navy felt humiliated because they were beaten by a crew from the Royal Naval Reserve in the Fleet Rowing Race. The Admiral's Cup is nowadays competed for annually by yachts at Cowes, Isle of Wight.

There is no reliable record of the actual number of Western islanders who served with the Royal Navy and the Royal Naval Reserve in WWI. The figure of around 3,500 is normally the one quoted for Lewis but, if we add men from Harris, Uist, Benbecula and Barra, we can be fairly sure the number is probably in excess of 4,000. This figure must, of course, have been much higher, as it does not take into account all the islanders who were resident in many UK cities, nor those, (and there were many) who were domiciled overseas.

Many islanders travelled at their own expense from overseas so that they could enlist. Some of them, like John MacDonald, from Balallan, did not even make it to our shore. He was drowned on the way home from Patagonia in 1914 on *SS Vine*. He, like many others, has not been listed amongst the war dead, but it's my belief that these men should be honoured in the same way as any soldier killed in the front line.

In WWII, Donald MacLeod, from the same village, returned home from Peru, and was drowned on *SS St Sunniva* in 1943. His brother, Angus John, was drowned a year later on the naval tug *Adherent*.

The islanders flocked to the Navy and the true level of their losses is harrowing. Eleven Lewis reservists were drowned when *HMS Clan Macnaughton* mysteriously disappeared in the Atlantic in February 1915. One of those lost was 17 year old Dugald Kennedy from Calbost, who had been a survivor from *HMS Hermes* four months earlier, when barely 16 years of age.

At the Battle of Jutland in 1916, one of the worst of the British losses was that of the battle cruiser *HMS Invincible*. This ship took over 1,000 men with her to the bottom of the sea, including 11 Lewis reservists.

One of only 6 survivors from the *Invincible* was Murdo MacLeod, from 10 Aird, Point. Having survived this calamity, he was drowned in the *Iolaire* disaster coming home on leave after the war had ended. Ten men from this Aird croft served in the war; eight of them with the British and Canadian Navies. One of them was lost, two were severely wounded, three survived being torpedoed at sea and one was decorated by the Norwegian government for bravery at sea.

In the Imperial War Museum, London, there is a painting, 'The last of the Invincible' by Robert H. Smith, showing the ship sinking and six men on a raft. One of those on the raft is E.R.A. Murdo MacLeod, one of the youngest seamen decorated for bravery at the Battle of Jutland. Murdo, from Shawbost, was awarded the Distinguished Service Medal for bravery on *HMS Princess Royal*. In WWII he was a survivor from a destroyer sunk at Narvik in 1940.

In one day, the Battle of Jutland left 16 children fatherless in North Tolsta, Lewis. This is a colossal number of children from a small village left to depend on their mothers until adulthood.

In WWI, fifty per cent of the able-bodied men in Lundale, Uig, were killed or badly wounded. On a population basis, if the Lundale figures had been replicated throughout the U.K., the British war casualties would have been virtually inestimable.

With so many men killed or wounded, many family fishing boats could not be manned, and were left to rot on the seashore or used as fence posts. The *Iolaire* disaster was another nail in the coffin of the Lewis fishing industry, as the majority of those drowned were ex-fishermen.

The MacLeod family, of 12 Portnaguran, lost three sons during WWI and their fourth son was drowned in the *Iolaire* disaster; William, RNR, drowned on *HMS Lydian,* Angus, RNR, was interned in Holland and died from illness, Alexander, Gordon Highlanders, was killed in France and 20 year old Norman, RNR, was drowned in the *Iolaire* disaster coming home on leave from *HMS Venerable.*

Kenneth MacPhail, RNR, from Arnol, was the sole survivor from *SS Cambric* torpedoed in 1917. He swam for over thirty hours before coming ashore on the coast of Algeria. It is indeed poignant that this powerful seaman, after so miraculous an escape, drowned within a few yards of his native island coming home on leave on the *Iolaire.*

Warrant Officer Alex. MacDonald, RNR, of New Valley, was decorated more than once during the war for bravery at sea and again for services during the Great Halifax Explosion in 1917. A Master Mariner in the Australian merchant navy, he was coming home to visit his widowed mother before returning to Australia, only to be drowned on the *Iolaire.*

Mate Angus MacKay, RNR, from Shader, Point, was awarded the D.S.M. for outstanding bravery when *HMS Plumpton Pedlar* was blown-up by a mine near Ostend harbour. He was not only decorated but also given the honour of hoisting the British flag on the wreck of *HMS Vindictive.* He received the further honour of hoisting the Flag over Ostend on the occasion of the entry of the King and Queen of the Belgians after the Germans had retreated. Drowned on the *Iolaire,* he left a widow and four children. His body was recovered and his remains are interred at Eye Cemetery. The Western Isles fishing fleet has never been able to make up the manpower lost in the two World Wars.

In 1938, Mr Duff Cooper, First Lord of the Admiralty, in a House of Commons reply stated that, out of 6486 seamen in the Royal Naval Reserve, 1634 came from the Western Isles. It is truly amazing that the Outer Hebrides, the least populated area of the country, should be in the position of providing over 25% of Britain's naval reservists. Even before war was declared in 1939 reservists from the Western Isles were mobilised. The figure I have seen quoted is 1,700. In the book, 'The Proudest of Her Line, the Story of HMS Veteran', John Lawton, referring to these islanders states,

'They were used as a nucleus of professional seamen to assist and train conscripted 'Hostilities Only' men with their duties on board naval ships. At the outbreak of war, they were amongst the first into action; before one English soldier had been killed, over thirty of these Lewismen were dead.'

In 1939, proceedings in the House of Commons were suspended in order that the Prime Minister and the House could pay tribute to the naval reservists of the auxiliary cruiser, *Rawalpindi,* in her heroic fight against the most powerful battle-cruiser in the world, the *Scharnhorst.* In his speech the Prime Minister stated, *'These men might have known, as soon as they sighted the enemy, that there was no chance. But they had no thought of surrender. They fired their guns until they could be fired no more, and many of them went to their deaths.'* Twelve of these fearless and gallant gunners were from the Isle of Lewis. Eight of them were killed and four became German prisoners of war.

In January 1940, the *Daily Herald* ran a feature with the banner headline, 'I Sailed with Angus MacLeod,' written by their naval correspondent. In the report he asks,

'Do you remember the peace-time story of Angus MacLeod? I wrote it more than five months ago on the sunny after- noon of a fine summer's day when the first of the naval reserves were being called up as an emergency measure. We weren't at war then. I went to Portsmouth to watch the first arrivals, answering the emergency summons to

serve their country.
In a crowded room at the RN Barracks a petty officer bel-
lowed the name Angus MacLeod. And ten men stepped
smartly forward. They all came from the Hebrides.
There are now another 200 Angus MacLeods playing their
part in Britain's war at sea.'

I am sure just as many if not more Angus MacLeods served
with Merchant Navy.

In June 1941, photographs in the national press showed lifeboats in the Atlantic with survivors from the Armed Merchant
Cruiser *Salopian*. Over 40 of these survivors were reservists from
the Isle of Lewis. If they had been lost, Lewis would have suffered
a disaster more poignant than that of the Titanic. When one thinks
of the huge population in our large cities, why on earth did the
Admiralty draft over 40 Lewismen on to the same warship?

Many of those who made the supreme sacrifice from the Hebridean diaspora are not included in the Western Isles or even the
British war losses, although they are commemorated on memorials overseas. To illustrate my point I would like to mention
two men; Leading Seaman Donald McIver, who died in WWI
and is counted amongst the Canadian war dead. His parents are
shown as Malcolm and Margaret MacIver from Great Yarmouth,
England. Knowing that hundreds of islanders fished and settled in
Great Yarmouth, and bearing in mind the surname, I am positive
that McIver is a son or grandson of a Lewis fishing family resident
in Great Yarmouth. No war historian would come to this conclusion and, on the information shown, would automatically assume
McIver is of English origin. Secondly, Norman A. MacInnes, killed
in WWII, is commemorated in South Africa. He was the son of a
ship's captain from Scarp who was living in Durban. MacInnes
is not even honoured on the Harris War Memorial.

Commemorated on the Huron and Ripley War Memorial,
Ontario, Canada, are many of the grandsons and great grandsons of the Lewis people evicted by Sir James Matheson in 1851
and 1852. Lewis surnames are prominent on this memorial and
many of those who do not bear island surnames are maternally
of Lewis descent.

There are Campbells, MacAulays, MacDonalds, MacKays,

MacKinnons, MacIvers, MacLays, MacLeans, MacLennans, MacLeods, Martins, Mathesons and Smiths.

The Western Isles losses in the world wars, per head, are reputed to be the highest losses for any area of the British Empire. Did the islanders ever receive any reward from the British government for their valiant service in Britain's wars? I personally do not think they did.

Many of the island villages that provided the 'War Heroes' are now depopulated and derelict. For example, the island of Scarp in Harris, and the village of Ungishader in Uig, between them in the World Wars provided the Allied forces with approximately 100 men and women. Both places are now uninhabited.

During the Highland Clearances those who had fought at Waterloo and Trafalgar were evicted with the rest. The widows and orphans of the men from South Harris who were killed at Waterloo were forced into fetid emigrant ships and transported to the backwoods of Canada.

In the three years following the end of WWI, around 3,000 Lewismen, mostly ex-servicemen, left the island for Canada under the pretext of being given good jobs. The *'land fit for heroes'* for which these men fought was not to be in the land of their birth.

These heavy war losses make up one of the factors that has led to the steep decline of the Hebridean population, which has virtually halved since 1890. In the same period the population of Iceland to our north has increased four fold.

Since the Act of Union in 1707, the Hebrides has made a military contribution greatly above her due share, having regard to the Hebridean proportion of the British population. I view the Hebrides as a versatile area that has been to some extent exploited (as other areas have been) and often used as a reservoir to provide fighting men for the British government.

The incredible loss of ten Merchant Navy captains/chief officers from the island of Tiree just beggars belief. With a population of only around three thousand, Tiree should not even have had ten captains/ chief officers, never mind so many making the supreme sacrifice. It would be interesting to learn what percentage of the population of the London suburb of Chelsea was lost in the Merchant Navy.

As a token of respect to these gallant captains I give you their names and where they were lost at sea,

> Chief Offr. Malcolm Cameron, *M.V. Wellfield (Newcastle).* Drowned Atlantic Ocean.
>
> Capt. John Kennedy, *SS Emerald (Glasgow).* Drowned near Beachy Head.
>
> Capt. Malcolm Kennedy, *SS Denham (Liverpool).* Killed in air raid on River Mersey.
>
> Captain Donald MacCallum, *SS Designer (Liverpool).* Drowned Atlantic Ocean.
>
> Captain Donald MacCallum, *SS Baron Dechmont, (Ardrossan).* Drowned north-west of Cape Roque, Brazil.
>
> Chief Officer Charles MacDonald, *SS Derrynane, (London.).* Drowned near Azores.
>
> Captain John MacCorquodale, *SS Rio Blanco (London).* Drowned off Cape Hatteras, Carolina, USA.
>
> Captain Hugh MacLeod, D.S.C., *SS Dan-y-Bryn (London).* Died from war service.
>
> Captain John MacNeil, *The Monarch (Glasgow).* Drowned Bay of Biscay.
>
> Captain Donald Sinclair, *SS Empire Eland, (London),* Drowned North Atlantic.

This heavy loss of captains from one small island reminds me of the use and abuse suffered by Highland troops in the Seven Years' War, as reported in the 'Edinburgh Courant', in July, 1763, *'Were not Highlanders put upon every enterprise where nothing was to be got but broken bones.'*

In WWI, Mrs Donald MacLeod, Balallan, a blind and widowed mother, was left alone and helpless in a croft house when her last and fourth son was called up to the Colours. Three of her sons and a 17 year old grandson died in WWI. One of her sons survived the war but sadly his two sons were lost at sea in WWII; Donald on *SS St Sunniva* and Angus on HM Tug.

In WWII, the six sons of Mrs Angus MacDonald, Tobson, were conscripted into the Navy, leaving her, an elderly widow, to toil and work the croft alone. An application was made to have one son exempted from service to help his mother work the land but the request was refused. She could not manage the croft on her own. This was at a time when the British government urged people to make use of all the land in their possession. However, it appears the British government wanted as many islanders as possible for the front line. The MacDonald family were extremely fortunate in that the six sons survived the war. However, Donald was more providential than most having survived both the sinking of the armed merchant cruiser, *Comorin*, and being badly wounded on *HMS Sirius*. His most traumatic escape, and a situation that must have been on his conscience for the rest of his life, was not joining *HMS Hood*.

Donald, with his shipmate and pal, John MacKay, Tolsta Chaolais, were serving on a naval vessel when they were told they were being transferred to *HMS Hood*. On reporting to the drafting officer, Donald was told there was some discrepancy in the crew numbers and that he was to report to another ship. His pal John MacKay boarded *HMS Hood* and Donald was never to see him again. There were only three survivors from her crew of 1,419. John MacKay did not survive. Alex Sim, Kirkibost also perished on the *Hood*.

Angus MacDonald, a cousin and neighbour of these MacDonalds, was an only son whose father had been drowned in the *Iolaire* disaster. He was also conscripted and his widowed mother left to toil on their croft. Angus was drowned on *HMT Northern Princess* in 1942.

In WWI an elderly widow from North Tolsta, Mrs John Martin, lost her only son, her two sons-in-law and her three nephews. We know about the death of men in the front line but no mention was ever made of the island pillows drenched nightly by the grievous tears of mothers, wives, aunts, grandmothers, cousins and girl friends for those who did not return.

When it comes to war service and losses I need look no further than my own family; my great, great grandfather, Macaoidh, Valtos (MacKay) was in the ill-fated expedition to Egypt in 1807, serving with the 78th Highlanders in *Cogadh an Turc* (The Turkish War). Like many of the Lewis soldiers in the regiment he became blind through disease. How these blind soldiers got back to Lewis is a mystery to me.

My kith and kin have been in action in the British forces down through the centuries. Twenty-eight of my relations were killed in action in the World Wars with nearly double that number wounded, and eleven others were very fortunate to survive the abominable horrors of German and Japanese prison camps. At least eleven relations were decorated for bravery, serving with all branches of the armed forces and the Merchant Navy. Sixteen of my relatives lie at the bottom of the ocean, surrounded by nothing except the wind, the wave and the seagull's wail, with no stone to mark their grave.

I think that in all honesty I can humbly state, that if blood is the price of war then my family has paid more than the full ransom. These excessive losses have been of no benefit to my family. Many of the villages where my relations were reared are now totally depopulated; the rabbits scurry around the uncultivated lazy beds, the bracken covers the brae, the village burn is choked by overgrown weeds and the Gaelic song of the crofter's boy is gone forever.

The Westminster government has neither recognised nor appreciated the part Hebrideans have played in Britain's wars for the past three hundred years. However, they have freely sacrificed the lives of our kith and kin and used our valour in active theatres of conflict around the globe. I agree with the words of the late James Shaw Grant, of the Stornoway Gazette, on the Lewis contribution in war, *'Two centuries of honourable service for the British Empire has not added to the material or cultural wealth of the Island as much as a single song.'*

THE FIRST WORLD WAR –
THE OUTER HEBRIDES

Malcolm MacDonald

An assassination in the Balkans was the catalyst that led to mobilisation for the great confrontation that was to become the First World War. Britain had been involved over the previous eight years in an industrial battle to maintain her superiority at sea. The new dreadnought type battleship had rendered all others obsolete and Germany saw an opportunity to challenge Britannia in an arms race for sea power.

On 4 August 1914, Britain declared war on Germany and her Austro-Hungarian allies, but despite having the most powerful fleet in the World and an advantage in dreadnoughts, the strength of the Royal Navy was not matched by the strength of the Army. In 1914 there were only 247,432 regular soldiers and of these only 120,000 were available for the British Expeditionary Force that was to cross the English Channel to fight alongside French and Belgian allies. The British Army was therefore, woefully short of men in comparison with the land armies of the continent – France for instance, had 3,500,000 men. On 7 August, Field Marshall Lord Kitchener famously appealed for volunteers with his 'Your Country Needs You' campaign and got 500,000 recruits by mid September.

Private cars were commandeered to travel to rural Post Offices throughout the Western Isles and printed notices went up notifying the islands that they were at war. Despite the relative remoteness from the continent of Europe it was from blackhouses with no water, electricity and sanitation that men sprung to action. Nearly all the fishermen and crofters of the isles were reservists with the Royal Navy or the Militia (Reserve Battalions of the Seaforths and Camerons receiving a retainer for annual training was attractive as it supplemented the meagre income to families). The muster in the Western Isles called up the reservists from villages where often no roads existed and in even remoter locations like St. Kilda and the Monach Islands (Heisker), the men that were mobilised had even greater difficulty in getting to Uist than in reporting to their depots throughout the United Kingdom. Gordon Macleod at the Port of Ness Post Office used his Marconi system to the benefit of all the Ness RNRs and persuaded the Admiralty to send a drifter to the Port of Ness to collect the Reservists and their kitbags, saving them all a trek of up to 28 miles to Stornoway.

As fast as these men were trained and uniformed they were mustered by the authorities, resulting in countless wooden fishing boats left to rot on the shore. Many were used later as fence posts. Such was the scarcity of trained soldiers that the Royal Navy used some of their strength in helping the Army by forming the Royal Navy Division and many islanders were temporarily drafted to act as soldiers in the Anson, Collingwood, Drake, Hawke and Nelson Battalions. The Lewis seamen had been drilled with rifles at the RNR Battery in Stornoway and knew how to use them with bayonets. The Division fought bravely against heavy odds in the defence of Antwerp in 1914, but a number of them were forced in retreat into Holland where they were interned for the duration of the war at Groningen.

By April 1915, many men of the Outer Hebrides wore khaki or naval uniforms and following state of affairs existed:

In Lewis, 2350 men were with the RNR, 782 were with the county regiment the Seaforth Highlanders, 206 had joined the Queens' Own Cameron Highlanders and 193 were enlisted with the Gordon Highlanders. From the Stornoway Drill Hall a total of 153 artillery men left to link up with the mainland units of the Ross Mounted Battery; 304 Lewismen who had emigrated pre-war were with the Canadian regiments and 314 others wore the uniforms of an assortment of regiments such as the Lovat Scouts, Scots Guards, Royal Engineers, Royal Army Medical Corps, Royal Artillery, and the regiments of the other colonial countries. A small number of nurses were in service but that number was to rise once the nature of the conflict became apparent.

In North Uist, Grimsay, Benbecula, South Uist and Eriskay, a total of 344 were with the county regiment, the Queen's Own Cameron Highlanders, 188 were with the Lovat Scouts, 64 wore the bib and tucker of the RNR (half from Eriskay), 38 wore Canadian uniforms and exactly 100 wore an assortment of uniforms including one with the Royal Flying Corps.

I have not been able to access figures for Harris, Scalpay, Scarp

and Berneray but the percentages of those serving and their dispo-
sition would have been much the same as the other Inverness-shire
islands.

That is unless we take Barra into account, for no numbers have
been given for those serving in what became known as the Fourth
Service – The Mercantile Marine – later known as the Merchant
Navy. In Barra, for both wars, the vast majority of men sailed
with the various merchant shipping lines with few venturing into
khaki or navy blue uniforms. In the First World War however,
a fair percentage were in the Camerons and, when on 16 April
1915, the *HMY Vanessa* arrived from Stornoway, local fishermen
from the southern Hebrides took the King's shilling with the RNR.
Along with 32 Eriskay men, 58 men from Barra and 10 Vatersay
lads enlisted for naval training.

It is hard to calculate how many men from Lewis, Harris,
Uist, Benbecula and Barra were with the Mercantile Marine, as
they travelled to and from home and over the sea with only deck
officers and the recently introduced radio officers in uniform. It
would be difficult to argue that at least 500 men from the Western
Isles had served in their various capacities with the Mercantile
Marine by April 1915.

The vast majority of these islanders who donned uniform, or
indeed continued as regulars in all the armed services on land
and at sea were in action within the bat of an eye; such was their
readiness to be available when called on. The total lack of prepa-
ration for war amongst those who made up the vast majority of
the population of the United Kingdom was in stark contrast to
that of the windswept Outer Hebrides, who had fishermen ready
to react immediately to the Kaiser and his contemporaries. These
descendants of Viking and Celtic blood were natural seamen,
hardened to the Atlantic rollers and the vagaries of The Minches
when fishing for a livelihood.

During the war, islanders paid the ultimate price on oceans all
round the World, in an effort to protect convoys, to sweep mines,
to support landings or to engage the enemy. In addition to those
lost in accidents aboard ship, many others died of illnesses such
as pneumonia or tuberculosis. Inoculations to prevent diseases
with known cures were in place, but so many diseases remained
untreatable by the medical fraternity.

Many Hebrideans served on the capital ships: the dreadnoughts, pre-dreadnoughts, cruisers, and destroyers and were involved in occasional sea actions, but for the most part remained aboard ship at Scapa Flow, Invergordon and Rosyth. When the German High Seas Fleet did come out, the Home Fleet fought actions at Coronel, the Falklands, Heligoland and Dogger Bank before the major confrontation at the Battle of Jutland on 31 May 1916. The Germans had a slight advantage in capital ships sunk and in lives lost but the Germans had turned and ran, never to emerge from Wilhelmshaven again. This allowed the British blockade to continue. As a result, the battle tends to be viewed as a stalemate, but Admiral Sir John Jellicoe undeniably missed a great opportunity to hit German morale hard by using his superior numbers (3:2) to better effect.

Due to having good sea legs, many islanders found themselves allocated to lesser ships such as armed merchant cruisers, used to patrol and stop enemy blockade runners supplying the enemy via the Atlantic routes. But it was in the smaller vessels such as trawlers, requisitioned for war use as minesweepers/anti-submarine vessels and latterly as convoy escorts that most Reservists served. Large minefields were laid by the enemy off the British coast and it was here that our men, with paravanes, small boats and rifle fire, destroyed countless mines to keep the vital shipping lanes open. The U-boats had operated clandestinely in all areas, but challenged first the areas off St Kilda, the Flannans and the Butt of Lewis, which proved to be 'killing fields' close to island hearts. Unrestricted U-boat warfare took place in 1917 and ship losses multiplied at an alarming rate, but Coalition Prime Minister David Lloyd George's involvement in forcing the Admiralty into the convoy system brought immediate dividends and losses dropped, although individual shipping times increased as they waited for numbers and escorts. Fewer ships sailed independently and were therefore much less vulnerable, despite guns aboard; the clandestine Q ships that sailed to trap U-boats proving to be less than satisfactory.

Generally Royal Navy boys had a reasonably easy life in port, with naval rituals keeping things 'ship-shape and Bristol fashion', plus innumerable inspections and practice. At sea, coaling was an arduous and filthy business, unless one was on one of the new oil powered battleships of the 'Warspite' class. Tots of rum, spells ashore and navy morale worked wonders for the boys of 'Nelson's Navy' who even sang *'Roll out the Barrel'* when they had to abandon ship! The German Navy suffered from low morale after Jutland and mutiny had to be stifled.

In the Mercantile Marine, the privately owned businesses had been run for profit pre-war, with little thought of the deck and lower deck crew. Conditions were primitive and food was generally poor, unless one was in port, where drinking was rife and appetites only picked up with the good 'scoff' received the day after leaving port. Fruit and local produce made up for the Cook's normal menu of 'Not Much' and 'Not Much' again tomorrow! Ship's biscuits were allegedly of the same type as the famous 'Roigan's biscuits' from Ness, thus satisfying the countless Lewis sailors, who thrived on them! The Mercantile Marine crews were undoubtedly the unsung heroes of the war, sailing their 'rust buckets' with food, ammunition and troops from Canada and the United States. These supplies brought succour to the British Isles and added fuel and manpower to a war effort that ultimately achieved a successful outcome, concluding the most grotesque war that mankind ever wrought.

My researches reveal that upwards of 330 Hebrideans died aboard more than 150 lost ships. In addition some 140 seamen died serving their country in various other capacities. The *HMY Iolaire* disaster compounded the losses experienced in 1914-18, with another 181 men drowned at Holm. In terms of numbers of islanders lost in a single vessel, excluding the *Iolaire*, the record is eleven men lost on the battlecruiser *HMS Invincible*. The *Invincible*, pride of the Battle of the Falklands, exploded and broke in two during the Battle of Jutland, leaving only six survivors from her large compliment, one of them a Lewisman, who was then tragically lost on the *Iolaire*. The nearest challenger to the *Invincible* was the armed merchant cruiser *Clan McNaughton* which disappeared with all hands, including ten Lewismen, during a gale off the coast of Northern Ireland in February 1915.

In the Mercantile Marine, only those seamen killed directly as a result of war were treated as war dead. Those dying of natural causes, of accidents on board or in port were not classified in the same way as personnel in the armed services. They were treated as unequals, and even men dying of wounds or pneumonia in hospital after surviving a sinking were not recognised as war casualties. This continued in the Second World War. The five Barra seamen lost on *SS Curaca* were not recognised by the Commonwealth War Graves Commission, as it was due to an accident. The catastrophic explosion of the ammunition ship *Mont Blanc* at Halifax, Nova Scotia, was reported to be the largest man-made explosion until Hiroshima, bigger than the Messines Ridge mine and one that saw a ship's anchor flung half a mile across the flattened city.

France and Flanders, the area that is forever associated with the First World War, witnessed the goriest battles of the conflict. The vast number of soldiers and sailors killed, lost, maimed or gassed in the entrenched stalemate far exceeded previous conflicts. For four long years soldiers on both sides had to endure artillery bombardments, snipers, heat, cold, rain, snow and the mud that made living in the trenches and fighting on the battlefields so difficult. The trenches, with their sandbags, duckboards and primitive latrines, had sleeping areas dug into their sides. The Highlanders, with khaki aprons covering their kilts and puttees to prevent water and mud going down the tops of their boots, were still prone to infection, due to the congestion of the living quarters, and trenchfoot was rife. When orders came to go over the top, the whistle blew, the bagpipes sounded and after climbing up the escarpment they faced barbed wire obstacles, shell craters at their feet, shell bursts above their head, rifle fire and the constant chatter of the Spandau machine guns that decimated the advancing ranks. These brave assaults led to the slaughter of fine human beings who attempted to break the deadlock in a war of attrition that stymied both sides. Cups of tea, meal breaks, cigarettes, mouth organs and singing kept the morale up in the trenches with a letter or parcel from home being eagerly accepted. The Sergeant Majors and junior NCOs kept the men on their toes in case of attack and supplemented this with extra duties, such as night patrols to reconnoitre the enemy trenches or collect the dead and wounded. Those that were found alive in No Mans Land were taken to Field Hospitals and the dead were buried in temporary graves and marked with crosses (many became permanent graves as they were not found again). When relief troops arrived and the Battalion could re-muster behind the Front Line to accept fresh recruits from 'Blighty', it was an opportunity to mentally and physically wind down, clean both body and equipment and hope it was their turn for a spot of home leave.

The campaign in the Dardanelles saw the Ross Mounted Battery landed with their horses, ammunition limbers and light guns. Heavy artillery could not be deployed by General Hamilton as the terrain was not suitable on the Gallipoli Peninsula. The Battery's guns could be easily manhandled and even dismantled, like those that one used to see at the Royal Tournament. This was the only artillery protecting the infantry from the Turks, who occupied the high ground and therefore the advantage. The Royal Navy used their heavy guns in support early on, but minefields and Turkish gun emplacements forced their withdrawal. As in north-west Europe, the fighting was trench based with the cavalry consigned to history. Churchill's initiative, to strike at the soft underbelly of Europe, was a flawed one and withdrawal proved the only sensible option.

The Turks were also the opposition in Mesopotamia, now Iraq, where the 1st Battalion of the Seaforth Highlanders was deployed in 1916 to fight in the heat and dust of the desert. Large numbers of British and Indian troops had surrendered earlier at Kut-el-Amara. Experience of the heat of India helped, but logistically the Seaforths were at a disadvantage, with stretched supply lines. In addition, as well as the temperature of 120 degrees Fahrenheit, the arid desert was prone to flash flooding in the delta areas. Add in the desert flies, mosquitoes and other vermin and it was little wonder that disease was rife, affecting large numbers of the troops. Nevertheless, the Allies pressed on from Basra, taking Baghdad in 1917, but when the Armistice was signed the Turks had hardly capitulated and could have fought on for longer.

Countless families lost two sons in the conflict on land and sea and the following households all lost three of their sons:

8 Aignish – Murdo, Malcolm and Roderick Mackenzie
56 North Tolsta – John, Alexander and Angus Macleod
41 Habost, Ness – Malcolm, Norman and Alex John Campbell
19a South Dell – Angus, Alexander and Finlay Morrison
24 South Bragar – Malcolm, John Murdo and Donald Morrison
21 Callanish – Donald, Kenneth and Finlay Maclean
3 Lundale – Donald, Angus and John Macaulay

14 Plantation Road, Stornoway – Alex Dan, John Murdo and Robert Nicolson

7 Balemartin – Alex. Snr., Alex. Jnr. and Donald Archie Macdonald. They were lost serving with the US, Australian and Canadian armed forces, showing that the will to fight for the homelands was retained following emigration.

Worst of all the losses was at 39a Balallan where three sons (Donald, John & Roderick) and a nephew (Donald Macleod Sneddon) brought up by Donald and Marion Macleod as a son all died. Young Donald is referred to as Snaddon in military records and was only 15 years-old – the youngest from the Outer Hebrides to die in the war.

At 10 Portnaguran, Donald and Christina Macleod's war was equally tragic, compounded by the fact that their fourth son to die, Norman, was lost on the *Iolaire* (William, Angus and Alexander had all died of wounds and injuries before him).

Lewis had 6,172 men in the forces by the end of the war, out of 13,750 men of all ages. Unfortunately figures for the other islands are not available.

Hebridean Days of Sorrow – several lives lost with the same unit in the same action

1. First World War on Land

11th November 1914 – At the First Battle of Ypres, the 1st Camerons lost 19 islanders in crucially repulsing the Prussian Guard at the Menin Road (two from Lewis, three from Harris, five from North Uist, four from Benbecula and five from South Uist). They were:

    Alexander Shaw – 15 Newvalley
    George Mackenzie – 46 Balallan
    John Macdonald – West Tarbert
    Donald Macleod – East Tarbert
    Donald Montgomery – Diraclete
    Roderick Morrison – 16 Grenitote
    Norman Macdonald – Crossroads, Grenitote
    Roderick Macdonald – Claddach Kirkibost
    Donald Ewen Maclean – Baleshare
    Donald Macdonald – Field Illeray
    Norman Macleod – Uachdar
    Donald Ewen Mackinnon – Griminish
    John MacCormack – Muir of Aird
    Angus John Wilson – Liniclate
    Archibald Bowie – 99 Carnan
    John Macphee – Iochdar
    Roderick Norman Chisholm – Grogary
    Duncan Blair – Daliburgh
    Donald Steele – Garryhallie

22nd December 1914 – At La Bassée, as part of 1st Division, the 1st Camerons lost 12 islanders (seven from Lewis, two from South Uist, two from Benbecula and one from Harris). They were:

    Murdo Macdonald – 7 Ballantrushal
    John Macaskill – 23 Lower Shader
    Norman Smith – 29 Lower Shader
    John Macdonald – 13 New Shawbost
    Angus Mackenzie – 1 Callanish
    Murdo Mackay – 2 Achmore
    Finlay Nicolson – 13 Ranish

John Angus Chisholm – 8 Lemreway
William Macdonald – 4 Finsbay
Donald MacCormack – Mill Gate, Liniclate
Michael Macdonald – Torlum Gate, Liniclate
Neil Morrison – West Gerinish
Donald Archie Mackay – 62 Bualuachrach

25th April 1915 – Near Hill 60, the 2nd Seaforths lost 17 Lewismen in action. They were:
Alexander Montgomery – 6 Sheshader
Kenneth Macleod – 14 Sheshader
Alex Dan Macleod – 38 Point Street, Stornoway
Alex Dan Graham – 34 Newmarket
Donald Mackenzie – 3 Knockaird
Dougald Mackenzie – 36 Eoropie
John Smith – 19 Habost, Ness
Murdo Morrison – 31 Cross
Donald Mackay – 27 Arnol
Donald Mackay – 29 Arnol
Finlay Mackay – 18 Carloway
Donald Mackay – 48 Carloway
Donald Macgregor – 12b Tolsta Chaolais
Malcolm Maciver – 14b Callanish
Malcolm Macdonald – 25 Valasay
John Macaulay – 4 Hacklet
Alexander Montgomery – 27 Laxay

25th September 1915 – At the Battle of Loos, the 5th Camerons lost 25 islanders in an otherwise successful advance – the Germans retreated, with General Sir John French impressed by the orderly advance (four soldiers were lost from Lewis, four from Harris, six from North Uist, five from Benbecula, five from South Uist and one from Barra). They were:
John Macdonald – 34 Lower Shader
Malcolm Macleod – 1 Crulivig
John Macleod – 20 Leurbost
Murdo John Macleod – 17 Balallan
John Morrison Snr. – 9 Quidinish
John Morrison Jnr. – 9 Quidinish

Angus MacCuish – 30 Northton
Donald Mackenzie – Borve, Harris
Malcolm Macdonald – Scolpaig
Alex MacCuish – Balelone
Neil Boyd – Hougharry
John A. Macdonald – Field Illeray
John Archie Macpherson – Carinish
Captain Alexander Morrison – North Uist
Donald Macleod – Uachdar
Neil Wilson – Griminish
Murdoch Johnstone – Balivanich
Donald Macisaac – Balivanich
Archibald Macphee – Aird, Benbecula
John Morrison – 67 Ardnamonie
Alexander Macdonald – 70 Ardnamonie
John Macdonald – Inver, Iochdar
James Macdonald – 18 Gerinish
Archibald Macphee – Garryhallie
Archibald Mackinnon – Bruernish

7th January 1916 – At the Battle of Sheikh Sa'ad, Mesopotamia (now Iraq), the 1st Seaforths lost 10 Lewismen in action against entrenched Turkish positions:
Donald Macleod – 51 Upper Bayble
Peter Graham – 9 Maciver's Buildings, Stornoway
Murdo Macleod – 34 Coll
Murdo Macleod – 54 Coll
Angus Mackenzie – 36 Back
John Macleod – 16 Lionel
Alexander Macdonald – 21 Lionel
Angus Mackay – 20 Cross
Donald Maclean – 21 Callanish
Donald Nicolson – 21 Ranish

22nd April 1916 – At the Battle of Sannaiyat, Mespotamia, the 1st Seaforths lost seven Lewismen on a 300 yard front surrounded by swamps, as they tried to relieve Kut-el-Amara from the Turks:
John Macdonald – 15 Aird, Point
Angus Macdonald – Flesherin

Angus Macleod – 13 Benside
Norman Morrison – 7 South Dell
John Maciver – 31a Breasclete
John Maciver – 21 Kirkibost
Angus Macaulay – 3 Lundale

1st July 1916 – On the first day of the Somme, the 2nd Seaforths lost 14 Lewismen as they moved forward in the second wave at 9am, attacking Beaumont Hamel, with the Redan Ridge their ultimate objective. They reached the third line of German trenches and one of their colleagues won the Victoria Cross:

Alexander Macleod – 30 Lower Garrabost
Evander Mackenzie – 5 Upper Garrabost
Murdo Macleod – 65 Back
John Macleod – Hill Street, North Tolsta
John Morrison – 16 Skigersta
Alexander Morrison – 14 Eorodale
Malcolm Gunn – 15 Eorodale
Murdo Macleod – 19 Eoropie
Allan Macdonald – 18a Habost, Ness
Malcolm Campbell – 26 Cross
Kenneth Graham – Aird, Dell
Murdo Macgregor – 12c Tolsta Chaolais
John Macleod – 24 Tolsta Chaolais
Kenneth Smith – 25 Leurbost.

Two Tolsta boys with the 2nd Gordons and a James Street HLI lad succumbed to the vicious enemy fire on that fatal day on the Somme – the blackest day the British Army endured. The saddest day of all for the Outer Hebrides was on 9 May 1915, when 39 islanders did not survive an early morning assault on the German trenches at Neuve Chappelle. The heavy machine gun fire took a grim toll on the Seaforths, fighting alongside the Gurkhas in the Dehra Dun Brigade. Of this total, 22 Lewismen were with the 1st Seaforths, one Lewisman was with the 1st Black Watch and six were with the 1st Camerons, who came up in support later that day. Colleagues of these six Lewismen were four soldiers from North Uist, two from Benbecula and three from South Uist. One soldier from Barra was with the 21 above in the Seaforths, who suffered 509 casualties in the attempted advance; the Camerons enduring 249 casualties.

Seaforths:
Donald Macdonald – 4 Portvoller
John Macleod – 15 Lower Bayble
John Shaw – 15 Newvalley
Angus Macleod – 12 Tong
Donald Macdonald – 8 Aird Tong
Angus Macdonald Snr. – 6 Coll
Donald Maclean – 6 Back
Donald Mackenzie – 50 Back
Murdo Mackay – 17 Skigersta
John Gunn – 5 Knockaird
Donald Smith – 14 Habost, Ness
Angus Campbell – 16 Habost, Ness
Donald Morrison – 4 South Dell
Murdo Murray – 5 South Dell
Donald Graham – 18 South Dell
Murdo Mackay – 7 South Shawbost
Norman Macarthur – 26 Knock, Carloway
Murdo Macleod – 12 Garenin
Murdo Macleod – 4 Tolsta Chaolais
Neil Maclean – 8b Breasclete
William Macneil – 1 Carishader
Murdo Macinnes – 5b Crossbost
George MacCormack – Brevig, Barra

Black Watch:
Malcolm Macleod – 8 Tong

Camerons:
Alexander Mackenzie – 3 Castle Street, Stornoway
Alexander Macgregor – 21 Newton Street, Stornoway
Alexander Smith – 22 Fivepenny
Donald Macdonald – 12 Habost, Ness
George Mackenzie – 30 Callanish
Alexander Mackenzie – 35 Ranish
Malcolm Macaulay – Claddach Illeray
Donald Archie Macdonald – Ardnastruban, Grimsay

Donald Ewen Nicholson – 14 Kallin, Grimsay
Murdoch Maclellan – 3 Scotvein, Grimsay
Donald John Campbell – Uiskevagh
Malcolm Joseph Macpherson – Bridgend, Torlum
Ronald Macintyre – 66 Ardnamonie
Donald Currie – Iochdar
Allan Mackay – 303 Kilphedar

2. First World War at Sea

17th September 1914 – Two young Ness boys were drowned when the training ship/workshop *HMS Fisgard II* foundered when being towed in a gale off Dorset:
Donald Macleod – 7 Lionel
John Macritchie – 42 Swainbost

30th October 1914 – HMS Hermes, a seaplane carrier, was sunk north-west of Calais by U-27 killing two Lewismen:
Norman Macinnes – 1 Breaclet
Donald Macleod – 30 Cross

26th November 1914 – The pre-dreadnought battleship *HMS Bulwark* blew up in an internal cordite explosion at Sheerness, killing three Lewismen:
Malcolm Mackenzie – 5 Portvoller
Murdo Macritchie – 37 Swainbost
Norman Macleod – 13 Brue

13th January 1915 – Three Lewismen were lost when the elderly armed merchant cruiser *HMS Viknor* hit a mine or suffered a structural fault:
Donald Finlayson Jnr. – 11 Brue
Duncan Mackinnon – 18 Brue
Alexander Maciver – 26 Leurbost

3rd February 1915 – The armed merchant cruiser *HMS Clan McNaughton* disappeared off the north-west coast of Ireland with ten RNR men lost (nine from Lewis, one from Harris):
Donald Martin – Portvoller

Donald Finlayson – 19 Aird, Tong
John Macleod – 25 Aird, Tong
Donald Murray – 33 South Dell
Donald Morrison – 41 Borve
Donald Campbell – 26 North Bragar
Kenneth Macaulay – 3 Breasclete
Dugald Kennedy – 2 Calbost
Neil Morrison – 9 Calbost
Ewen Morrison – Outend, Scalpay

11th March 1915 – Four Lewismen were lost off Corsewell Point, Stranraer when U-27 sank the armed merchant cruiser *HMS Bayano*:
John Campbell – 13 Aird, Point
George Graham – 1 Flesherin
Roderick Smith – 20 South Bragar
Donald Murray – 12 Coll

13th May 1915 – The pre-dreadnought battleship *HMS Goliath* was sunk by TCG Mauvenet off Cape Helles with the loss of two Lewismen:
Donald Smith – 43 South Bragar
Kenneth Nicolson – 24 Lemreway

25th May 1915 – The pre-dreadnought battleship *HMS Triumph* was sunk by U-21 at Gallipoli with the loss of two Lewismen, the first named being of an extremely rare breed among islesmen – a regular stoker:
Hugh Mackenzie – 46 Laxdale
Malcolm Mackay – 3 Achmore

31st May 1916 – At the Battle of Jutland a total of 19 islanders were killed or drowned. The battlecruisers *HMS Invincible* (11) and *HMS Queen Mary* (1); the heavy cruisers *HMS Defence* (4) and *HMS Black Prince* (2 including one from South Uist); plus the destroyer *HMS Broke* (1). There were only six survivors out of *HMS Invincible's* 1,025 crew when she broke in two. One of them was Murdo Macleod of 10 Aird Point who was drowned in the *Iolaire* tragedy below.

Invincible:
  Angus Graham – 4 Lower Garrabost
  Malcolm Murray – 5 Lower Garrabost
  Allan Macsween – 2 Newton Street, Stornoway
  Murdo Murray – 27 North Tolsta
  John Macleod – 56 North Tolsta
  Angus Maclean – 17 Habost, Ness
  Donald Smith – 11 Cross
  Norman Macleod - 28 Lower Barvas
  Finlay Macritchie – 46 Lower Barvas
  John Macarthur – 8 Cromore
  Donald Morrison – 9 Calbost

Queen Mary:
  Roderick Macdonald – 9 Gravir

Defence:
  John Carson – 13 Keith Street, Stornoway
  Murdo Macritchie – 48 Keith Street, Stornoway
  Alexander Macarthur – 48 Lewis Street, Stornoway
  Murdo Macdonald – 41 Leurbost

Black Prince:
  Donald Macleod – 1 Arnol
  Fred Matthews – 2 Kilaulay

Broke:
  Angus Maciver – 33 North Tolsta

25th August 1916 – The armed boarding vessel *HMS Duke of Albany* was sunk by UB-27 off the Orkneys with two Lewis Seamen lost:
  John Macdonald – 9 Kirkibost
  Donald Macaulay – 3 Lundale

25th September 1915 – The armed yacht *HMY Sanda* was sunk by the Blankenbergh Battery off the Belgian coast killing two Lewis men:
  William Macleod – 10 Portnaguran

Murdo Mackay – 50 Leurbost

5th November 1916 – The patrol trawler *HMT Cantatrice* was sunk by a mine laid by UC-18 off Winterton-on-Sea. Two young men from Scalpay and Berneray lost their lives:
Norman Macleod – Scalpay
John MacCuish – Borve, Berneray

18th December 1916 – *SS Opal* of Glasgow with her cargo of limestone struck a mine laid by U-80 off the Isle of Man. The Captain, from Lewis, and the Lamp Trimmer, from Vatersay, were lost with 10 others:
Donald Martin – Stornoway
Roderick Campbell – Caolais, Vatersay

20th January 1917 – *SS Bulgarian* of Liverpool with her cargo of iron ore was sunk in the North Atlantic by the enemy submarine U-84 with the loss of two Lewis gunners:
Alexander Morrison – 10a South Dell
Evander Macdonald – 15 Coll

25th January 1917 – *HMS Laurentic* struck a mine laid by U-80 off Fanad Head and foundered with the loss of 3 Lewismen:
Angus Macdonald – 7 Tobson
Norman Macdonald – 5 Breaclet
Duncan Nicolson – 22 Gravir

26 January 1917 – *SS Ava* of Glasgow was sunk in the South Atlantic by U-45 with 92 lives lost. Among those lost, the Quartermaster and Carpenter were Lewismen:
Murdo Smith – 25 Leurbost
Thomas Macleod – Stornoway

6th February 1917 – *SS Ilvington Court* of Liverpool was sunk off Cape Cherchel by a U-34. The Bosun, from Eriskay, and a Seaman from Harris were lost:
Norman Macdonald – Drinishader
Kenneth Gillies – Baile, Eriskay

18th March 1917 – The paddle minesweeper *HMS Duchess of Montrose* was sunk by a mine laid by UB-12 off Dover. A Harrisman and a crewmate from Lochboisdale were lost:
   Donald John Maclennan – Govig
   Norman Macdonald – Lasgair, Lochboisdale

1st May 1917 – *SS Bagdale* of Whitby was lost to a UC-66 off Ushant with four islanders (three from Barra, one from Eriskay) among the 23 casualties:
   John Macdougall – Coilleac, Eriskay
   John Macdonald – 14 Cleat
   Donald Macneil - The Square, Vatersay
   Michael Macneil – The Square, Vatersay

17th May 1917 – *SS Dartmoor* of South Shields, with her cargo of ore, was sunk by UC-50 south-west of Fastnet, with three Barra seamen drowned and another who had been rescued died of pneumonia in Devonport:
   Donald Mackinnon – 10 Ardveenish
   Neil Maclean – Brevig, Barra
   Simon Macneil – 6 Grean
   Archibald Mackinnon – Upper Borve, Barra

16th July 1917 – *HMS Newmarket*, a requisitioned minesweeper, was sunk in the eastern Mediterranean by UC-38 with four Lewismen lost:
   John Macleod – 25 Lower Shader
   Colin Macdonald – 2 Brue
   Norman Maciver – 34 Coll
   Donald Maciver – 17 North Tolsta

29th July 1917 – The patrol trawler *HMT Robert Smith* disappeared north-west of the Shetlands, with a sailor from Vatersay and a Point lad among those missing. It transpired later that U-44 had encountered the unfortunate trawler:
   Norman Graham – Flesherin
   Roderick Graham – Caolais, Vatersay

22nd July 1917 – *HMS Otway* was torpedoed and sunk off North

Rona by UC-49 with a total of 12 men lost. Five Lewismen drowned almost within sight of their native isle:
Peter Stewart – 3 Lower Bayble
Donald Campbell – 54 North Tolsta
Murdo Macdonald – 9 Eorodale
Donald Macphail – 24 North Bragar
Murdo Mackay – 55 South Shawbost

9th October 1917 – The deck gun of the enemy submarine UC-75 sank the collier *SS Main of Cardiff* off Drumore, Luce Bay. Two naval gunners from Lewis and Harris were lost:
John Maciver – 15 Benside
John Macleod – 5 Kyles Scalpay

6th December 1917 – At Halifax, Nova Scotia the ammunition ship *Mont Blanc* collided with the *Imo* and exploded with catastrophic severity, severely damaging the town of Halifax itself. The *SS Curaca* of London was one of the ships sunk, killing five Barra seamen. They are not commemorated on the Tower Hill Memorial in London to the Merchant Navy:
Michael Macneil – Balnabodach
Malcolm Maclean – Ledaig
Donald Mackinnon – Upper Borve, Barra
Donald Mackinnon – Kinloch, Tangasdale
Donald Campbell – Vatersay

13th December 1917 – *HMS Stephen Furness*, an armed boarding steamer was sunk off the Isle of Man by UB-64. A Barra sailor and a Ness sailor were both lost:
John Morrison – 18 Upper Adabrock
Alexander Macrae – Bruernish

15th January 1918 – A South Uist sailor and his Barra crew-mate were killed in action on the minesweeping trawler *HMT Rodino*:
Archibald Macrae – Smerclate
Archibald Macpherson – Craigston

2nd February 1918 – *SS Avanti* of Copenhagen was sunk by UB-59 off St Alban's Head. The Third Officer from South Uist and an

AB from Vatersay were lost:
    Alexander Macphee – 6 North Frobost
    Michael Campbell – 17 Vatersay

4th February 1918 – *SS Lofoten* of London was sunk by UB-59 off Start Point. An AB from South Uist and two Barra seamen were drowned:
    Donald John Macintyre – 2 South Locheyenort
    William Mackinnon – Balnabodach
    Joseph Macdougall – Earsary

12th February 1918 – *SS Eleanor* of South Shields was sunk off St Catherine's Point by UB-57 with two island gunners lost:
    Angus Thomson – 3 Habost, Ness
    Kenneth Macaskill – 6b Gravir

21st April 1918 – *SS Normandiet* of London was sunk off the Calf of Man by U-19. Two Lewismen and a Harrisman perished, along with 16 others:
    John Murdo Nicolson – 14 Plantation Road, Stornoway
    William Macdonald – 18 Garenin
    Donald John Macdonald – 3 Kyles Scalpay

13th September 1918 – *SS Buffalo* of Whitehaven is lost to UB-64 off Corsewell Point with 5 islanders (three from Harris, two from Lewis) among those lost:
    Alexander Macrae – 23 Upper Bayble
    Donald Morrison – 3 Cross
    John Mackinnon – Stockinish
    Finlay Morrison – Stockinish
    Malcolm Macleod – Leac a li

30th September 1918 – The torpedo boat/destroyer *HMS Seagull* sank after colliding with *SS Corrib* on the River Clyde. Two Lewismen were among the casualties:
    John Macleod – 14 South Bragar
    John Macdonald – 27 Coll

1st January 1919 – *HMY Iolaire* disaster with 181 islanders drowned (174 from Lewis, seven from Harris including two from Berneray). The 181 quoted does not include the 20 crewmen lost who were not from the Western Isles.

See Stornoway Historical Society website for details of those lost.

9th January 1919 – *SS Northumbria* of London was sunk by a mine off the River Tees with 4 islanders lost (three from Barra, one from South Uist).

John Maclennan – Manish
Peter Macintyre – 351 South Boisdale
John Maclean – Tangasdale
Neil Mackinnon – Kentangaval
Joseph Macdonald – Brevig, Barra

14th June 1919 – Two recently demobbed RNR men from Lewis were lost when the *SS Talus* from Canada disappeared off Iceland:

Hector Ferguson – 1 Portvoller
John Macdonald Jnr. – 17 Back

8th January 1920 – The minesweeping trawler *HMT St Leonard* disappeared when sailing from Inverkeithing to Dundee and two Nessmen were lost:

John Murray – 21 Swainbost
Roderick Gillies – 20 South Dell

HMY Iolaire Disaster – 1st January 1919

The loss of His Majesty's Yacht *Iolaire* in the early hours of New Year's Day 1919 is undoubtedly the most tragic single occurrence to befall the combined island of Lewis and Harris. That it happened within sight of the Stornoway harbour lights, as families waited for their loved ones to come home (many had not been home for a year or more) is doubly distressing. Many of the sailors aboard were demobbed and ready to resume their peacetime occupations, while others were receiving a well-earned leave after the strife of 1918. All had presents for their loved ones and each were longing to see their families after the deprivations of war.

The *Iolaire* stuck the rocks at the Beasts of Holm at 1.55am on New Year's Day 1919, as she transported home Royal Navy and Mercantile Marine personnel to their homes. The rending of the ship's hull on the jagged rocks was a frightening sound to those aboard and was replaced in the days to come by the wailing of families who lost loved ones. Despite the proximity of the shore, a gale blew up as the yacht approached Stornoway, the ship was in an exposed position and the sea was a boiling cauldron that even experienced swimmers could not survive in. Men were dashed on rocks and the lifeboats, which were launched, were quickly swamped in the darkness of the night. Although there was a radio aboard, the operator could not generate enough power to transmit due to water in the batteries and although the ship's rockets fired, and were spotted by the Royal Navy base (also named Iolaire), this did not generate the speedy rescue that was necessary before all was lost. When the yacht's lights failed, those left aboard must have felt a shiver as they clung perilously to the railings, with the roar of the waves crashing on the rocks and the rending of the hull on the Beasts piercing their very souls. A total of 181 islanders were drowned, along with 20 of the 27 man crew. The bravery of John F. Macleod from Port of Ness, who swam ashore with a line which he attached to the rocks saved most of the survivors, who used the rope to clamber onto the dark rocks on the shore. Eventually though, the vessel heeled over and it was realised nothing could further be done. Nothing remained but her masts above water. The survivors clambered up the rocks, reaching the shelter of Anderson Young's farm. As dawn rose, one sailor, Donald Morrison from 7 Knockaird, was rescued from a mast; shortly before, another mast held onto by three others had been broken by the storm. Bodies were washed up on Sandwick shore and as news of the tragedy spread from Stornoway to the various districts, the relatives of those lost came to the shore and to the mortuary at the RNR base at Battery Point to identify their loved ones. The sea shall give up its dead on the final day, it has been promised. What was sad for so many in 1919 was the fact that despite the proximity to the shore, a total of 64 bodies were either not recovered or identified. A row of ten *Iolaire* graves at Sandwick Cemetery contains six unidentified graves interred on 14 January 1919. The headstones, all neatly aligned, are inscribed at the bases, "Known Unto God."

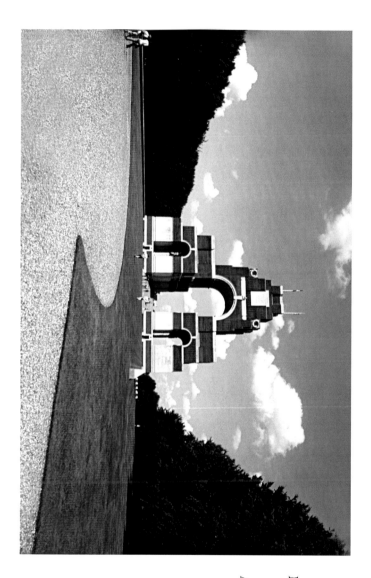

1. Tiepval Memorial to the Missing of the Somme. 73,000 are named on its panels

2. BEAUMONT HAMEL, MEMORIAL TO 51ST HIGHLAND DIVISION

3. Inscription on the
51st Highland
Division Memorial

4. CARBOST, WE WILL REMEMBER

5. SEAFORTH HIGHLANDER GRAVESTONE AT LE TOURET

6. Le Touret Cemetery, where many Islanders are both buried and listed among the missing on wall panels

7. MENIN GATE, MEMORIAL TO THE MISSING OF THE YPRES SALIENT, WITH OVER 56,000 NAMES

Winners of Fleet Rowing Race.

FINE ACHIEVEMENT BY LEWIS CREW.

Back Row :—Standing (Left to Right :—Angus Macleod (Kenneth Back; Donald Nicolson; stroke oarsman, North Tolsta; Murdo Macdonald North Tolsta; John Macdonald, Shewbost; Donald Macleod, 45 North Tolsta; Jack Kelly, Ireland; Heritt Bonham Carter, the Racing Officer.
Sitting Row :—Angus Macleod, Keose, Lochs; Donald Macleod, Lochs, Andrew Coull, A.B., coxswain, Montrose; Alexander Mackenzie, Lochs; Torquil Mackenzie, Aignish
Lying on Deck :—John Benton, Lochrove; Donald Patience, Balintore

8. WINNERS OF THE FLEET ROWING RACE
(FROM THE LOYAL LEWIS ROLL OF HONOUR, '1914 AND AFTER')

9. 'The Last of the Invincible', watercolour by Robert H. Smith, RNVR. Murdo MacLeod of Aird, Point, is one of the survivors on the raft

10. Murdo MacLeod of Aird, Point, one of only six
survivors from HMS Invincible drowned in the Iolaire
disaster of 1 January 1919

Seaman John Macdonald, R.N.R., 16B Tobson.

Norman Macdonald, R.N. H.O., 16B Tobson.

S.B.A. Johnnie Macdonald, 16B Tobson.

S.B.A. P.O. Malcolm Macdonald, 16B Tobson.

Seaman Murdo Macdonald, R.N.R., 16B Tobson.

Seaman Donald Macdonald, R.N.R., 16B Tobson.

11. THE SIX MACDONALD BROTHERS OF TOBSON (FROM THE ROLL OF HONOUR, NESS TO BERNERA, 1939-45)

12. Iolaire Memorial at Holm, Isle of Lewis

13. RAF PERSONNEL
EMBARKING AT
LOCHBOISDALE

14. Off-duty RAF aircrew exploring Benbecula

15. B17 FLYING
FORTRESS OVER UIST

16. WARTIME SHOT OF A FAMILY ON THE ISLAND OF LEWIS.
THE SON IS SERVING WITH THE RAF

17. 518 Squadron, the only RAF squadron in WW2 to have a Gaelic motto. The squadron was founded at Stornoway and served almost two years on Tiree

18. RAF GROUNDCREW AND WAAF AT STORNOWAY, 1944

19. RAF MEN
SERVING AT
RADAR SITE ON
LEWIS WW2

20. 'The Rock Dodgers'. RAF Communications Flight based at Abbotsinch flew various aircraft including this De Havilland Dominie to RAF units and airfields (and beaches) on many Hebridean islands

21. BRITISH SOLDIER TRYING OUT RECONNAISSANCE IN THE FAROES

22. A lot of the soldiers' time in the Faroes went into training. Here some soldiers from the Lovat Scouts train in camouflage in the village of Syðrugøta

23. In addition to military matters, a big part of the soldiers' job was to make sure that the British forces and the Faroese population were on friendly terms. This is just one of many pictures that gives us a sense of how successful they were in doing the latter part of their job

24. THE PLAYING OF THE PIPES ALWAYS ATTRACTED MUCH ATTENTION FROM THE FAROESE, AND THE PIPEBANDS WERE GREATLY MISSED WHEN THE WAR ENDED. HERE A HANDFUL OF LOVAT SCOUTS PLAY ON THE HARBOUR IN TÓRSHAVN

Diver Victor Gusterson, of *HMS Iolaire* base, never dived again after releasing bodies from the saloon of the sunken yacht. My father, who was eleven years old, had travelled from South Bragar to identify his own father but was unable to find him. Many carts returned empty, as the sea held onto a third of the victims, another crushing blow to the families of the island sailors that had once sailed so proudly under Admirals such as Jellicoe, Beatty and Sturdee.

A three-man Admiralty Enquiry came to no conclusion, as all of the officers and those at the helm had perished. The Public Enquiry that followed did not apportion blame either and talks of conspiracies, drunkenness and incompetency permeated local discussions. There is little doubt that the latter played a large part, with the yacht *Almathaea* and her crew only recently taking the title *Iolaire* when the yacht of that name, called after the Stornoway Naval Base, left for repairs. Commander Mason collided with the quay at Kyle when the yacht called to collect the sailors that the mail steamer *Sheila* was unable to carry along with the soldiers. He and his navigating officer Lt. Cotter set course for Stornoway when the night was fine. As the *Iolaire* neared Lewis, the wind that was to turn into a gale had risen. It must be assumed that the yacht had sailed on further than intended before the turn to port that would lead her into Stornoway. This brought her too close to the Holm coast; the crew did not react to steer her away from the shore and the yacht struck the Beasts before they realised the danger they were in. Countless survivors spoke of the sobriety of the officers and the rocks showed clearly on the naval charts, so therefore this tragedy of all island tragedies must surely be categorised as pure human error on the part of the officers.

Some 80 men were rescued, but little thought was given to them by a community in shock. All attentions were towards the affected families. The disaster left 221 dependent children, aged from 3 to 19, nine young adults, 67 widows, 53 mothers, 66 fathers, 8 sisters/ aunts, one grandmother aged 77 and a grandfather aged 83. The source of these statistics come from the *Iolaire* Disaster Fund report of 9 March 1922, therefore babies born after their father was lost were aged three by the time of the report. The fund, administered by John Maclean, National Bank, then stood at £24,906.

Lewis had already lost a thousand war dead from a generation in their prime before that fatal night and so this unexpected blow struck a dagger in the backbone of the island, as scarcely a house was unaffected in one way or another. Harris had lost 121 men, but five more were added to the roll on the war memorial later erected at Tarbert. The Isle of Berneray (Harris) lost two more, to add to the sixteen who had succumbed earlier.

All of the officers of the yacht were drowned and so the rumours spread, but Commander Richard Mason and his navigating officer, Lieutenant Edmund Cotter were both considered proficient seamen by colleagues. That they made a mistake cannot be denied, especially as they were new to the route from Kyle of Lochalsh, but to suggest that they acted negligently cannot be proven as all witnesses at the enquiry swore to their sobriety.

The *Iolaire* tragedy cast a shadow over the islands that remained until well after the Second World War and in some ways it still remains. My father never spoke about it, like many who experienced the grief of the time, but he did name me after his lost father. Silence, weeping and bitterness permeated the communities, along with the question as to why such a devastating final blow could hit such a God-fearing people after the blood of over one thousand souls had already been spilled in France, Flanders, Turkey, Greece, Mesopotamia and the oceans of the World. The *Iolaire* has one rather unusual connection to the other largest maritime catastrophe that the islands of the Outer Hebrides have witnessed. The *Annie Jane,* bound from Liverpool to the New World of America in 1853, sank off the shores of Vatersay, with the loss of some 300 souls (the children aboard were not registered). There were 102 survivors. The Master's name was Mason – the same surname as that of Lt Commander Robert Mason, the skipper of the *Iolaire*! This coincidence is remarkable.

There is so much one could write about the *Iolaire* and the effect it had on the island. James Shaw Grant has written about it and the sinking itself has and will be further addressed, both in book form and in songs and poems. However, over 40 years had elapsed before a book appeared and a memorial to those lost was unveiled at Holm. A generation had remembered in silence before the island felt they could talk a little bit about it. The words of Vic Morrow, the US War correspondent, summed it up for countless islanders, *'For most of it, I have no words!'*

Memorials and Cemeteries

When one attends an Armistice Day Service, passes a War Memorial or visits a cemetery containing war graves, the question, 'why?' is always prevalent in the mind, especially during the one-minute silence. Wars have been waged for centuries and have been depicted as both glorious and hell on Earth; but the harsh reality that both winners and losers must respect is that lives are lost on both sides. Each November, as we wear our Flanders poppy, immortalised in John McCrae's '*In Flanders Field*,' what is really meant when we remember them – as in Laurence Binyon's '*For The Fallen?*'

Long lists of names on memorials or blunt inscriptions on Commonwealth War Graves Commission style headstones do not tell us much about the individuals; their families, their desires, their hopes, their beliefs. The grief and suffering that each loss brought to each household touched by the sword of death can only be imagined, unless one was from one of the families affected. In the First World War, 126 households were given sad news more than once, 10 of them three times and, in the case of that at 10 Portnaguran, four times (the fourth following the *Iolaire*). The late Donald James Stewart, Freeman of the Western Isles, was born in 1920 and named after his two uncles from 10 Bells Road, lost with the Seaforths and Canadians. His father died in 1944, when serving with *MV Jaccinth* in the Merchant Navy. Marriage and in-laws could be covered in detail here. The marble and stone edifices, erected to honour the fallen, do serve a purpose, and our strong Hebridean feelings for our War dead see continual additions to their number, with new memorials having been built or being planned. The first was unveiled at St Moluag's Church, Eoropie on the 18th of August 1918, and with the unveiling of the Callanish one, the number in the Western Isles has reached 22 according to my records:

Lewis (Cnoc nan Uan, Stornoway)
Harris (Main Street,Tarbert)
Isle of Berneray (Quay)
North Uist (Clachan na Luib)
Benbecula (Griminish)

South Uist (Bornish)
Barra (Nask)
North Lewis (Cross)
North Lewis (Borve)
Carloway
Tolsta Chaolais
Isle of Great Bernera (Breaclet)
Uig (Baile na Cille)
Tolsta (North Tolsta)
Back (Back)
Branahuie/Melbost
North Lochs (Crossbost)
Pairc (Kershader)
Point (Garrabost)
Kinloch (Laxay)
Arnol, Bragar & Shawbost (Bragar)
Loch Roag (Callanish)

Memorials that do not bear a list of casualties, such as the *Iolaire* Monument, Ross Battery cairn, RAF Plaque, Seaforth Highlanders Plaque and plaques that may exist within local religious establishments/village halls/museums and schools have not been referred to.

In addition, 44 locations in the Outer Hebrides contain Commonwealth War Graves Commission gravestones. These symbols of national and community loss convey the bravery and sacrifice made in circumstances we all pray will never happen again. Uniquely, interred near one Royal Navy man on the Monach Islands is German machinist Otto Schatt, from U-110, lost on 15 March 1918. Although the Monachs are included in the 44 locations, William McNeill of *HMS Laurentic* has a metal plaque attached to a rock, while Schatt has a standing plaque. All other headstones are almost all standard type and found in cemeteries from Habost (Ness) down to Cuier (Barra), which has a stone for three Chinese Merchant Seamen interred on Vatersay.

Despite being from the remote Hebrides, the record of service and sacrifice made by our men and women is second to none in the Commonwealth and in both World Wars. Our Royal Navy Reservists were at sea before the first shot was fired and our soldiers, fighting with the County regiments, the Seaforths and Queens Own Cameron Highlanders, were among the first to fight in France. In the last war, the 4th Battalion of the Camerons were Territorials (Harris, North Uist and South Uist), as were the Ross Mounted Battery (Stornoway – with rural detachments) and both were deployed with the 51st Highland Division before some regulars were organised. The Admiralty filled Armed Merchant Cruisers and naval trawlers with Reservists that could serve in action from day one. Over both wars the kilt ceased to be worn, supposedly to counter gas attacks, and new methods of fighting and equipment evolved. The kilt was attractive in a romantic way, but was quite impractical for trench warfare, where the hems were often frozen or soaked and chafed the brawny knees of the braw lads!

The best example of the local ability to adapt and diversify in warfare is undoubtedly the Uist and Benbecula detachments of the Lovat Scouts, which started the First World War on horses and ended the Second World War as Alpine troops on skis in Italy.

The First World War was one that has been seen as being based in the gory trenches of Northern France and Flanders, but it was truly a worldwide war. Today British troops patrol the streets of Basra in Iraq, but in 1916 that country was called Mesopotamia. There the 1st Seaforth Highlanders lost 48 Lewismen in battle with the Turks (39 in moving north from Basra) and 3 other Lewismen in other units were also lost (2 RNR/1 RAMC). The Basra War Memorial has recently been moved outside the city, but it is in Europe today that the scale of death suffered in the mud of France and Flanders in the First World War can be viewed and still comprehended, up to a point. The vast cemeteries, with row upon row of headstones, covering acres of Northern France and Belgium still send chilling messages. Countless numbers of bodies were never recovered from the mud churned up in the incessant bombardment of the trenches. Those soldiers who did not receive an individual burial are commemorated on huge edifices, of which the Menin Gate at Ypres is the best known. Name upon name is engraved in columns that appear never ending. On that individual memorial alone there are 250,000 names of Commonwealth soldiers who have no known grave and of that number 59 are from Lewis, 6 from Harris, 14 from North Uist, 8 from Benbecula and 12 from South Uist.

For those at sea, the Royal Navy bases at Portsmouth, Chatham, Devonport and Lowestoft have memorials to those lost on active service, with the Tower Hill Memorial in London paying homage to the crews of 8,091 ships sunk in the wars. Standing sentinel over the Tower Hill Memorial in London since its unveiling on 5th of November 1955, are two sculpted figures. One is an officer, and the seaman on his left was modelled on Bosun Kenneth Stewart MBE of 11 Tong, chosen for his rugged features and for his 30 years sterling service to the New Zealand Shipping Company.

1. Comparative Losses with Commonwealth Countries

	Population 1911	Losses WW1	% Loss
Australia	4,455,000	61,859	1.388
New Zealand	1,058,308	18,042	1.704
Canada	7,207,000	56,500	0.784
UK	40,831,000	908,371	2.225
Western Isles	46,732	1,797	3.843

2. Western Isles War Losses – First World War

Approximate Number serving – 9,500
(19.26% of Population)

	Army	RNR	MM	RM	RAF	Civ/NK	Total
Totals	1,120	549	116	4	2	6	1,797

3. Losses by Clan

Western Isles – First World War

Macleod 297, Macdonald 267, Morrison 113, Mackenzie 86, Maclean 78, Campbell 65, Mackay 62, Maciver 61, Murray 53, Macaulay 48, Smith 48, Mackinnon 46, Nicolson 26, Macrae 24, Macaskill 21, Graham 20.

119

THE HEBRIDES AND NORTH WEST SCOTLAND DURING WORLD WAR TWO

Mike Hughes

The story of the Hebrides and North West Scotland in WW2 is a story of two very different cultures coming together. On the islands in particular, many locals spoke Gaelic and lived a lifestyle which, for some, approached self-sufficiency. Travel had nothing like the ease and immediacy of today. For some islanders there had been little or no experience of cities, large shops and trains. Also, for some, English was very much a second language.

Into their midst came soldiers, sailors, airmen from 'a' the arts and parts' that the Allied world could offer – England, Wales, Ireland, Canada, Australia, Poland, Rhodesia, the USA and at least a dozen other nations, grand or grander still.

As with World War One, in purely statistical terms, perhaps even cultural terms, World War Two was to see the Islanders sacrifice themselves in far greater numbers than any others partaking in this noble cause. When war broke out, enormous numbers of Hebrideans were already serving in the Royal and Merchant Navies. Many more were in the Royal Naval Reserves and others quickly volunteered. On top of this, with so few opportunities for leisure and recreation in the 1930s, many Highlanders and Islanders had joined the pre-war Territorial Army. This brought opportunities for socialising, sport and even some travel. So the declaration of war on 3rd March 1939 had an immediate impact on these parts of the country.

However, the whole world knew from day one what sort of war it was going to be. In late 1917 the U boats had came close to winning the First World War for Germany. On the morning of 3rd September 1939 the SS *Athenia* (of the Donaldson Atlantic Line, built at Fairfield's, Govan) was making her way quietly between Northern Ireland and the west of Scotland. She was packed with anxious Canadians and Americans hoping to reach home before hostilities became a certainty. Also on board were many British women and children, perhaps having anticipated what dreadful conditions war might bring, fleeing across the Atlantic in the hope of finding safety. Of course the crew contained many men from the west of Scotland and the islands. Without warning she was attacked by U-30. Some of the press reports of the times even have the U boat surfacing and firing indiscriminately on the lifeboats. So the *Athenia* was the first major casualty, and it brought a foreboding warning of the type of unrestricted warfare that was to come. Britain, a collection of islands on Europe's north west extremity, would be dependent on the sea, and the extreme peril of keeping the nation fed, armed and assisted by Allies would inevitably place an onerous burden on her seafarers.

What kind of environment prevailed in north west Scotland and the islands in late 1939 and early 1940? The culture was distinctive. The majority of rural/island homes had no electricity or running water. On some islands peat was the staple fuel. On some crofts chickens had the run of all areas including the dwelling spaces. Gradually, the military occupied more and more locations, initially around harbours, and then fields were requisitioned for the laying of runways. The immensely robust and utilitarian Nissen hut sprung up in a variety of guises. Not surprisingly, there were locals who feared for their culture, land and livelihood. Not surprisingly there were servicemen (and later women) who wondered where on earth they had been posted. Many found a landscape, unkindly called lunar by a few, which was unlike any they had ever previously witnessed (in a time before TV documentaries and geographic magazines).

One chap stationed on a South East England RAF airfield was told he was being posted to RAF Benbecula. '*Sounds great,*' he said, '*I have an image of a south seas island, with dusky maidens in grass skirts.*' '*You got the island bit right.*' said the posting sergeant.

The languid journey to and from the islands by the wonderfully unhurried MacBraynes vessels and their crews, was also something of a shock to big city types. In places like Oban and some of the larger islands, the numbers of military personnel would grow to many thousands at one time. This meant an enormous exercise in logistics; to feed and shelter these new inhabitants, while attempting not to seriously destabilize the local economy and infrastructure. However, enterprising crofters soon found there was a tremendous desire for 'off-ration' eggs, from the visitors. So much so, that some Islanders referred to them as the REF (Royal Egg Force). The ancient art of bartering was given renewed vigour and copious amounts of bully beef tins, to say nothing of ammunition for poachers, found their way into local homes, in return for eggs and other off-ration goods.

The waitresses at Kennedy's tearoom in Oban had to make a drastic change of strategy. For a time these delightful young ladies (many of them islanders) would discuss the handsome RAF customers, quite freely, in their native Gaelic tongue. However, this practice came to an embarrassing halt when, after sitting quietly for half an hour or so, some Canadian airmen asked for their bill in fluent Gaelic. The waitresses, who had been loudly telling each other which one they fancied, ran screaming into the backshop. Every word had clearly been understood!

As these two communities slowly began to come together in relative harmony, out at sea the U boats wrought havoc. The Germans called the first couple of years of the war 'The Happy Times'. The Royal Navy and the RAF had ships, aircraft and equipment which at first were ill-suited to pursuing the elusive U boats. The dangerous climate was added to by the fact that a huge proportion of local young men were not present. Many were at sea, many posted overseas, many were prisoners of war (after the 51st Highland Division held the rearguard at St Valery – Dunkirk), and of course, many were never to return. The potential was there for social disaster. That it did not occur – despite the presence of unduly glamorous visitors like Yanks, Canadians, Australians, Poles and Norwegians – is enduring testimony to the standards of those times.

One of the most surprising arrivals in the Highlands, as early as June 1940, were the newly-formed parties of commandoes, finding the ideal environment for secret exercises and other ordeals. These incredibly brave young men were preparing for the fight to liberate Europe from the middle of 1940 onwards; quite a remarkable fact given that the retreat from Dunkirk was barely over and that the free world was reeling from one Nazi blitzkrieg victory after another. Yet here was this country preparing for the fight-back; astonishing. When I speak to the veterans of World War Two, a hundred times or more I have felt incredible pride in the never-say-die attitude, which saw this country prepare for victory, when all around there was capitulation, neutrality and appeasement.

On the islands, the first large-scale presence was the Royal Navy, with Fleet Air Arm seaplanes at Stornoway in summer 1940. The RN and FAA made good use of Stornoway harbour to provide mine-laying in the North Western Approaches and to support the ill-fated Norway campaign. They were followed shortly afterwards by the RAF, hoping to assist the fledgling convoy system. The RAF commandeered the golf course, near Stornoway, and aircraft took off from an improvised runway/fairway! Desperation may have been in the air. The Germans had won the day in Norway and further south, the Battle of Britain was raging. Invasion no longer seemed a mere possibility, but imminent.

The sturdy old Avro Anson was utilized by 612 Squadron RAF. 612 was one of the pre-war Auxiliary Squadrons, and this group of men had strong ties with Aberdeen. They did their best to seek out and harass the deadly U Boats, within the limits of the technology then available. Four or five hour flights were the norm, and it was a choice between extra fuel tanks or bomb capacity (no depth charges at this stage in the War), and no radar. How the necessities of war would gradually enhance the capacity to engage the enemy and inflict maximum harm.

Before the war, the Air Ministry and Admiralty had envisaged flying boats as being the most likely provider of airborne assistance to the Atlantic supply route. For the first couple of years, this was undoubtedly the case. RAF Coastal Command had access to few, if any airfields in proximity to what became the Battle of Atlantic. Also, the Short Sunderland, followed by the US-built Catalina, were among the very best options for pursuing and attacking the enemy before long-range, land-based aircraft designs came into operation. RAF Oban flying boat base (with a presence at other west coast locations, including Islay) was very much to the fore in the period 1942/3. In the period 1943-1945 Oban continued to play a valuable role in helping train flying boat crews for the ever expanding theatres of war in the South Atlantic, Indian Ocean and Far East.

By 1941/42, Lockheed Hudson aircraft (converted passenger aircraft) had replaced the Anson at Stornoway, and then 48 and 224 Squadrons RAF used Islay and Tiree. Improvements in fuel and bomb loads ensued, but still the U Boat very much had the upper hand.

In the early days especially, RAF men were billeted with families, and lifelong correspondence and friendship often followed. To this day, ageing but often agile WW2 veterans can be seen in quiet dignified contemplation, staring wistfully into empty spaces which were perhaps long-gone sites for Nissen huts, NAAFIs or canteens, where many a pleasant evening was spent by youths, hundreds if not thousands of miles from home, entrusted to the thoughtful care of our least-acknowledged, least-praised volunteers of WW2; the women's and church groups, who struggled to care for their own, often ration-blighted homes, while still finding countless hours for the needy (someone else's lonely sons and daughters).

We almost had some truly exalted visitors to the Hebrides. Almost, but not quite, thankfully. Had Britain fallen to Nazi invaders, plans appear to have been in place (according to many Islanders and RAF personnel stationed on the Island) to fly the Royal family and Winston Churchill to exile in Canada. Such a flight could not, in 1940/41, have been achieved without re-fuelling. Therefore Tiree appears to have been chosen as the first staging post. This eventuality was never put to the test, as we know. However, evidence of tunnels from the airfield and deep, fortified, underground chambers, are testimony and legacy to what might have been.

Conditions were not easy for the airmen posted to the islands at any time, especially in the earlier years of the war. Some could not believe they did not receive an overseas posting allowance. Unless one was lucky enough to pay for a spare seat on a transport/communications aircraft, then the journey on leave, to places in the south of England, could take 36 hours or more on storm-tossed ferries and over congested wartime trains.

As technological advances progressed, radar formed an integral part of the UK defences. Coastal areas hosted these camps, with their strange, tall, strutted structures and naturally, careless talk certainly was not common about this 'weapon of war'. If towns and ports of the north and west were remote postings, then radar bases were inevitably, well and truly off the beaten track. Airmen at these postings did however often gain a much clearer insight into rural Highland and Island life.

If life was taxing on land it could be even more arduous for those at sea. One airman, flying out of Benbecula in 1942/43, summed things up well for me. Ted Nelson was a wireless operator /airgunner with 206 Squadron. As his aircraft scoured the Atlantic on lengthy patrols, he was thankful to set foot on land at the end of these ten/twelve hour Coastal Command convoy protection patrols. He did however have great sympathy for the men of the Merchant and Royal Navy who they saw day after day, being pitched and tossed around on the unforgiving Atlantic. Some days they would be flying low enough for the sailors to wave to them and offer a 'thumbs up', in thanks for their vigilance.

Flying over a convoy for the first time, perhaps there might be 30 or more ships heading for home ports. Re-joining that convoy a day or so later, there might now be only 24 or 25 vessels having survived the U boat 'wolf packs'. And, if the RAF crews were detailed to cover the same convoy a day or so later, there could be less than 20 ships still surviving, and ploughing slowly homeward to safety, or at least a brief respite from the war at sea.

One thing which has saddened me greatly was the discovery that for the greater part of the war, many merchant seamen had their wages stopped as soon as their ship was sunk. They could be drifting around in a lifeboat or clinging onto a raft for dear life, but not a penny was paid until they found another ship to join when or if they returned to port.

The shores of the islands and west coast were littered by much wartime debris, from the re-usable spoils of war to bodies. On one occasion, bodies were washed up in huge numbers, in many locations, from one particular ship, *HMS Curacoa*, a profoundly sad event. Little was revealed about these terrible disasters at the time due to wartime censorship, and many families were never to discover the fate of their loved ones. In October 1942, the mighty and majestic *Queen Mary* was making its way at speed across the Atlantic, with perhaps 15 or 20 thousand troops, to support the war effort. A number of warships would have provided her with an anti-U boat shield, as they zigzagged to and fro in front, to the side, and behind the great liner. It appears that the *Curacoa* may have mistimed such a manoeuvre, and she was impaled on the bow of the *Queen Mary*. The hapless ship was carried for some time until she eventually split in two and sank. Those on board the *Queen Mary* were sworn to secrecy, but many were haunted by the terrible cries for help from the sailors on board the stricken *Curacoa*. The *Queen Mary* would have been strictly forbidden from stopping, even in these circumstances, as she would have presented the most spectacular prize for any lurking U boat.

Another occasion was the sinking of the *Arandora Star* on July 2nd 1940. This Blue Star passenger liner was involved in ferrying Italian internees and German POWs, among others, to Canada. Their vessel was torpedoed and sunk with great loss of life. It was particularly sad because many of the Italians on board had no love for Mussolini, and indeed some even had sons and brothers in the UK, who were happy to be members of the British forces. Another sad aspect to this story was that among the British troops onboard were Lovat Scouts, drawn mainly from the Highlands and Islands. This west coast, Battle of the Atlantic frontline, saw much flotsam of these two tragedies, and countless others, washed up on her shores.

The west coast had numerous Royal Naval facilities to assist with convoys, minesweeping and minelaying, and many other activities. Among these were Loch Ewe, Kyle of Lochalsh, Fort William and Tobermory. Loch Ewe provided a secluded gathering point for Russian and other crucial convoys. It proved a lonely but well sheltered haven in the North West. Tobermory, under the famous Vice Admiral Gilbert Stephenson (the Terror of Tobermory) became a tremendously successful 'working up' base for a whole range of vessels, well suited to U boat hunting and detection. Tobermory provided a genuine 'short sharp shock' for the young crews of sloops, corvettes etc. before they ventured out into the vast Atlantic. It is said that despite the massive dangers ahead, many sailors were delighted to face the terror of the U boat, rather than the 'Terror of Tobermory'.

As the war progressed a greater range and diversity of RAF units proliferated on the western seaboard.

RAF Air Sea Rescue units were to be found at Oban, Lochboisdale, Tiree, Stornoway and other harbours. Construction personnel, military and civilian, were constantly in demand.

There are many tales of individual fortitude, bravery and endeavour to be told, but only a couple will have to suffice here. A Sunderland flying boat, from 228 squadron at Oban, attempted to land at Lochboisdale in May 1942. On board was a young wireless operator named Eddie Chadwick, from Bury in Lancashire. The pilot attempted to abort the landing when he spotted rocks. He tried to climb away and gain height, but unfortunately stalled and crash-landed. The last thing Eddie recalled, before passing out was the Sunderland slowly sinking, himself trapped, and the hands of crewmates reaching down to pull him to safety. When he came to, he wondered, *'Did I make it, I'm only 19. I hope so.'* He looked around to find himself surrounded by nuns. *'Oh no,'* he thought, *'I'm in heaven. I didn't make it.'* On seeing him awake, the excited nuns began chatting. Eddie was shocked to discover they did not speak English in Heaven! Of course he wasn't in Heaven, he was in the Sacred Heart Convent Hospital in Lochboisdale, and of course the nuns were speaking Gaelic (surely the language of Heaven, some will say)!

Tom Blue was an RAF corporal in the transport section of RAF Benbecula. Tom got the job of 'rounding up' young ladies from out-lying crofts on Benbecula and South Uist to take them to one of the first big dances which the RAF organised on the Islands. Somehow, between Tom's broad Glaswegian accent, and the ears of suspicious, Gaelic-speaking crofters, there were misunderstandings, and Tom found himself more than once staring down the barrel of a shotgun, or being chased by an angry father with a pitchfork. It seemed the men had failed to fully comprehend Tom's assurances that he'd *'take away their lovely daughters, but bring them back safely'*. I am pleased to say that intermediaries and interpreters righted the situation, and many a wonderful evening was had, with a splendid fusion of big-band swing music and ceilidh rhythms.

Another occasion when an interpreter proved invaluable was when Italian POWs were given free rein to work and wander on Benbecula. Many had 'trustee' status, as they were anti-fascist anyway, and eventually Italy was to pull out of its partnership with the Nazis. Some bright spark at the RAF had an idea to put red lights outside houses in the proximity of runways, so that RAF pilots might spot them as they came in to land. Unfortunately, some Italians misunderstood the nature of these red lights. After some unpleasantries, this tricky example of poor communication was righted.

As the war continued, more and more women volunteered and were even conscripted. A great range of tasks were performed by the WAAFs, WRNs ('Wrens') and ATS. They did this with distinction in every location where war work was necessary and the west coast and islands were no exception.

MacBraynes, as already mentioned, did stalwart work as ever, providing for islanders and military alike. Unfortunately one of their vessels was lost, with a number of the crew, in January 1942. The *Lochgarry*, enroute from Glasgow to Oban and then the Faroe Islands with war supplies, ran aground and sank off the Rathlin Islands. Many other well known vessels 'did their bit', such as the stately *King George V*, which served with honour at Dunkirk, and then was employed supplying troopships anchored off the 'Tail of the Bank' at Greenock.

I have been such a lucky, lucky man to correspond with and meet so many wonderful people of that special generation who served and indeed saved us, in WW2. I could name hundreds, literally. Here are a couple I would like to mention. Fred Styles, a corporal on Air Sea Rescue launches at Oban was considered '*a character to be treated with suspicion*' by a few officers. Why? Because he spoke articulately at gatherings of RAF personnel about the need to ensure their generation did indeed get their '*land fit for heroes*' after the war, as their fathers were promised, then denied, after WW1. Fred was on a launch one freezing November night in 1943, when a Catalina made a poor landing and began to sink. Fred's officer said '*Nothing we can do, those lads have had it*.' That wasn't good enough for Fred. He stripped off his coat, boots and jacket and dived into the waters of Firth of Lorne. Three men were pulled to safety but still he would not give up. Fred lost nearly every nail on his fingers and toes as he struggled around inside the slowly sinking flying boat, looking for its unconscious crew. However, there were still men to be rescued. Fred would not leave the water until he was thrown a rope, which he tied around the tail of Catalina. Only then did Fred allow himself to be pulled aboard his launch, suffering from hypothermia. Unfortunately the rope snapped and the plane and remaining crew were lost. Some time later, Fred learned that he had been awarded the British Empire Medal (and his 'file' had been binned). He was too brave to be a suspicious character!

Eddie Kilshaw was co-pilot on a Catalina which was flying out of Oban in the spring of 1944. Eddie was an excellent foot-baller, as was his skipper, David Clyne of Glasgow. David was the captain of Queens Park FC and also captain of the Scotland Amateur national team. Sadly, one night their Catalina crashed on high ground on the Island of Vatersay. Three crewmen died (including Clyne) and Eddie seriously injured a knee. After the war Eddie was transferred from his local team Bury, to Sheffield Wednesday for the then enormous fee of £20,000. Because of his war-time knee injury Eddie was sometimes unavailable to play for Sheffield Wednesday. Feeling self-conscious about the large transfer fee, Eddie didn't lift his wages on the weeks he didn't play. Compare this, if you will, with the vulgar mercenary attitudes of some players involved in professional football today.

At Benbecula there began to be ample evidence of how the war was changing. Boeing B17 'Flying Fortresses' were supplied to 206 Squadron and 220 Squadron RAF, who were based on the Island from late 1942 on into the summer of 1943. This in fact coincided exactly with the turning of the tide in the Battle of the Atlantic. By now the Admiralty and Coastal Command were working effectively in partnership. New Royal Navy tactics, and long-range aircraft, were making the difference. U boat losses escalated dramatically. Benbecula certainly played its part in this momentous victory in the Atlantic, with ten successful U boat attacks in this period.

As there would have been at all wartime bases, there were numerous great characters at every level of the hierarchy of the forces on the Hebrides. Two great friends, pilots Willis Roxburgh (of Glasgow) and Johnnie Owen provide one insight into the fortunes of war. Willis played rugby for Scotland and he and Johnnie were inseparable from their days in training onwards. On March 25th 1943, Roxburgh became one of the successful RAF skippers at Benbecula, when he sank a U boat. He actually spotted the U boat directly below his aircraft. Casting aside normal attack instructions, he turned the B17 into a dive bomber, literally. The huge beast of an aircraft plummeted towards the sea before the U boat could spot them and hide beneath the surface. With every nut and bolt screeching, Willis and his co-pilot managed to pull the mighty Fortress out of the dive just in time to release the depth charges, and then skim away over the surface (the tail-gunner swore to me there was seaweed all over the rear wheel). Around the same time Johnnie spotted and attacked not one, but three, U boats on a single patrol. Many vigilant crews spent up to a 1000 or more hours flying with Coastal Command and never sighted a single U boat. On this particular day, Johnnie Owen spotted and attacked a surfaced U boat, dropping seven depth charges. Luckily he saved one depth charge, which he dropped when he saw a second U boat, sometime later. Finally, when he was almost back at Benbecula, he saw a third U boat. Not content to simply log its position, he dived with open bomb doors, but he had only machine gun bullets to make his attack. Johnnie knew that if, as was likely, the U boat dived to the seabed, it might stay there motionless for a day or two, in case the RAF and Royal Navy were scanning the area. This in turn might well allow a convoy to pass by unmolested by the hiding U boat. Two outstanding pilots, they obviously were. Willis gained a DSO, and survived to live until the 1990's. Johnnie was lost a few days after his 'hat trick' of attacks. Despite countless hours of searching by Willis and other crews, nothing was ever found of his aircraft or crew. Could it have been a U boat? Well-armed, some were choosing to stay on the surface, and fight it out with the RAF aircraft. Was it the wild Atlantic weather? We will never know, but this gallant crew were gone, like so many others, with no known grave but the sea.

Not all technological advances in wartime were to prove purely destructive. Another fine member of the RAF at Benbecula was Dr Ian Donald. Captivated by radar and sonar, Dr Donald, who was the Medical Officer at RAF Benbecula, would spend every spare moment pestering the technical chaps for details of these wondrous new inventions. After the war, as Emeritus Professor of Midwifery at Glasgow University and Rottenrow Hospital, he helped use his wartime-gained expertise to develop ultrasound scans for pregnant women.

Many other islands also made tremendous contributions towards the war effort. Barra, Coll, Colonsay, Skye, Harris and South Uist all had RAF units at one time or another. Tiree and Stornoway however, deserve special mention here. As the tide of war turned, and the Allies moved from the defensive to the offensive, these islands made outstanding contributions to the actual winning of the war. Tiree had RAF squadrons deployed on anti-U boat activities; 304 (Polish) Squadron RAF being worthy of particular note. These brave men contributed to Bomber Command operations with fortitude and courage, and then transferred to Coastal Command, serving at Tiree and Benbecula, among other locations. How sad then, that having fought from day one of the War, the Poles were unable to return to a free homeland in 1945. The 'Iron Curtain' descended, and the men who had served with the RAF were not welcome in a communist-dominated country.

518 Squadron, which formed at Stornoway in 1943, then moved to Tiree, where they remained until 1945. They patrolled the Atlantic with the usual Coastal Command duties, but it is their role in gathering meteorological data which set them apart. They gathered all sorts of information (such as barometric pressure readings, temperature and humidity readings etc.) at dangerously low levels of 50 or 60 feet above the waves, before climbing up to 20,000 feet to continue this task. They flew out deep into the Atlantic on these patrols, and many crews perished. However, the intelligence gained proved invaluable to all sorts of Allied personnel (e.g. Bomber Command, commando-raid planners and most notably the Supreme Headquarters Allied Expeditionary Force). No less than General Eisenhower himself benefited from data gathered by 518 Squadron crews. D-Day, in June 1944, had been postponed once due to unseasonably poor weather. With hundreds of thousands of invasion troops ready to embark in southern England, it was possible the Germans would discover the build up. It was imperative that the right decision was made about when to launch the invasion armada. The weather was a major problem, however, when 518 Squadron provided information about a possible weather window on the 6th June, Eisenhower made the decision to go, and the rest, as they say, is history.

RAF Stornoway also contributed to the anti-U Boat war, but again, made its most vital contribution in another sphere. Like 518 Squadron, who flew Halifax bombers, 58 and 502 Squadrons used this mighty aircraft to good effect. In the final year of the war there was a tremendous amount of German Army and Navy activity around the Skagerrak and Kattegat seas between Norway and Denmark. Patrols from RAF Stornoway flew over the north of Scotland, and then crossed the North Sea, to launch attacks on German shipping in these waters. It is only in recent years that the German plans have come to light and so we now know how crucial the work of the Stornoway based aircraft was. The Germans planned and then launched a massive final offensive of the War in winter 1944/45, in an area of the Ardennes Forest in Belgium. Subsequently, this became known as the 'Battle of the Bulge'. A whole German army of 200,000 winter–trained men, was to be transferred from Norway to Belgium, to supplement this big push. Thanks in part to 58 and 502 Squadron crews, who paid a heavy price, this transfer of troops never actually took place. The Germans attempted to carry out much of the work by sailing under cover of darkness. But these crews from Stornoway were specially trained for night-time flying. Recently, I had the honour of working on a book with John Davenport, who won the DFC for his outstanding contribution while flying with 502 Squadron from Stornoway on operations such as these.

My research now leads me on to challenges new and the gathering of material on many other western and northern Scottish locations in WW2. To mention just a couple; Inveraray; where over 400,000 men trained for D Day, and other vital landings, which were to free Europe and North Africa from Nazi domination. Prestwick (with links to Stornoway), where the 'Transatlantic Ferry' terminated, was absolutely crucial in the supply of US-built aircraft to the Allies in Europe. There were as many as 1000 flights in and out of Prestwick in a day being logged in early 1944, as aircraft crossed the North Atlantic to join in the Allied war effort, as victory began to look possible.

So what remains today? What legacies of WW2 are visible? Developments in landing craft were well suited for inter-island ferry initiatives. Many Nissen huts became byres or holiday homes! Perhaps the biggest change was in attitudes. Scottish servicemen and women had travelled extensively and acquired a taste for emigration. A second 'Highland clearance' seemed a possible threat in post-war years. People had served in Scotland from the world over, and unquestionably this gave a boost to tourism, which continues to grow in importance, for the Highlands and Islands communities to this day. Wartime long-range aircraft developments opened up the world to an increasingly mobile clientele. Highlanders had served alongside Australians,

Americans and Cockneys, to name but a few. It is certain that their outlook would have influenced the naturally reserved and deferential Scots.

It has been my great privilege to attend reunions of wartime personnel, making returns to the Highlands and Islands. Perhaps late in the day, some welcome cairns and memorials are being put in place (usually thanks to efforts of a few hard-working individuals). Museums in these parts are acknowledging the outstanding role played by Hebrideans and Highlanders in WW2, while at the same time, recognizing the decisive contribution this area played as the frontline in the Battle of the Atlantic. The last words must be these though. So many victims of Battle of the Atlantic have no known grave but the sea. Please remember and honour them, and encourage younger generations to do likewise. Their memory and our freedom deserve nothing less, and a lot more than one day per year.

STORNOWAY AIRPORT IN
WORLD WAR TWO

John Davenport DFC

I was an RAF pilot of 502 Squadron, flying Long Range Halifaxes of Coastal Command, first on Anti-Submarine Operations from St Davids, SW Wales, then based at Stornoway in the Hebrides from September 1944. It is a great privilege to be invited by John Randall to return to RAF Stornoway after 63 years! It was a strange feeling approaching to land at the airport, having made perhaps 80 landings myself in the last nine months of the War.

I look back on my posting to Stornoway as the last of a series of milestones in my flying career. Having volunteered with my twin brother Peter to be a pilot, the first must have been my first solo in a Tiger Moth on my 19th birthday. The second was being awarded my 'Wings' in Canada flying Oxfords, then being selected for Coastal Command to fly Mitchells & Liberators at RAF Nassau, Bahamas. The next came at the tender age of 21, making an attack on a German U-Boat in the Bay of Biscay, my first action of any kind, against fierce flak opposition in bright moonlight in a white Halifax Mark II of 502 Squadron, staying at the controls at the request of my American Captain.

Finally to Stornoway in September 1944. 502 came with 58 Squadron, the only two Operational Halifax squadrons in Coastal, to take a completely new role in the maritime war. The experience of night attacks in the Bay of Biscay found us ideally equipped to take the offensive against German shipping movements between Norway, Denmark and the Baltic.

We would use Radar to find them, employ flares or moonlight to illuminate them, finally drop six 500lb bombs to damage or sink them. Until then ships had been able to move unscathed under cover of darkness, free from threat of attack, carrying troops, vehicles, artillery, horses etc., or raw materials such as iron ore, sulphur, coke etc., across the Skagerrak or Kattegat, or up the Norwegian coast to Bergen or Trondheim, supplying U-Boat bases.

Stornoway airfield was very suitable – no land hazards, except a 800ft hill due North, which required care taking off on Runway

36 on a shallow fully loaded climb at night on instruments. It was
fairly free from weather problems of snow or fog, but it was often
wet and windy, as it is now! I see Stornoway on the TV weather
maps – it's strange how the blue areas of rain seem so often to
be covering the Hebrides!

Accommodation was in Nissen huts with a central stove and
separate toilet/shower facilities – primitive by comparison with
pre-war permanent RAF stations. The Officers Mess and Sergeants
Mess were more civilised, though rather overwhelmed at first with
the number of Aircrew arriving.

We thought that St Davids was the back of beyond, but Stornoway seemed remote in the extreme. Seven hours on a train from
London via Inverness to the Kyle of Lochalsh, followed by an eight
hour trip on the ferry made for a prolonged return from leave.
There was hardly an enticing night life, few pubs, one cinema, a
quiet Sabbath, no tourism as there is now, but there were compen-
sations. As aircrew we had extra leave, supplementary pay, and
always slept between sheets, even when training. We didn't have
to fight in blood or mud; casualty rates were lower than in Bomber
Command, and as we were attacking German supply ships we
were not involved in 'Area Bombing' with its inevitable mass of
civilian casualties. WAAFs on the station helped to give an air of
normality. We hardly had any contact with the local population,
although my Navigator, Johnny O'Kane, has just written to tell
me that he met the Macleod family at the Star Inn on the harbour
side who made him and some of our crew very welcome.

Stornoway's contribution to anti-submarine activity started
with the Avro Anson in 1940, using the Mark I 'Eyeball' (no
radar), followed by Hudsons in 1942 and the early days of the
Radar Mk II-the fixed beam system adopted in the Battle of the
Atlantic by VLR Liberators, using the 'Leigh Light' for night
attacks, when U-Boats would normally have been using their
diesel engines to charge batteries, travelling at speed on the surface.

The real advance came with the introduction of the rotating
beam short wave Mark III Radar fitted to Liberators, Halifaxes,
Wellingtons and Fortresses. Known as H2S in Bomber Command,
it was superb for detecting surfaced U-Boats and effective in the
victory in May 1943, when for the first time U-Boat losses in the
month exceeded the number of ships sunk and Doenitz conceded

defeat. Halifaxes of Coastal had this Mark III from 1943, but no Leigh Lights and relied on flares or moonlight for attacking U-Boats at night, and later at Stornoway for the campaign versus German shipping.

Morale at Stornoway was very high – superb leadership and training in the air and on the ground really helped. There was a plentiful supply of wartime low strength beer to contribute to a number of rough games, bawdy songs and topical limericks rounded off by singing the 'Sash'; 502's Squadron song arising from its Ulster origins. The prospect of frequent action led to an expertise, refined by a bombing course at Leuchars when we practised on trawlers in the North Sea. We developed a night technique of constant angle radar homing, wind finding by the use of flame floats to measure drift on three courses at intended bombing height (possible with shipping – not U-Boats), setting the wind on the automatic bombsight. If no moon, we'd return to the target to drop six delayed action parachute flares, make a timed detour around to the opposite side to see the ship(s) silhouetted in the beams on the sea for the approach again on a constant angle for the attack. This need for a Constant angle approach, e.g.7 degrees starboard, compensated for the wind and the moving speed of the target and led to accuracy in our next attack on the *Pergamon* in Jan 1945, when we obtained three direct hits and sank it!

In the early months, we flew the Halifax Mark II in white Coastal camouflage, most unsuitable for Night Operations as it was so conspicuous in moonlight (I'm sure it contributed to our losses), but it was fully equipped for our purpose with radar, Gee navigation, radio altimeter (used for flying at 100ft at night to avoid enemy radar), extra fuel tanks, the Mark XIV bombsight, flares, flame floats, even a camera with photo flash to record results! In February 1945, we converted to the Halifax Mk III with the more powerful Bristol Hercules engines, but a startling difference was the Black camouflage, which must have saved many lives.

The Squadrons made well over 200 attacks on German ships. Results were often impossible to see, but one of our first, on the *Palos* in November 1944, was reported in a Swedish newspaper. The next two, on the *Pergamon* and T/16 Torpedo Boat had to await confirmation from the Air Historical Branch of the MOD in 1993! The last and probably the most dangerous, was on the *Neukuhren* in April 1945, at Frederikshavn, Northern Denmark, against heavy 88mm land flak, radar directed, lighter flak from ships and shore aided by a dazzling searchlight. Having reported two hits, we were able to find the wreck aground and photograph it on a post-War daylight recce. We could even read its name! The two sinkings were quoted in the citations for my DFC and the DFM for my Navigator in April 1945.

Most of the lost aircraft from Stornoway were shot down by German night fighters flying from Grove, Northern Denmark. Fortunately, they were seriously short of fuel which limited their capability.

By the end of the War, there were over 2000 staff on the Station, a considerable increase from the early days, when Ansons were flying from Melbost Golf course. With the activities of 502 and 58 Squadrons I realise now what a noise we must have made, day and night, and I apologise for the disturbance we must have made to the quiet of the locality.

RAF Stornoway made a significant contribution to the War effort by its successes in the blockade of German shipping. The Casualty list totalled 27 in 502 Squadron and 60 from 58 Squadron, a total of 87 in eight months flying from Stornoway, details recorded on a plaque at the Station entrance and in St Martins Church. They were the real Heroes.

"WE WILL REMEMBER THEM"

APPENDIX

Extract from the 'Dagens Nyheter'(Swedish Newspaper) for Nov
6th 1944:

'GERMAN IRON ORE BOAT BOMBED OFF VARBERG.
VARBERG, 5TH NOV 1944

*At about 20.30 hours on Sunday 4th November, the German
steamer 'Palos', of Oldenberg, was attacked by Allied aircraft
just west of Varberg, only one sea mile outside Swedish Territorial waters.*

*The aircraft, presumably British – dropped flares before it
attacked, and then dropped five bombs and opened machine
gun fire. None of the bombs hit, but the 'Palos' was so badly
damaged that she had to request the help of a pilot to take her
into Varberg harbour.*

*When the flares were dropped, the roar of an engine was heard,
and many of the people of Varberg rushed out to watch. They
could clearly see an aircraft machine gunning a steamer, which
gave return fire. The action continued for about a quarter of an
hour, when the aircraft flew off.*

*The 'Palos' was en route from Norway to Germany. She was
badly damaged astern and amidships. The crew stated when they
came ashore, that two of the five bombs dropped exploded only
a few metres from the ship. The 'Palos' is 2000 tons d.w.*

*During the attack, a 16 year old seaman was thrown overboard
by the blast from a bomb explosion. Nothing could be done to
save him.*

*Eight members of the crew of 20 were taken to hospital, six
on the Saturday night, and two on the Sunday.*

*The 'Palos', which was loaded with iron ore, carries one 20mm.
Flak gun and other armament. She may remain in port for 48
hours.'*

This extract refers to an attack carried out by Halifax captained
by F/0 J. K. Davenport, at 2030 hrs on Nov 4th. He reported
at the time that the bombs fell along the port side of the vessel,
approximately 30ft away. No other results were observed.

Postscript

Island Heroes – The Hebrides and UK Military History

I was invited to contribute a talk on RAF Stornoway in World War Two, which involved a return to Stornoway after 63 years! It was a pleasure to meet members of the Islands Book Trust and to be given such a very friendly welcome.

We were agreeably surprised to discover areas of picturesque scenery in the Isle of Lewis. My wife and daughter found time to make the run northwards to the Butt of Lewis lighthouse, finding very pretty secluded sandy bays – open to the Atlantic, in the most remarkable fine warm weather. Quiet roads, few cars, no pedestrians; the only hazards were sheep on the highway and blind summits on straight narrow roads!

Stornoway airfield hasn't changed much since 1945. The long N/S runway has been extended at each end by about 200 yards – the NE/SW (07/25) is still used by light aircraft but the SE/SW one is no longer in use, being occupied by a Coastguard Rescue helicopter base in a new hangar.

We were given a special opportunity to visit the Flying Control building, the same one as in 1945, used as a focal point for airfield movements, with the hospitality of the Station Manager. I was able to go up the same staircase to the first floor viewing gallery, in 1944/5 occupied by WAAF R/T (Radio/Telephony) operators and Flying Control duty staff.

On the approach to the modern terminal building, the coach party stopped at the RAF Memorial plaque. Although 125 names of known war dead are listed in a Book of Remembrance at Martins Memorial Church (closed on later visit) these were not listed at the Airfield. Before leaving Stornoway I was able to discover another fully detailed Book of Remembrance at the Arts Centre behind the British Legion, beautifully presented, with a page for each individual, and spent some time turning the pages, which gave details of colleagues and friends, most of whose names are also recorded at the magnificent Runnymede Memorial, west of London.

The effect of the blockade of shipping movements in Danish/ Norwegian waters by 58 & 502 Squadrons has been researched by the Danish historian Carsten Petersen, who looked me up at Lymington in 2001. He had gained details of highly secret wartime documents addressed to the Operational Intelligence Centre, listing ship's names, positions and sailing dates. He also found that the German 20th Mountain Army of 200,000 men was urgently required to assist in the Ardennes offensive, the battle of the Bulge. Shipping was needed to transport all the troops, artillery, tanks, vehicles, even horses from Norway to Germany.

This movement, and that of many supply ships, carrying iron ore, chemicals, timber etc., plus supplies in the reverse direction to the U-Boat bases in Bergen and Trondheim, were hampered by over 200 attacks made by 502 & 58 Squadrons, which apparently led to a 'Go Slow' and reluctance to sail by German crews.

RAF Stornoway made a marked contribution to the aggressive conduct of the War from its early days in 1941, with Ansons flying from the Melbost Golf course through stages of enlargement with tarmac runways, using Hudsons versus U-Boats in the Battle of the Atlantic, to the last nine months of operations with Halifaxes active in night attacks on German shipping.

I was privileged to join the Islands Book Trust Conference and to make my short addition to the subject of Island Heroes – the Hebrides and U.K. Military History. My talk was a minor section in the context of the longer history of the contribution of the islanders and I was proud to take part.

J K Davenport

RADAR, THE SECRET, SILENT SENTRY AT RODEL

Ken Watson

Having been in on the early stages of radar technology, when bread boards, thermionic valves, string and chewing gum were involved, I have witnessed staggering advances to the range of the means of communication available today. I remain faithful to the traditional mode of public speaking, preferring to rely on the human voice unaided by artificial amplification, so let us set the microphone beyond its eavesdropping range.

At the outbreak of war, the coastline of the British Isles was defended by radar stations with 360 feet high static aerial structures. They were aptly known as Chain Home stations (CH). Brenish, on the west side of Lewis was one such. Enemy aircraft had found a means of avoiding detection by flying just above sea level, under the radar beam. Hence the development of stations with 50 feet high revolving aerials, known as Chain Home Low (CHL). There was one at Rodel in Harris, the focal point of my talk today, where I served for 8 months in 1943.

Over the years, I have been back several times, most recently this April (2008). The domestic site is on land adjacent to the Rodel Hotel. The Nissen-hutted accommodation has long since gone, but the concrete foundations remain, as do the intersecting pathways that link them. A single gatepost remains to identify the original five-barred gate entrance. Passing this, I followed the path to the foundations of my erstwhile home, which brings me to the word 'secret' in the title.

Radar was essentially ultra secret. At Rodel, radar mechanics occupied one Nissen, radar operators another alongside. The rest of the personnel were housed elsewhere and knew nothing of what went on at the technical site, which was a mile or so up the east coast road to Tarbert, on a commanding height. Among my fellow radar mechanics were several Canadians, one of whom established proprietary rights by chiselling into the threshold paving stone the legend, 'Canada House'. Sixty five years later, pushing back the lichen with my foot, I was gratified to discern the faint, weatherworn evidence of his patriotic handiwork. Furthermore, flanking the concrete foundations, marking the very spot where my bed space had been, was a Scottish thistle, flourishing despite the elements. It gets better. A grassy mound separates 'Canada House' from the NAAFI, where the love I developed for all things Hebridean evolved into something more personal. Three years after being posted from Rodel, I celebrated VE Day with a mobile radar unit, sited in Bavaria, from where we had shortened the war with a devastating 1000 bomber raids on Berlin and other major cities. My celebrations were personal as well as national. I had proposed to the NAAFI Manageress, Annabella Gillies of South Dell, Ness, and to my great joy she had accepted.

Sadly, she was called home in 1974, aged but 58, the victim of cancer. A headstone marks her passing in Hartlepool, another on the family headstone at Habost. There is a third, which serves for me as a shrine. On the concrete foundations of the NAAFI quarters at Rodel stand the rusting remains of the kitchen stove on which many a scone was baked. The personal significance of this for me is immense. As is its social evaluation; I know of no other place in the U.K. where scrap metal can lie undisturbed for sixty five years.

Within the next few days I shall be visiting Rodel again to say a word or two alongside that rusting stove. With me, as always will be, in spirit, the girl I met there, who was to be by my side for 28 companionable years. I shall be carrying a photograph of her. You can take the life out of my Annabella but you cannot take Annabella out of my life.

Let us now move up the Golden Road to the technical site. I know of no other radar site where sufficient evidence remains on which to reconstruct, in the mind's eye, the station as it was in its heyday. The solid stone walls remain, as do the concrete foundations within them, ducts clearly visible where cabling connected the operations room with ancillary accommodation. Outside, rusting iron hoops, embedded in concrete, recall nights of Atlantic gales, when we had to lash the aerial array with steel hawsers, two at each end, to restraining iron hoops in the ground. It is time now to take you into this secret world, using a passage from my *World War Two Memoirs—Radar, Reminiscence and Romance*,

144

'The heart of the CHL system was its receiver unit, a package that housed two cathode ray tubes (CRT) – known today as television screens – ancillary circuits, and a console shelf at the front with operator controls. The CRT on the left was circular, that on the right rectangular. Each CRT was manned by a separate operator. A line on each CRT was known as a time base and differed, one screen from the other. On the left hand screen, known as the Plan Position Indicator (PPI), the time base was a rotating radius, revolving round a central axis. It was fluorescently white and easily observed as it swept the circumference. The rotation on the screen was synchronised with that of the aerial array, mounted on a 50 foot gantry outside. This array swept through 360 degrees continuously, detecting any object within range, transmitting the information to the screens below. On The PPI this showed as a fluorescent white arc. As soon as that appeared, the operator flicked a strobe switch in front of him. This left a radial time base afterglow as the time base itself continued rotating. The circumference of the screen was etched with azimuth readings. Noting the reading from the afterglow, the operator would call it out.

The second CRT had a horizontal time base, calibrated in miles with a range up to 300. Its colour was green. When the fluorescent arc appeared on the PPI, and its operator flicked the strobe switch, a downward blip appeared on the second screen, remaining a few seconds as an afterglow. The operator was now able to call out the range. In practice, the bearing was called out, followed immediately by the range. At a Perspex covered table with a grid referenced map of the area under observation, a third operator placed an indicator that coordinated the two pieces of information called out. Successive revolutions of the aerial array produced new data. Thus was added to the information the direction of travel and estimated speed of the object detected.

This information was passed to Ground Control Interception stations (GCI), responsible for the defence of the area. Knowing the whereabouts of their own aircraft, they very quickly identified hostiles. Once detected by one radar sta-

tion, a hostile quickly came under the scrutiny of others. If necessary, fighter planes were scrambled to intercept and engage. It was this system that safeguarded us all, vigilantly, round the clock, and won for us the crucial Battle of Britain.'

Not all who served at Rodel fell under its benevolent spell. For some the isolation was unbearable. A service policeman blew his brains out one lonely night watch. Another airman was found at the foot of the cliffs, having been missing all day. For those debarred from the secrecy of the technical block, life must have seemed pretty pointless. There was nowhere to go. If you left camp all you met were sheep. We had a standard diagnosis of stages of madness at Rodel: 1. You talked to yourself. 2. You talked to the sheep. 3. The sheep talked to you and men in white suits came to take you away. To help maintain morale, I produced a camp magazine, issues of which have survived. Two poems encapsulate the acceptance of the way of life,

Ode To Beauty by Rodel Romeo

As in a dream I saw her there
The sunlight shining in her hair
Tinting it a glorious shade
Like Autumn leaves in a grassy glade
A smile played softly round her lips
Alluringly she swayed her hips
The love light glistened in her eyes
For all the world like the sunrise

Her pearly teeth she boldly bared
Her beauty left my breath impaired
And when she showed her shapely leg
I fell in love with little Meg

Her bosom heaved with heartfelt sighs
The fires of love still ruled her eyes
I looked her o'er from head to feet
And thought my heart would cease to beat

I left her by the light of dawn
My love for her I'd softly sworn
Her slave for life I fell asleep
And dreamed of Meg – my favourite sheep

A Beautiful Memory

Last night I held a little hand
So gentle and so sweet
My little heart it nearly burst
So loudly did it beat
No other hand in all the world
Could greater solace bring
Than that little hand I held last night –
Four Aces and a King

There was a serious motivation behind this seemingly frivolous levity. Those two airmen who had found real life so unbearable that they were driven to end it would have been better advised to have sought an alternative solution. Far better to create and dwell in an imaginary world, where dreams take over from harsh reality, where you shape your own sense of belonging, than succumb to the harsh reality imposed on you. For the non technical personnel at Rodel life very probably seemed pointless. Unaware of the ultra secret world inhabited by the radar staff, they must have pondered on the point of serving on a camp situated at the far end of nowhere day after dreary day. We all need to feel useful. Some of them patently did not.

A chance posting had taken me to the remoteness of Rodel. An equally random decision had placed Annabella Gillies there. So began my abiding love affair with the Outer Hebrides. During twenty eight years of happy marriage and beyond, I have integrated into the community of Ness and have recorded the process in memoirs entitled '*All Isles Excelling – An Appreciation of a Community and its People.*' Full of interesting characters, it builds on relationships that began at Rodel. One of these was with a radar operator who shared with me many a watch. He was more at home than most, coming from Bayble. A year older

147

than I, he provided glimpses into a culture that was increasingly to capture me. His name will be familiar to many in this audience. Derek Thompson went on to become a Gaelic scholar of note, a university professor of renown, and a prolific contributor to Gaelic poetry and prose. At Rodel, he was part of a watch that safeguarded his homeland in the role of secret, silent sentry.

It was similar watches around the coastline of the British Isles that narrowly won the Battle of Britain, removing the threat of German invasion. This was radar as a defensive weapon. I was posted from Rodel as new offensive technologies were being developed and spent a fortnight at Land's End, confined to a Nissen hut, committing to memory details of this embryonic new weapon. No written evidence was permitted to leave that hut. Theory was well ahead of practice and it was some months before I joined a fully equipped mobile radar unit at Swanage. From here we directed devastating air raids on German industrial centres, and it has to be said, on city civilian populations, before targeting coastal defensive gun emplacements in the run up to D Day.

In September 1944 we crossed the Channel to take up a position in the Ardennes from which we could target the German hinterland. Our mission was abruptly interrupted by the Battle of the Bulge at Christmas 1944, forcing a retreat to Mons. It being December and approaching the shortest day, it was still dark at 3 a.m. as we began the withdrawal. A damp, swirling mist hampered visibility. About 6 a.m. we heard on our portable radio that the German advance was rapidly developing and that American troops were everywhere in retreat. Shortly after dawn we received orders to get our unit on the road and head west. Approaching the log bridge that gave access to the road, we learned that German Panzers had overrun a sister unit some 15 miles to the east. A continuous flow of trucks with unused ammunition, Press jeeps and vehicles with staff officers passed as we edged our Matador and trailer on to the road. It was noon precisely. The Panzers arrived at 12.15. It was a close run thing.

A few weeks later we returned to the site to resume the offensive, before crossing the Rhine at Remagen to venture a few hundred miles deep into Germany itself, establishing a position from which we launched devastating raids on Berlin, Hamburg and Hanover among others, bringing the end of hostilities in

Europe to a conclusion. It was here that we celebrated VE Day in spectacular fashion. It began with an address by the C.O., '*Gentlemen,*' he announced, '*on the back of AMES 9412 is a large carboy of full strength Navy rum, which we have transported from the beaches at Arromanches to its present location, for use in cases of emergency. In my view, such an emergency has now arisen, and I have a strong premonition that the said carboy will fall off the back of the trailer at precisely 18-00 hours. I am sure you will agree with me that it would be a tragic waste of good spirit were it to drain away into the parched earth, and German soil at that. I would therefore urge you to prevent such a calamity by presenting yourselves, armed suitably with regulation issued mugs, outside the orderly room at the appointed hour.*'

To a man we responded, transferring the contents of our brimful mugs to any receptacles we could find for future use. An inch in the bottom of the mug was enough to see most of us off, so potent was the brew, and every time we filled our mugs with hot tea in the days that followed we were quite merry again. In the meantime, uninhibited celebrations erupted. A nearby castle was rumoured to harbour a collection of mediaeval theatrical costumes. These we purloined, along with an oxcart found alongside. A newly established strolling players group toured the village, giving impromptu inebriated performances at every street corner. There was no audience, save for those behind twitching curtains as locals struggled to take on board the fact that, for them, as for us, the long, bitter conflict was over.

This victory was achieved only in the nick of time. German V2 rockets, launched from mobile platforms, were raining down on London. The final victory, like that of the Battle of Britain, was a close run thing. A brief description of radar's offensive characteristics is apposite at this juncture. Mobile units worked in pairs, separated often by hundreds of miles. One operated as the cat, the other as the mouse, the roles being interchangeable. The cat operated with the pilot, the mouse with the observer/bomb aimer. The pilot flew along a radar beam, invisible to the eye but audible in his headset which emitted a continuous whine while he was on it. Deviations to either side were indicated by morse code dots or dashes. Pathfinder pilots were adept at initial weaving on both sides before settling on the beam. Their job was to stay there till bombs had been dropped. The observer/bomb aimer's headset was connected to a stream of information that coordinated all the data essential to precision bombing in all conditions. He received checks at 12, 9, 5 and 2 minutes from bomb release, after which computer fed flight information was transmitted. On precise instructions he pressed his bomb release button, assured of pin point accuracy. These highly skilled manoeuvres were carried out by Pathfinders flying Mosquitos, who dropped marker flares that lit up the target area. Close on their tails came 1000 fully laden Lancaster bombers.

Since publishing my War Memoirs in October 2003, I have received letters, e-mails and telephone calls from diverse sources. The latest arrived but a fortnight ago, from an eighty-seven year old whose daughter-in-law had bought my book for his birthday. His RAF career was almost a mirror image of mine. He'd missed the joy of a posting to the Outer Hebrides, but had spent a year at Point of Stoer. More significantly, he had been with the only other mobile radar unit to operate so deeply into Germany in the final stages and had shared with my unit those radar directed raids that shortened the war. He was about to enter hospital for an exploratory operation and ended his letter with '*per ardua ad astra*'. I do hope he recovers. There aren't many of us left to tell the tale.

The theme of our conference has been the disproportionate contribution and sacrifice of the Hebridean islands in U.K. military campaigns. This has been demonstrated by a succession of contributors, each from the specific perspective of individual expertise. I have found the proceedings educative, engaging, occasionally emotional, above all enjoyable.

For my part, I am pleased to have had the opportunity to reveal that, during the absence of islanders from their homes, serving their country around the globe, their coastlines were assiduously defended round the clock from any threat of enemy incursion by a radar network, manned in many cases by others who had also crossed oceans, and had in some cases made the ultimate sacrifice.

Finally, the main tourist attraction at Rodel is St. Clement's Church, which attracts regular visitors. The domestic site of the wartime radar station is but a stone's throw away, the technical site but a mile up the road, easily located by the existence of a mobile phone mast alongside, and visible from the road. The track leading to it is steep and rough. A vehicle with good tyre tread and adequate suspension can negotiate it. Otherwise it's shanks' pony. The views from the top are spectacular and well worth the effort. Binoculars will afford instantaneous pleasure. A camera will create a memory to be cherished at leisure.

If you are lucky you may experience something I did on occasions when the wind was in the right direction and I had slipped out of the claustrophobic heat of the technical block for a few lungfulls of fresh air. Floating up on the breeze from the crofts below wafted the evocative sound of a Hebridean crofter at work on his loom: 'clickety-clack, clickety-clack, clickety-clack'. I remember thinking then that I knew why I was in that isolated radar station. With others, serving on sites around the coastline, we were defending that crofter's way of life from alien forces intent on its destruction. To remind me of that fact I have a wardrobe of seven Harris tweed suits, one for every day of the week. That wartime posting to the Hebrides has a lot to answer for.

May I conclude by thanking John Randall and all at the Trust for inviting me to contribute towards the invaluable aims it continues to pursue and to wish it every success in future ventures. For my part, I wish we had had another day or two to develop relationships that have just begun to blossom. It has been a pleasure to meet you all.

LEWIS AND ATTITUDES TO THE MILITARY – AN AFTER-DINNER GALLIMAUFRY

Sheriff Colin Scott Mackenzie D.L., FSA Scot.

"ARMA VIRUMQUE CANO," with which often quoted words began Publius Virgilius Maro his Aeneid, – and so I thought might I – but you can relax: I will not tread further into the realms of the classics. Many of my generation, at least, will understand the reference in the current context. For others into whom Latin was not thrashed at school, it simply indicated that Virgil was going to write about matters martial, as I intend – eventually. Also, of course, it may give my musings a gloss of erudition, however unmerited, though I make no claim for them to be in a Virgilian league.

I hope you have all had a good meal and are well-watered and feeling content and well-disposed towards your after-dinner speaker. My 'slot' in this medley of lectures is minor. All I have to do, if I understand my task correctly, is to entertain rather than to instruct. That rather lets me off the academic hook and may allow me to wander off on a frolic or two on my own. Furthermore, as this day marks the opening of the grouse season, I hope I can also indulge myself in a brace or two of perhaps controversial grouses without too much let or hindrance.

Starting off on an entirely serious note I had hoped to look at recent recruiting figures so that I could compare and contrast the situation now with that of about a hundred years ago. I did write to the army records people in Glasgow for some statistics but alas nothing of value transpired from that correspondence. Indeed I had difficulty in obtaining any current information at all. Those who could tell me were somewhat evasive in their responses – prevarication as we call it in the trade. The army records people I wrote to for information at their Glasgow HQ replied to me at some length, saying effectively 'No'. They went on to say that they were treating my query as a request for information in terms of the Freedom of Information Act and that they had interpreted that Act as not applying to them. I wonder why they bothered to say that? In any event, I went so far as to look up what the Act actually says. I have not been addressed on it, of course, but I

153

did not see any exemption for the military in its terms – so what are they trying to hide, I wonder. Being stymied in that important direction I must now present to you my other straw-challenged bricks, though the local TA PSI and its Inverness HQ have indeed been helpful as far as they could go.

Before I turn to such figures as I have, perhaps we should look at a little bit of our local military history, doubtless at no small risk of merely repeating what you may have already heard during this seminar.

As you will know the Territorial Army is one hundred years old this very year (2008). There have been and are to be throughout the land various celebrations – including the Beating of the Retreat by a band of TA pipers, performing from Shetland to the Borders. Rather strangely, given our not insubstantial contribution to the TA in the past, the powers that be are seemingly bypassing Stornoway altogether. That is not, I must add, in any way the fault of the local TA unit. Here, I hope, in September, there will be a slightly belated TA100 celebration in the Stornoway Town Hall for all who have ever been associated here with the TA and it is hoped that the Lewis Pipe Band will be able to provide the missing pipe music as it frequently did in the past – so, it is trusted, all will be made well again.

Of course military service and volunteering did not come into existence in the islands just 100 years ago. The whole island race was pretty well permanently on a war-footing throughout the early, mid and high middle ages. The clan chiefs demanded and got military service as part of their social compact with their clansmen – who were, one may be reasonably certain, usually only too happy to join in a raid or *creach*. That ancient word *creach*, by the way is still quite frequently heard today in Gaelic as an exclamation of dismay. The expression '*mo chreach*' is still used by Gaels, day in daily, (though I suspect few would necessarily appreciate its aetiology or origins) and the fuller phrase '*Mo chreach 's thainig*' or simply '*Mo chreach*' means 'My raid has arrived (upon me)'. It is the sort of thing one's forefathers or perhaps more probably one's fore-mothers might have said when they saw the war-galleys sweeping silently up the firth towards them – naturally a matter of great concern for all the watchers – and, once discerned, would certainly have inclined them to take to either the hills or their heels as rapidly as possible.

In the days of the Vikings, raiders did not give you warning of their murderous or piratical intent and only fairly substantial settlements could be expected to muster any kind of effective response in a hurry. The isolated settlements along our Highland and Island coasts were particularly vulnerable to sea attack – and the Vikings were as murderous a group of thugs as ever existed. They have had far too good a press for far too long from unthinking romantics. It should be remembered that these and other pirates only came into prominence after the Roman Navy abandoned the North Sea. A regular defence force long long ago proved its worth as a deterrent and that lesson is ignored at one's peril.

In these far off days and for centuries afterwards the locals themselves did not need much encouragement to go on the warpath. As Samuel Johnston said once – '*A martial people is quarrelsome.*' The warrior was then a highly respected member of Gaelic society – and he tended to know it. The arms bearing man was towards the top of his tree. The ordinary agricultural labourer, far less the *sgallag* at the bottom of the heap, was for most of that time simply not allowed to fight or bear arms. I am in no doubt that the actual fighters were, for most of our history, to be found in the higher ranks of society – related to or nearly connected with the chief or other important personages of the day. The man-rent bonds mentioned by Mr. Maclean-Bristol were as effective in Lewis at one time as elsewhere in Gaeldom.

Once, however, traditional Gaelic society had been dealt its mortal blow after 1746 the door was opened to lesser mortals to find their character and fortune as professional fighters. Perhaps the older ways continued for some decades longer in places like the Isle of Coll but the imperial demand for men and more men to serve in the military was insistent. Those newly eligible to bear arms were not all necessarily very keen on that change and though the pressures from family and clan were very strong to follow the chief abroad in his new-fangled regiment some were not persuaded easily. One may expect that those with a family tradition of learning how to be a warrior just joined up without a second thought whereas those without such a tradition were less in favour of being blown to bits on some foreign field of endeavour.

The much later, surprisingly often bloodless, raids by one clan upon another – where you stole back the black cattle which had been stolen from you last year – or the more serious raids on the neighbouring fat-land farmers of Lowland Scotland, were also described as *creachs*. To be on the receiving end of any kind of *creach* would have been no laughing matter but it did keep the boys who dished it out fit and active and well adapted to guerrilla warfare.

To join in a raid or *creach* on the richer lowland regions of Scotland or Ireland with the hope of a consequent share of booty was long considered by the average island warrior a more or less respectable way of earning some badly needed capital. From that more or less constant state of affairs can be said to have developed all later military proclivities.

What follows here is an outline (and nothing more) of some of these military matters – with more emphasis on the voluntary side of things than on anything else. Though it is just an outline it still goes on for quite a number of pages, principally because I have not had time to compress it. but also because the background is, I believe, essential to any understanding of the current situation. What I touch on will, you must understand, only be one strand of many which could be followed. I will not read out all my thoughts on the matter to you, mainly for lack of time but also because you would soon tire of the sound of my voice. It will all the same, I am told, be available to you afterwards in print should you want to look a little further into it all. What I will do, however, is speed-read parts of my distillation out to you and you can catch up on the detail later, if you wish.

By the 1600s, modern times were catching up with the islanders and their fights tended to be more organised from afar. Our foray to distant Auldearn in Moray in 1645 on behalf of the Covenanters was a bit of a disaster for us – we were totally outmanoeuvred by that master Royalist tactician of the day, Alasdair Macdonald, better known as Alasdair Coll Ciotach, and only three Lewismen out of several score made it home alive. The more widely famed Marquis of Montrose gets all the plaudits for the Royalist victories of that era but it is arguable that Alasdair Coll Ciotach was at the very least his equal, if not his master. Presumably the Alasdair's name has been eclipsed because the Lowlanders, who have in general written the history books, did not know how to pronounce his name. The Battle of Auldearn is slightly odd because in spite of its relative importance no one seems to know on which precise day it was fought, other than it was sometime in May of 1645.

George, the Second Earl of Seaforth at that time, was a most important fellow, with probably more acres and swordsmen to call on than anyone else at the time – though his rival Campbell of Argyll is often given that pre-eminence, possibly incorrectly. The Seaforth family, particularly in the early days of their ascendancy, were well known to be very clever and "subtill" – which is how they acquired Lewis in the first place – and not good enemies to have. Seaforth was dynastically connected with anyone who was anyone in Scotland and far beyond. His 'empire' at its height stretched from sea to shining sea – from the Black Isle to Lewis itself – and like many in that sort of position, he naturally never had quite enough and was always looking to improve his own position. Auldearn nearly proved the very end for himself and his ambitions, but he was a consummate politician. 'Very fickle,' his enemies quite rightly said – his politics changed with the wind – but he always managed to escape with his head, unlike many others. His son, the next Seaforth, nearly lost his, as he had been rumoured to have been engaged or about to be engaged to the daughter of the Lord Protector, Oliver Cromwell. Like father like son: he, no doubt, had his eye on the main chance of the day, but after Charles II was restored to his throne in 1660, the young Seaforth was called to the royal presence and required by an irate and irritated sovereign to account for himself. Naturally he denied ever having had any remotely honourable intentions towards the lady, whatever else he had had in mind, and he seems to have been let off with a warning.

Be that as it may, distant government was becoming ever less distant and always more effective – and it has inexorably tightened its miserable grip ever since. So far as the warriors were concerned, however, they had no option but to make their fighting abilities pay through grabbing for themselves what they could carry while the action was hot – and, indeed, why not? After all, no one at all in any of the Highland armies got paid anything like what we would recognise as a wage until as late as September 1715 (when the Jacobite Earl of Mar first shelled out his largesse).

157

During the time of the Jacobite rebellions of 1715 and 1745, the whole of Gaeldom was in uproar. Most historians ignore the one in between – that of 1719; largely hatched in Stornoway and which again involved a large number of Lewismen, a few Spaniards and not many others, but was led or fomented by a perhaps surprisingly large number of top European names of the day. Charles XII of Sweden had promised 10,000 troops to help but was unhelpful enough to die before these could be embarked. The only relevant footnote I have been able to discover about Swedish Charles is that there is an obscure Highland step-dance called after him. There was only one battle – that of Glenshiel, just outside of Dornie, by Kyle of Lochalsh, and that was the end of that rebellion – but it was for all that very important as it proved sufficient to discourage the island's chief, the then current Seaforth, from risking his neck again in 1745, he having been by then pardoned twice before. The consequences of that may arguably have had a most significant effect on the end result of that final Jacobite rebellion. The whole future direction of the UK then all hung in the balance after Derby and a further Jacobite regiment of Seaforth's men might well have swung things for Charlie. They didn't, so we had to thole the duller Hanoverians instead – which is probably just as well.

Incidentally, while Seaforth, as a result of his various misdemeanours, was suffering exile in Paris, his loyal Lewismen not only paid their rent to the Commissioners of the Forfeited Estates (of which Lewis was one) but they collected amongst themselves the same sum again so that their exiled chief need not let the side down in Paris through impecuniousness. There were no banks as we know them to facilitate international trade, nor indeed was any kind of financial transaction other than handing over gold or silver even possible outside of Edinburgh, and the islanders sensibly decided they would accompany the cash to the south, just in case. The sudden appearance in the douce, if malodorous streets of Edinburgh of 400 Lewismen armed to the teeth, gave the citizenry and their magistrates grievous palpitations, but before they could recover from their panic the money was handed over by its guardians, to be sent to Paris in the usual way and the Lewismen departed home utterly peacefully, having behaved impeccably during their city sojourn – just as one would have expected. It would not be the last time that they would be underestimated.

The Gael had for centuries bled loyally for his chief, who in turn had organised protection against the inevitable human predators always circling around the clan territory and interests. That was, as I have indicated above, their social compact – and it worked and kept everybody happy for a surprisingly long time. Once, however, the native order of things as exemplified by the Lordship of the Isles had been broken and the chiefs who arose on its ruin subverted, he, the Gael, scarcely had time to consider whom next he should follow. He had barely got used to the idea of a Scotland encompassing the Lowlands far less the very recent United Kingdom, before the sky fell in on him post Culloden. His subsequent pacification was brutal even by the standards of a not particularly fussy age. Probably half of the Highlands had not turned out for the Stuarts but that didn't do them much good, as the royal Duke of Cumberland did not distinguish much or often between friend or former foe.

Lewis was to a considerable extent protected by the fact that Seaforth had not 'come out' for Charlie, but in reality a major factor there might also have been the mere presence of the Minch. The government troops were more urgently required on the mainland and sending any significant number across the water to a place that had not 'come out' was not seen as being cost-effective – or whatever was the buzz-phrase of the day.

These factors combined for once to protect us. In general, however, the newly disarmed Gael all over the Highlands and Islands pretty quickly and wholeheartedly transferred his affections and unstinting loyalty from his chief, not to the crown, nor yet to the still new state, but astonishingly enough, to the British Army itself. After all, where else could a fellow acquire arms nowadays? After a short period of uncertainty on the part of southron politicians he was made full use of, as you can imagine.

Post 1745, there were generally three kinds of soldiers in the UK; the regulars, the militia and the volunteers. The regular and volunteer forces scarcely need any explanation. Naturally the harsh terms of the Disarming Act of 1747 did not apply to the regular soldier and to take the king's shilling was an acceptable way for a young man to make his way in the world. The Gael still thought in terms of a warrior caste. The young man's family would usually approve of an army career and he would have the chance to wear the kilt and show off his brawny legs to the delight of any passing damsels. The uniform then as now *did* attract many of the fair sex.

By and large the Gaelic soldier was a sophisticated cut or two above his lowland counterpart and played an inordinate part in the creation of the British Empire. Even Britain's quondam jewel of India could be said to have been finally won for Britain (if for only a mere couple of centuries) largely through the endeavours of the basically island raised 78th Regiment of Foot (later called the Seaforth Highlanders) at the Battles of Seringapatam and Assaye. Our warriors accordingly and understandably thought even more of themselves and, it has to be said, of many of their fiercer and worthier opponents – and they were held in equally high regard at home.

It was quite otherwise in England. Even well into the next century the Duke of Wellington, England's favourite general (called the 'Iron Duke' not because of his character but because he had iron shutters on his London home to protect himself from the mob) would describe his English troops as *'the scum of the earth, enlisted for drink.'* No wonder he needed protection. That was definitely not how the Highlander thought of himself nor indeed how he was described by others.

As well as the full-time regular soldier, there was in the 18th century a 'second-line' infantryman called a 'fencible'. There were – perhaps as far back as the 1760s – companies recruiting in Lewis (as elsewhere) for such fencible troops – but almost everything before then and for some time afterwards relating to formal units recruiting on the island (as opposed to the irregular and sometimes haphazard recruitment of earlier days) is pretty hazy so details are hard to come by. The records of the Fencible Units which we know recruited in Lewis are, however, inextricably combined with the mainland part of the former Shires of Ross and Cromarty (of which Lewis once formed part) and are not easily disentangled and so for our purposes they have to be rapidly passed by.

Initially the fencible soldier was merely a part-timer, but later on he became full-time and was trained and paid in the same way as a regular soldier – save only that he had a home defence commitment, presumably with a lesser pay. Fencibles as a special category of regular troops disappeared in 1802, when they were disbanded following a mutiny in the Netherlands. They had then expressed their contempt for the Grand Old Duke of York and their dislike of enforced foreign service. He it was who marched them endlessly and pointlessly wherever – though I doubt if they actually had many hills to climb in the Netherlands. They were all quickly disbanded in disgrace. Later units may also have been called 'Fencibles' but that was only an echoic name and not a categorical description.

The next most common type of soldier to appear on the military stage was the Militiaman. Now, that term, in the English language at any rate, has totally vanished from our scene. It went through various stages. Initially the militia was just another name for the 'host' – the body of able-bodied men called out in emergency ever since the dark ages – but the term 'militia' used to describe such a national armed body was recorded in Scotland only from about 1663. That militia, however, was so surrounded by rules and regulations (demonstrating that bureaucracy is nothing new) that it proved far too cumbersome to embody. It faded quite away after the Jacobite rebellions. In spite of all the Jacobite unrest in the first half of the 18th century only *one* unit – that organised by the Duke of Argyll, a perfervid Hanoverian – ever managed to take the field and that was in late 1745! Its inbuilt bureaucracy and dilatory nature meant that that Scottish militia was never called out again.

However, a new 'improved' kind of Militia was brought into being in England in 1757. Service in that force was *partly* compulsory for all able-bodied adult men – you were balloted for it if otherwise eligible and you took your chances that way - though if you had some money you could buy yourself out or pay for someone else who had not been balloted to go in your stead.

The government of the day was nervous about re-arming the Scots, however, and that particular type of local armed force was not introduced into Scotland until some fifty years after the Jacobite threat had been quashed at Culloden. *All* Scots were regarded by the English with a post-'45 jaundiced eye, irrespective of where they had stood in the rebellion (other than, of course, those who had joined the regular army and were fighting for

Britain, mostly overseas and well out of harm's way). In 1797, however, the UK parliament, to meet the new impending threat of Napoleon, finally introduced into Scotland the same 'new' kind of balloted-for Militia.

Neither that new Militia nor its companion organisations – the Supplementary Militia and the short-lived Local Militia – were *ever* popular with the public. In fact they were distinctly unpopular. They were a kind of selective National Service operated by the local Lieutenancy and were not seen as being 'fair'. One little known advantage of being in the militia was that you could claim exemption from being 'pressed' by the Royal Navy – not that the senior service always paid much attention to that if they thought they could get away with it.

The Hebrideans were, I think, seamen par excellence. They served at sea in considerable numbers, both in the Royal Navy and in merchantmen. There were, I understand, a number aboard Nelson's flagship, *HMS Victory*. It was a Stornoway lad by the name of John Robertson who is said to have run up the famous signal, '*England expects....* ' The story of these seamen, however, seems to be pretty well unsung for some reason. *Pace* the stories recorded by James Shaw Grant and Angus 'Ease' Macleod about press gang activities in Lewis, I have the feeling that fishermen in the Western Isles were exempted from the naval press gangs for quite some time (unlike the Northern Isles) principally because the men were mainly monoglot Gaelic speakers and 'Erse' was forbidden on HM's warships. I suspect that there really were very few such raids in these parts. There may be some confusion in the popular mind because the recruiting bodies sent out by the chiefs and landowners were also demotically if improperly called 'press gangs' – though they had *none* of the compulsory powers of the naval variety. They had to rely on persuasion and when recruiting became sticky, possibly veiled threats. My own people were tacksmen in the early days of Stornoway itself – I could do with some of what the tack covered today, even in the current economic clime. As far as I know we had almost no connection with the navy – though I did have a step-great-grandfather who achieved the rank of Rear-Admiral. You can see a cannon which he, while still a Captain RN, gifted to Sir James Matheson, lying in front of Lews Castle, painted most inappropriately in aluminium silver on a concrete block plinth. It was taken in battle in I think Hangkow – there is a legend inscribed deeply on it.

To return to the military, there were two ordinary Militias which recruited in Lewis and possibly one Local Militia as well, but as time went by the element of compulsion disappeared and the Militia became essentially just another entirely volunteer organisation. However, they were then directly competing with a third force which had grown up over exactly the same period of time (since 1797) – namely the Volunteers (properly so called – and which I will distinguish with a capital 'V' – for by this time all soldiers other than the new Militia were in a sense volunteers, as hosting belonged to the past and conscription was many years in the future).

Volunteer companies were raised all over the UK in the years after 1797. They represented a genuine citizens' part-time army started by patriots to meet a declared French threat. Initially they wrote their own constitutions, laid out their own terms of engagement and designed their own uniforms – all for free and at no cost to the government! Some were little more than gun-clubs. They were in fact (and rather surprisingly, given the financial side of the equation) not very popular with the government nor with the regular army – probably because central authority had little or no control over them and they were thought to interfere with regular recruitment.

Being a populist movement, however, the Volunteers could not be ignored. Initially tolerated, they were eventually paid for parades by the government. There were two companies of these early Volunteers active in Lewis. We don't really know very much about what they did or even who they were – all we have is a handful of names.

These Volunteer Companies had their ups and downs and almost totally disappeared from the scene for several decades after 1808, by which time the first French threat had more or less faded away. They came back with a vengeance however, with the renewed French threat of 1859.

Tennyson's poem, '*Storm, storm, Riflemen, form*', published in the London Times on 9th May that year roused all the UK nations to a fever pitch of patriotic enthusiasm. It may be difficult to for us in modern times to appreciate just how roused everyone became throughout the UK, by a poet of all people – but roused they certainly were.

Lewis was one of the first areas to form a new approved Volunteer unit. It was embodied as The 1st Ross-shire Artillery Volunteer Corps on April 13th 1860 – though locals said they had really come into being in December of the previous year when the decision to form up had been taken. That is really where the history of our now local and properly organised defence force begins – at least in any detail. We know a great deal about that fine body of men. We know who was in it – and that was it seems anybody who was anybody– and we know more or less what they did. What we don't know is quite why the Corps was an *artillery* one. So far as is known there was no previous tradition of artillery in the area. We do not know if there was any other option available for the Volunteers – but of course we do know that most of the other small burghs dotted around the northern coasts of Scotland also were given artillery units so presumably it was all part of one grand government plan.

They had a fine time letting off their large cannons which made very satisfactory bangs down at the Battery Park in Stornoway. As an aside I may say that I always think it is grossly unfair that although Battery Park was named after *them* and their successors the TF Battery, the only plaque to be found there refers to a subsequent, albeit much larger, RNR battery which shared the site with them for a relatively short time.

Militarily speaking, all the Volunteer companies had an uneventful time throughout the ensuing forty or so years of their existence. None of them fell in battle and the highlight of their existence was to have attended the 'Wet Review' in 1881. That was held to mark the 'coming of age' (i.e. 21st anniversary) Review of 40,000 Volunteers held in the Queen's Park, Edinburgh before Queen Victoria herself, where a tremendous downpour soaked all present to the skin – save presumably Her Majesty. The Stornoway contingent, under the command of one John Norrie Anderson (a notary public of the burgh and later chief magistrate, whose name still shines out from the brass plate of Messrs Anderson Macarthur & Co., Solicitors, Stornoway) distinguished itself by *not* seeking to take avoiding action (as did everyone else) when an overburdened sewer burst in their path. They showed by such disdain that such things did not make them deviate from their duty as they saw it.

Would all that happen today I wonder? In any event, for almost all of its existence anyone who was anyone claimed to have attended the 'Wet Review' and survived. Actually the local lads were lucky – some of the other Highland units went all the way home in their dripping wet uniforms and tragically, a few developed pneumonia and actually died. This was averted for the islanders by the kindly action of a Lewiswoman who ran a public house in the capital. She went to the railway station to wish them a safe journey home and saw their bedraggled and miserable state. She immediately sent to her hostelry for bottles of whisky and dished them out to the goggle-eyed and incredulous troops. According to the late Rev. Roddie Morrison, sometime of the High Church Stornoway and himself a quondam Volunteer and who, as he was nearly 100 years of age when he passed on, can still be recalled by islanders of a certain age, the whisky was *not* for drinking, perish the thought (the Rev. Roddie being a lifelong, not to say rabid teetotaller) but for rubbing on their bodies the better to dry themselves. Maybe that's the yarn they told when they eventually got home. Even the Rev. Roddie was heard to say that never had there been such a monstrous waste of fine whisky in such a good cause.

The Volunteers were tremendously important on our social scene. I doubt if it is even possible to over-estimate their importance and influence. The Battery was usually referred to as just that – but pronounced in local style as the '*Baaaaatterrry*'. The town and island seemingly almost revolved round their annual balls and other similar events. Their gunnery competitions, both locally and on the mainland, were followed most assiduously by a knowledgeable crowd. Their annual review day attracted large crowds, the school got a holiday and the town was decked with bunting. They regularly entertained the citizenry with brass and silver bands and concerts. Their every activity seems to have been reported in minute detail by the press – almost as if they were truly important people like modern pop-stars or footballers. They were in fact very popular in their day and no one was too grand in civilian life to serve as a humble gunner in the Volunteers. There is nothing on the present scene to compare with them, alas.

That 1860 battery kept going until 1908. By all accounts the 1ˢᵗ Ross was a very efficient unit but, perhaps because of a basic lack of overall control, many other units in the deep south had fallen by the wayside in too many respects and had lost not only their own impetus but also the support and respect of both the army high command and the politicians. Those units which *were* efficient, such as the 1ˢᵗ Ross, were damned with the rest.

Various governmental reports were commissioned and those of Cardwell and Haldane recommended that the now generally looked-down-upon Volunteers be entirely replaced root and branch by a new much more strictly controlled and professionally trained body of men to be called the Territorial Force. The 1ˢᵗ Ross Volunteers accordingly held their last parade in June 1907.

Before we leave the old Volunteers, however, perhaps I should mention in passing an associated uniformed *Cadet* organisation which was run for youngsters in Stornoway to bring them up 'in the faith', as it were, and to provide a pool of new recruits when they became old enough to join the adult organisation. There was always a tendency then as occasionally now for underage youngsters to try to join the senior lads. Actually the lower age for joining the Volunteers varied from time to time and often enough overlapped the ages of the senior cadets (as does the current ACF and TA) but an interesting thing is that Stornoway had its own uniformed Cadet unit as soon as or possibly even before the other cadet units that were brought into being in London post 1860, by the redoubtable Mrs Octavia Hill. Mrs Hill founded Cadet Schools, of which there are said to have been six in England.

The Stornoway version, however, foreshadowed the modern version and was unconnected with any specific school (or at least not officially so) but was still informally associated with the local Volunteers. It was brought into being through the efforts of the island proprietor's mother-in-law Mrs Perceval (whose name is recalled in a street and a square in town and a plaque on Cuddy Point even yet). She too was a most redoubtable and energetic lady. Whether she was officially authorised to form that quasi-military organisation in term of the 1859 Act I do not know but form it and pay for it she did – uniforms, rifles; the lot. These cadets could thus merge almost seamlessly into the Volunteers once they were old enough. The local cadets may have petered out nearly fifty years later before the Volunteers themselves came to their end, but that does not detract from Mrs Perceval's far-sightedness.

The English Cadet Schools had ceased to function as such by 1908 when the CCF came into existence along with the TF. The ACF as we know it today took even longer to be organised UK-wide (though it claims an 1860 origin) and the present Stornoway unit was not formed or revived until 1943. Initially, however, we were right up there with the advance guard in cadet matters military. Major-General Grierson said in his seminal and much regarded history of the Volunteer Forces that though such units were formally authorised by the 1859 Act, none were actually formed in Scotland. In that he was quite wrong, not only regarding Mrs. Perceval's happy band but there were at least two others, one in Fife which rather incredibly ran to a couple of cannons in its armoury and one in Edinburgh; the latter attached to the 3rd City of Edinburgh Rifle Volunteer Corps. They all recruited between the ages of 10 or sometimes 12 and 15 years. The latter's uniform was distinctive, being a red Garibaldi shirt and a blue forage cap. Our local unit was rather duller, merely echoing that of their adult corps. There were three cadet units actually present at the infamous 'Wet Review' of 1881 but there would, I imagine, have been others spread around the country, not necessarily attached to an adult Volunteer Corps and were thus only semi-official.

One cadet unit (the 1st Cadet Bn. King's Royal Rifle Corps) even went to the Boer War with the City Volunteers and having served throughout the war *actually received a battle honour*. That is more than *any* of the Volunteers actually managed throughout their whole history. A few, a very few, Volunteers did serve in South Africa but they had first to go through the rigmarole of joining the regular army for a year 'and the duration', albeit they did so as a unit. Perhaps that could best be described as an exercise in semantics and a question remains whether they could still be classed as Volunteers. As far as the cadet participation was concerned, however, that, to an extent at least, got around the problem that no doubt upset many people then and later who doubted the wisdom of even teaching juveniles to fight, far less actually sending them off to war – not to mention the restriction on Foreign Service explicit in the Volunteers' conditions of enrolment.

Island Heroes

Nowadays the philosophy behind the cadet forces is much more to inculcate good citizenship into youngsters than to create a military machine, however embryonic, but in laying out the foundations for such good citizenship, the elements of discipline and training then will doubtless come in handy in any emergency – for themselves as much as for anyone else – should they when adult ever be called upon to defend our national interests.

Today the old cadet connection with the long defunct Volunteers can still be seen in certain of the badges used by the cadets to indicate, say, proficiency in certain ranks (such as the four-pointed star worn above the chevrons to indicate, for example, a sergeant's proficiency or the horizontal rifle with stars or crowns indicating degrees of marksmanship), just exactly as in the old Volunteers. For these examples, of course, the modern TA and the regulars nowadays employ just *slightly* different insignia.

I make no apology for mentioning the cadet organisations in this general context. There is really very little difference between a cadet and a TA soldier save that of age – as General Sir Derek Laing once said to me – and, as the Gaelic proverb says of anything that improves with repetition, *"'se 'n t-ionnsachadh og an t-ionnsachadh boidheach"* – which translates as *'the early learning is the pretty learning'* – or, perhaps, *'the sooner the better.'*

Anyway, to return to our fighting men, on 11th June 1908 the Left Section of the 6th Company of the North of Scotland Royal Garrison Artillery (Territorial Force) 3rd Highland Brigade came into being. It seems to have been fully recruited almost from the very start. All the fit young men from the now extinct Volunteers simply rejoined. They probably scarcely noticed the change. The older men tended not to rejoin – the conditions of enrolment were now rather stricter and more strenuous for everyone than they had previously been for the older members and the old soldiers probably thought it was time for them to hang up their sporrans – but that attenuation in strength was more than made up for by the youngsters clamouring to sign on. A glance at any of the unit's photographs of the era readily shows just how young so many of them were.

The new TF unit was still to be artillery – and a mountain unit at that. These were regarded as the cream of the artillery specialist units which pleased them immensely – though the new

168

unit was no longer to be an 'independent' one, complete in itself. Stornoway thus became the Left Half of the Battery – and the Right Half Sections lay in the village of Loch Carron where the Battery HQ and CO were also to be located. However, as you can imagine, Loch Carron has really got a very small population to draw on and the bulk of the men and almost all the many specialist trades required in a battery continued to come from Lewis. Lewisfolk, therefore, probably always thought of the Ross Battery – as it continued to be known as by the men – as being peculiarly their own. The mainlanders were (ultimately) accepted as being honorary Lewismen.

In the incomprehensible way of the military, the unit was renamed in September *of the very same year* as 'The Ross and Cromarty Mountain Battery RGA (TF) of the 4th (Highland) Mountain Brigade.' It was still demotically termed the Ross Mountain Battery or the RMB for short. Cromarty quickly slipped from mention, except on very formal occasions. Unlike every other mountain battery in the British and Indian armies, the three Highland Batteries in the Brigade (the Ross, the Argyll and the Bute) were all so named and not numbered. Mountain guns were the early 20th century equivalent of helicopter gun-ships. The field artillery laughed at the 'pop-guns' used by the mountain batteries but there was nothing more effective against, say, a machine gun nest than their demountable gun carried on pony-back. It fired a ten pound shell accurately over a distance of 1000 yards and was no slouch. Even one section of a Battery 'Half' could be largely self-contained and independently operational. They could go where no other artillery unit could venture – they were recognised as being a magnificent strike force and when available were naturally over-used.

Annual camp was the pay-off for many of the lads. Few of them took (or got) holidays as we know them and a paid fortnight amid the flesh pots of Blair Atholl or Barry Buddon were regarded as being well worth all the hard work they put in at weekly parades during the year. They were young, strong and idealistic; they enjoyed the work, however hard, and in addition the opportunity to play and win football matches was the icing on the cake.

1908 was a significant year as far as army reform was concerned and did not just affect the 1859 Volunteers. They had effectively ended up taking over the niche of the Militia – once service in the latter was no longer compulsory or balloted for. Militia units had co-existed of course since the time of the Volunteers' inception and were now voluntarily recruited, but their terms of engagement were quite different. In the 1880s, they had come to be treated as reserve units, from which pool regular forces could be supplied with trained militiamen all properly attested for General Service Overseas, for which the Volunteers (properly so called) were not. After 1908, all extant Militia units formally became known as Special Reserves and the term militia was no longer used by the Army.

However, therein lies a slight problem in this end of the country. Other than for the regulars, the Gael called just about every other version of the Army the '*malisidh*', pronounced '*maleeshee*'. Without known exception if you try to explain about the Militia, Volunteers or even the TF the response will be '*Ah yes – the malisidh*'. Even the TA is liable to be so described. It is pretty well hopeless to try to draw the distinction between them in Gaelic – not that it can't be done, the vocabulary is there – but the idea that first there is the regular army and then everything else is or was the militia, is so strong as to be pretty well nigh insurmountable. A further oddity may strike you, this time in English. Although the militia as such ceased to exist after 1908, the machinery for embodying it remained on the statute book until as late as 1953.

The regular army of course continued all that time to recruit in the islands – sometimes quite heavily even from the one village. A photograph is said to exist from about 1900 showing no fewer than 22 young Seaforths stationed in Egypt, all originating from the tiny village of South Dell in Ness. That is not a solitary example, I am quite sure. It would, however, require considerable research to dig out island recruiting statistics without further assistance from the Army which at present it is unwilling to give. Most of what I have been able to glean so far stems from the part-time voluntary sector.

My sole claim to literary fame is so far restricted to the considerable amount of research I carried out into the adventures of the Ross Mountain battery – the successor unit of the old Volunteers in Stornoway. The RMB RGA (TF) was almost Lewis' private army – just as the Volunteers had been. The stories about them are legion and most of them were true. Almost nothing was written down about them, however I managed to collect a few of the yarns from my father who served with the RMB at Gallipoli and Sinai. When the First World War broke out in August 1914, the lads had just come back from annual camp. A few days later they were back off across the Minch again, not to return until April 1919. The unit was not by any means alone in that – indeed it was dwarfed by the extent of the other Lewis war efforts – after all, the RMB barely mustered 150 men (and some of those were really only boys), whereas units such as the Seaforths had mustered 940 island men and other infantry units had attracted a total of 981 volunteers – and remember that they were all volunteers at that stage of the war. The Royal Navy had 149 tars and the RNR had a massive 3132. Lewismen flocked home from all over the world to enlist. According to Lord Leverhulme, speaking in 1919, Lewis had produced *'a higher proportion of volunteers for active service than any other identifiable part of His Majesty's realms.'* That was I think really saying something which is all too often forgotten nowadays, even in military circles.

All the island branches of the armed forces had their own war stories to tell, many of which were extremely dramatic, but as the RMB is the only unit I have researched to any extent, it is the only one I can really tell you about. It had as adventurous a time as any – its experiences could easily provide the basis for a Hollywood spectacular. The RMB was to a degree different from their sister batteries in Argyll and Bute. The latter were largely, though by no means solely, drawn from, can I say, the artisan class in their areas. The RMB was on the other hand largely drawn from the intellectual and academic cream of Lewis – though again not by any means solely so. Most of them were clever and literate and I was able to obtain several remarkable memoirs from ordinary gunners the like of which I doubt if many other units could provide. I could not find anything at all from any officer, however, which may say something about the latter.

The RMB was the first artillery and the first TF unit to land at Gallipoli – both at Cape Hellas and later at Suvla Bay, where they were in fact the front line for a time. Of all those who landed, they were they only part of the British Army at Suvla to accomplish its invasion goal, until they were chased back by a panicky infantry officer on horseback; apparently, *'the hill had not yet been taken!'* Extraordinary! It was also the last unit off when the order was given to go. They fought as part of the otherwise totally regular 29th Division and along with half a million others suffered extreme hardship and many casualties – but contrary to the defeatist tendency of many writers on that ever debatable venture *they* never ever thought they had been defeated – in fact they felt they had given the Turk the knock *every time* and were most disappointed when the order came to retire. A most pusillanimous order, they ever maintained. That said, however, they saw that the Gallipoli campaign knocked the stuffing out of their enemy and paved the way for the Allies' ultimate victory.

The bulk of the RMB troops were as I said, well educated men – some were still at school – the youngest boys, to their intense chagrin, were turned back from embarkation and not allowed to rejoin the battery until they had put in a year or more in the UK reserves. One can, perhaps, see a glimmer of social responsibility just starting to flicker on the part of the Army in that respect, but nonetheless a few of the more accomplished fibbers managed to slip though that net and serve on active fronts while still well under age.

A large proportion of the roll came from the senior classes of the Nicolson Institute, the local school. All or nearly all of the Lewis battery combatants had attended or indeed were still attending the Stornoway school – a school of both remarkable achievement and national repute at the time – and a still more remarkable number of them went on to join the professions once hostilities had ceased. Many of their detailed adventures have been delineated in my book, *'The Last Warrior Band'* (privately published and presently not in print, but available from the local library on loan) but many more yarns have just trickled into the sand of the passing years. I would refer you to my book for the bulk of their glorious story but I will incorporate here for your delectation a couple of episodes wherewith to whet your appetite.

Before I do so, may I remind you of the words, highlighted below, of General Sir Ian Hamilton GCB, GCMG, DSO, TD – the most decorated and shot at soldier of his generation. He was not only brave, but a clever and an erudite gentleman in the best sense of the word and was the Commander in Chief of the

172

Allied Expeditionary Force of 1915. He certainly knew what he was doing but may have been too diffident at times in passing on his orders to the rather thicker generals he had to deal with at Gallipoli. Anyway he got a great measure of the blame for the campaign's alleged failure, which I have to say was not all really deserved in my view. He himself was able to make splendid and literate judgements and observations about those below him in the Army's hierarchical chain of command and it is pleasing to note that he not only remembered the tiny RMB but held them in the highest regard. He came to Stornoway in September 1927 to unveil the Ross Mountain Battery Memorial which is to be found outside the local Drill Hall and proclaimed when carrying out that task what I think are immortal words,

'The story of the Ross Mountain Battery in the Great War is beautiful, so beautiful that you must be careful when you hand it down, lest you inspire the youth of the island with a cult of war'.

The Battery boys were indeed fine examples of islanders in their day. They acquitted themselves as men in every respect and were excellent templates for those who came after them. Their behaviour, no doubt, was at times not exactly as their ministers and elders at home would necessarily have wished and of course as Kipling said, *'Single men in barracks don't grow into plaster saints,'* but by all accounts they did not go mad in the brothels of Cairo nor were they ever needlessly cruel to their enemies. They did adapt their behaviour to the times they found themselves in, however, as several examples from the book might illustrate.

I suppose the one which best illustrates their coolness under fire is when, on 12th July 1915, they were engaged in a fierce fight for the hill the boys called Ali Baba and the Army called Achi Baba, but the Turks called something else entirely. Everyone was suffering from chronic dysentery by then. The heat was appalling, the food was worse and infrequent, water was scarce and precious, no one had had a good night's sleep for heaven knows how long, and Number 4 gun RMB lads were up front in the Worcester lines when they came under concentrated fire from the enemy. They had been well and truly spotted. All other guns bar another from the

AMB in the neighbourhood had been forced to fall back – but they didn't. They gritted their teeth and stayed put. It was calculated that their little mountain guns attracted 4 shrapnel and 1 HE shells *per minute for several hours on end.* The AMB gun was wiped out and the RMB captain was wounded. No fewer than 6 shells actually landed in the RMB emplacement but they kept on firing to such good effect that they were able to silence the opposition sufficiently to allow the infantry to overwhelm their immediate objective – though not alas the hill itself, which was never taken. The gun was kept going by Sergeant Alec Matheson. Later he was awarded the DCM for his actions that day. He was fine man in every way and became headmaster of Back School (and father of Iain Murdo Matheson, dentist, whom some of you might know).

The next excerpt is taken from '*The Last Warrior Band*', Volume 2, page 816, where RSM Mackenzie of the Argyll Mountain Battery (occasionally, as here, temporarily amalgamated with the RMB because of mutual casualties suffered during the campaign to together form the Highland Mountain Battery (HMB)) related a yarn concerning this kind of behaviour,

'*One pleasant walk we had along a shell-swept path at Suvla led us our way to collect our supplies. Half-a-dozen men and four ponies had gone to draw rations at the dump – life at the front seemed to be perpetually concerned with getting rations or digging holes with picks and shovels – and one of the ponies was playing up and kicking its heels. While the attention of the HMB lads was distracted by this display of bad behaviour four men passing by from an Irish regiment took advantage (or so they thought) of the situation and sneaked off with the HMB's four boxes of bacon. They were of course seen and the HMB quietly followed after them but saying not a word. The sun blazed above them and the flies buzzed around in their millions. Turkish shrapnel was searching that path all the time but we let the thieves sweat on. Each of them was carrying 44lbs of bacon. After a mile and a half had been thus travelled and it looked as if our paths were about to diverge, we quietly drew level with the Irish and thanked them profusely for having carried their bacon all that way in such circumstances but that we*

*would now carry our own bacon. The look on their faces
registered hate, but we were six to their four and so they
had to be content with the thanks tendered on behalf of
our pack ponies.'*

On another occasion, when the HMB came across an Australian unit repairing boats down by the beach, they discovered that
the Aussies had used one of them to send out a raiding party to
the island of Samothrace and had there collared a flock of some
25 or so sheep. These they corralled in a barbed-wire enclosure
well behind the lines. When it came to their attention, this was
too good a challenge for the HMB lads to pass up and in spite
of the fact that the sheep were now under the watchful eyes of
an armed Aussie guard, their expertise showed through when
they diverted attention sufficiently one night and liberated half a
dozen of the animals without even a baa and secreted them where
they could not be found. Presumably the Australians would have
noticed their loss in the daylight and they might have had their
suspicions as to who had been responsible, but as it was a case of
the biter being bit they could scarcely complain. On that occasion,
a fortunate few of the battery lads would have been better fed
for (it was said) some four days – but even half a dozen scrawny
sheep would not have gone very far among the perpetually raven-
ous HMB lads. Anything that was not actually tied down seems
to have been fair game to some of them and no doubt all units
had a few daring souls who were perpetually 'at it,' and not just
in the RMB or the AMB.

The next group are totally different in tone and come from
Volume 3 of the '*Last Warrior Band*', beginning at page 1097.
They relate to the final stages of the Salonika Campaign where
the RMB fought with distinction and this time indisputably won.
I make no apology for including them here although I have written
about them elsewhere. The excerpts illustrate how islanders were
deeply involved in a difficult, little known and under-appreciated
series of actions in that war to end all wars. I'd bet that few of
you are really aware how closely connected the RMB was to the
defeat of the Central Powers!

'Fourteenth September 1918

*The big push commenced on the 14th. It began with a main
artillery attack* 'with the roar of the guns echoing and re-echoing
through the mountains in an inferno of noise' *right across the 12th
Corps Sector. The HMBde was not called upon to advance at that
stage – no doubt to the great relief of the Bute Mountain Battery
(BMB) lads who had scarcely had any respite for a whole month.*

*The following day the French and Serbians stormed forward
at their part of the front. The Bulgarian front started to give way.*[1]
The longed-for great break-through looked distinctly possible.

*Over the next week or so attack followed attack. The HMB
were pulled forward. This time almost everything the Allies
essayed went according to plan – though success did not immediately come to pass, as a very great deal had to happen before
then. When it did, it all happened very quickly.*

*The Bute Battery had moved from Gugunci to Gokcelli. On the
17th they were again in action but this time the intended infantry
attack did not win through.*

*On the 18th they renewed their attack under heavy machine-
gun fire but again to no avail and the Battery withdrew to Gugunci
again having expended 1170 rounds.*

*On the 22nd they moved out of the 22nd Divisional area
and returned to that of the 27th Division via the Pyramids and
Guevgueli, Point, Pardovica, Gjavato and Mravinca and eventually were under instructions to rejoin the rest of the 4th (Highland)
Mountain Brigade (HMBde) then concentrating at Kosturino.
Before that happened, however, the BMB took part in the thrust
planned for the 12th Corps.*

*The rest of the HMBde had, meantime, received orders to move
to Ismaili to a camp with the unpropitious name of Cemetery
Wood. There they were told by the G.O.C. of the 16th Corps to
co-operate with the 8th and 9th Cretan Regiments of the Greek
Army in operations on the eastern side of Lake Doiran and the
Belasica Planina. These were to be in conjunction with an attack
on the western side of the lake undertaken by the 12th Corps
(still including the BMB), all with the object of forcing the so far
wholly undefeated, indeed totally unbudged, Bulgarian strong-*

---

[1] Rather to everyone's surprise, it seems.

holds of Petite Couronne and Grande Couronne. Thus it was that while the AMB and the RMB were on one side of the huge pincer movement, the BMB was on the other.

The main task of the British forces was then to attack the Lake Doiran / 'P-ridge'-position which was by far the strongest and most powerful and most heavily fortified of all the Bulgar hill sectors anywhere. These strongpoints had defied all that the Allies could throw at them, time after abysmal time. The Bulgarian 29th Division, which held the area, was experienced and believed the positions to be impregnable. The Allies had previously fought two very bloody and expensive battles for the 'P-ridge' position, to no avail whatsoever – prior to the involvement of the HMBde.[2]

The ground over which the attack had to be made is as tumbled and as broken and precipitous as any in Macedonia – and there can be little more difficult terrain anywhere else on earth. Four to five thousand yards away from the lake ran 'P'-ridge, a knife edge escarpment, four thousand or more feet high. It presents as massive a natural barrier as ever military men have had to face anywhere. Furthermore, between the plain and the ridge was a jumble of irregular hills broken by deep ravines acting as natural fortification ditches or moats. These were all themselves defended with various fortified posts and by the wire and the trenches of the front itself. It was all still just as formidable a proposition as it had twice before proved. The difference in strategy this time lay in the proposed attack by the 16th Corps around the eastern side of the lake.

The 4th (Highland) Mountain Brigade (less the Bute Battery) were, as stated, part of the 16th Corps, and in accordance with orders moved out of Ismailli, down to the plain. The first positions occupied were AMB at Brest Ruins, RMB at Brest Clump and the HQ at the unprepossessingly-named Mud Crossing.

Things thereafter happened very quickly, one on top of each other and it is often not too clear from the existing records what precisely transpired.

On 18th September the two batteries, AMB and RMB, were together acting in continuous support of the Greek infantry and were meeting considerable opposition as they advanced. Both

---

[2] Not that it is suggested that this time they were the utterly decisive factor!

batteries were heavily shelled at Orchard Wood.[3]

The Bute Battery, meanwhile, attached to the 12th Corps, was as equally intended, making its way around the west side of Lake Doiran. The 12th Corps was led by General Wilson who had at his disposal 231 guns of varying description, – in short every gun that could be spared – the 22nd Division, a Greek Division, 82nd Infantry Brigade, the 2nd Regiment of Zouaves and others. Two days of barrage followed which allowed the infantry to move forward. The Allied soldiers were not in good shape and were under strength – but they kept on going for a while. That western attack, however, soon stuttered to a stop and on "P-ridge" itself the 12th Cheshires lost the barrage and desperate hand to hand fighting took place. The Allies were being driven back and casualties were very high. A change of command and policy at that crucial time then took some of the western pincer artillery away to the west bank of the Varder, and that included the BMB.

At the same time as these difficulties were being faced on the west shore of the lake, the 16th Corps with rather fewer men and guns was working its way steadily around the eastern shore. The AMB and the RMB, as intended, were fully co-operating with the 8th and 9th Cretan Regiments and were involved in various actions directed against the Bulgar positions between Battery Cross and Lake Doiran. Only one Battery casualty[4] was reported on the 19th.

Generally speaking, that main attack of the 16th Corps was

---

[3] None of the Battery lads were too sure of the Greeks – and certainly not at that stage of the war. Probably the latter's lengthy period of sitting on the fence soured those who had borne the brunt of the fighting over the years. Some of their new comrades were obviously very acceptable but the general comments passed tended to be critical. Bill McWhirter (father of the Guinness Book of Records twins) recalled one occasion in the Struma Valley when the RMB, where he was a gunner as driver, were providing artillery support for a Greek cavalry unit which was all dressed in flamboyant colours, feathers and swords. A loud boom came from the far end of the valley indicating that the Bulgars had fired a large piece of ordnance, probably in their direction – whereupon without further ado, the cavalry reared round their mounts and fled the field never, so the story went, to be seen again! Possibly these gaily caparisoned troops had only ever previously experienced ceremonial duties.

[4] It is not shown who that was. No name is given in the HQ papers and the AMB papers do not mention it, so by inference it was an RMB casualty.

meeting fierce opposition. They found themselves being heavily shelled by enemy artillery from the heights 3000 feet above them. The fact that many of the Allied troops were suffering at the time from influenza and were simply no longer sufficiently fit for the immense exertions demanded of them, did not make matters any easier. Communications were bad. A bad grass fire caused many casualties in Allied men and horses and forced them to fall back – if only temporarily.

Everyone was stricken with great fatigue and weariness. The attacks, however, continued to be pressed forward – but it all yet again seemed to be to little avail. It must have looked as if the 'Great Salonika Break-Through' *was going to founder on the rocks of these powerful defences – just as all previous attempts upon them had done. In two short days of fierce and unrelenting battle, the British and the Greeks lost over 7000 men and 500 prisoners to an estimated loss by the Bulgars of just over 3000 – and the enemy seemed to be managing to sit tight as ever. There was at that point no sign of retreat by them from their fastnesses, far less any hint of collapse.*

However, that was not the only part of the front. To the west of the Vardar River, near to where the BMB had now been marched, our gallant Serbian Allies had just broken through. Normally that would have been dealt with by the Bulgars simply hurrying some reserves to the hole in the line – but all the Bulgarian reserves were now being tied down at Lake Doiran. None of them could be spared to stop the Serbs. The Bulgarians, moreover, were seemingly nearing utter exhaustion even quicker than were the Allies (who, moreover, had no idea of that situation in the enemy ranks). Still, some have recovered from worse situations before now and no outcome was yet certain.

Then the Bulgars suffered what might have been just bad luck. Considerable movements of their troops were spotted by the RAF, heading north along both banks of the Vardar, perhaps being redeployed to meet the new Serbian threat. The airmen took their chance and bombed the enemy to dreadful effect. That proved just too much for the enemy whose resolve at that point broke. They were seen to be in full retreat. That news destroyed the remaining morale of the Bulgars and their defence of P-Ridge and the Couronnes, which had until then held off all attacks, started to crumble.

General Milne reacted quickly. All forces, whatever their problems, were immediately to go on the offensive.

The heat was very great and very trying for the exhausted men – but victory was being scented and the adrenaline started to flow. By 24th September the 12th Corps were clearing the Blaga Planina and the 16th Corps was advancing along the Kosturino defile on the way to Strumica. On the same date the BMB crossed the Vardar and came into action near Bogdanci. The Bulgars were now retiring as fast as they could go, with the Allies in hot pursuit. Retreat became a rout.

The AMB and the RMB were instructed to push on as rapidly as possible. This was the sort of operation for which they were created. They could move as fast as the infantry – perhaps being self-contained, sometimes even faster. On the 23rd they set off in a North Easterly direction through Resili and Stojakova through the British system of defences, through the wire of the enemy front line, through Bogdanci and rested the night at Furka Dere. The march from the Pyramids to Furka Dere was most trying for all concerned, under very adverse conditions and through the full heat of the day. The HQ records noted that it was obvious that the enemy had made a hurried flight as large quantities of material and munitions had been simply abandoned, especially at Bogdanci, though their ammunition dumps had been blown up to prevent them falling into Allied hands.

On the 24th the Highland Batteries continued their pursuit to Causli. On the 25th September 1918 they crossed the plain to Valandova and co-operated with the 79th Infantry Brigade who were pushing the Bulgars in the latter's retreat over the ridge overlooking Rabrovo. The Batteries took up positions and shelled enemy detachments holding the crest – but a little later on the same day these Bulgar positions were observed to have been withdrawn from. The RMB accordingly moved forward and passed over the Bulgarian frontier line and into Bulgarian territory proper.

The RMB old soldiers always maintained that not only were they the first artillery into Bulgaria, they were also the first British or Allied troops to enter that country.

As Dr A.J. Macleod (Zadok) said later in his commentary on the actions of the RMB:[5]-

'When 'the day' came and the wall of the Belechitza Mountains was scaled and stormed and the Bulgar chased far into his own country, the men of the Ross Mountain Battery, were, as always, in the forefront – and on one particular occasion even in front of the cavalry. Although the C-in-C has credited an English Yeomanry Regiment with the honour of being the first British troops to enter Bulgaria, it is very doubtful if the honour does not belong to the RMB. Certainly they were the first artillery as they were at Cape Helles and Suvla. Unfortunately jealousy in high places came between them and the honours they so richly deserved ... but that is a small point when weighed against the fact that every man who has had any connection with the Battery or even any Regiment associated with it was always proud of that connection and association'.[6]

All was not yet over. There were hard blistering marches to be made and actions to undertake before they would get the order to halt.

The Brigade encamped that night at Kosturino and were at that stage rejoined by the Bute Battery, from the 12th Corps area. The same day the AMB had been told to co-operate with the Greek 14th Division. They continued to Tartarli, to Kajali and thence to Ormali.

Under Greek Command – Victory – and Surrender of the Turks!

The following day, the 26th of September, the whole of the 4th (Highland) Mountain Brigade was placed under the orders of the Commander of the 14th Greek Division. The Battery lads got on like a house-on-fire with their new comrades-in-arms when it came to the bit. They pushed on via the Tivoli track over the

---

[5] as published after the war in the Loyal Lewis Roll of Honour.
[6] Slightly paraphrased.

Belasica Planina on to the Strumnitza plain.

On the 26th or 27th September a section of the RMB had a most extraordinary experience. As they were pushing ahead, lickety-spit, near a place called Doleur, they saw in the distance something, they couldn't quite make out what, headed their way from an enemy direction. What could it be? That there was no one but Bulgars ahead of them, they knew quite well. 'Action Front!' – 'just in case.' Gnr D.R. Macaskill recalled the occasion:-

'We had recently had a gun duel – thick and heavy – and were making our way over some spring-water-logged ground. All of a sudden this thing was seen to be approaching. As it came closer we saw that it was a big black car bouncing and rattling across the rutted track. From it was flying a big white sheet, so we did not blow it to Kingdom Come. We were utterly mystified. They stopped beside us and we kept them covered while they spoke to us. It seemed that they were Bulgarians coming to offer terms of surrender. We had not the faintest idea what to do with them. We had no officer with us then and our sergeant reckoned, rightly or wrongly, that he could hardly accept the surrender of a whole enemy country. After a brief discussion amongst us we decided to send them on to another larger British unit which we could see above and behind us on the ridge – and off they went bouncing and lurching on their way. It turned out that they were in fact just what they said they were. We just continued with our pursuit.'[7]

The 28th of September found the HMB in position about Sekernik and Baldivico Selo shelling Bulgar infantry. The 29th

---

[7] There may (just possibly) have been two white-flag waving cars seen round about that time. One was said to have contained Bulgarian generals, the other to have been full of Bulgarian Parliamentaires who had ridden out of Strumica with a letter for General Milne offering an Armistice and terms. Equally, however, there may, indeed, have been only the one car 'claimed' by two different units. The boys of the RMB, however, reckoned that they had got in there first and liked in their lighter moments to interpret their encounter as an attempt by Bulgaria in general to surrender to the Hebrides in particular, even if the latter could not accept it. It all seemed quite right and proper to them, and just as it should be!

found the RMB continuing to support the Greek infantry and being heavily shelled by the Bulgars in return. The enemy retreated towards Petric.

The same day found the AMB heavily in action at Borisovo having marched there via Svidonica and Gubrovo. They then moved the same day to Mokrins where action was continued. They expended more than 200 rounds of shrapnel that day and 31 of HE.

That proved to be the very last day of hostilities in that war theatre. All was suddenly quiet on the Macedonian front and no more action took place. Early the next morning, the 30th of September 1918, came orders that a General Cessation of Hostilities had been arranged and all troops had to maintain their positions. As well as that remarkable success on the whole 94 miles of the Salonika Front and all that that implied, in Palestine General Allenby (El Nabi – the prophet, as the Arabs called him) had on the 27th wiped out two further Turkish armies on the plains of Megiddo, recapturing Nazereth and Damascus opening the door to take Syria. The Turks had no option but to throw in the towel.

Appreciations

No one would have been more thankful for the physical rest than the men of the 4th (Highland) Mountain Brigade. From 16th to 30th September they had been continuously on the move, hauling their guns, loading and unloading their pack-animals, and marching great distances, climbing up and down high almost perpendicular natural barriers, snatching what little sleep they could from time to weary time. Illness, mostly malaria, had affected large numbers of the Batteries' strengths, and the balance on whom the increased burden fell were not in much better strip. The continuous marching, day and night, had been a great strain on man and beast. The heat was almost unbearable and drinking water was scarce.

The Colonel was happy to sign his report for the period that, 'despite the adverse circumstances all ranks had shown great endurance and had kept up the reputation of the Brigade in advancing rapidly and getting in touch with the retreating enemy forces in a short space of time.'

A special appreciation of their support was given by the Greek commander of their 14th Division:-
'To Lieut. Colonel Kirby DSO, MC, Officers, NCOs and Men of the 4th Highland Mountain Brigade.

I wish to thank you all for the splendid support which your guns have given to my division – a support which enabled the 14th Division to be the first to enter Bulgaria.

The guns which were made for your Scottish hills, have proved their serviceability in the mountains of Bulgaria.

30.9.18 (Signed) John Th. G. Orphanides'.

A further appreciation was received from Lt-General C.J. Briggs, Commander of the 16th Corps:-
'On the conclusion of Peace with Bulgaria and the termination of the present Hostilities I wish to convey my deepest thanks to all Generals, Officers, NCOs and Men of the Units that have constituted the 16th Corps for their loyal support, energy and their fighting qualities displayed under most trying conditions. My thanks are particularly due to those who marched on their feet in the awful dust and great heat. The troops have something to be proud of viz.:- being the first to enter Bulgaria.'

General Walker, commander of the 27th Division in a letter to the CRA of the Division said in a letter dated rather earlier in the month:-
'The Divisional Artillery were splendid without exception, and in gallantry, endurance and accuracy of shooting, fully sustained the highest traditions of our Regiment. My thanks and congratulations are due to every officer and man under your command. These are not formal thanks, for, as a gunner, I know what they all had to do and (as you know) my standard is a high one. Will you please tell them this and say how proud I am to command them. Will you please tell the Mountain Battery[8] that I include them absolutely in all that I have said of the Divisional Artillery, and add that I should esteem myself lucky to have them in the Division for keeps.'

The ability of the Highland Batteries to work hard and fight

---

[8] The BMB.

well in all kinds of situations and conditions was well and truly noted and appreciated by many of their comrades-in-arms. They were indeed only very small units but they were seen to pull much more than their weight. That they were not thought enough of by subsequent reformers of the army even to be kept in existence, might sometimes lead one to think that they were, perhaps, just a little underappreciated at home!

Unheard of they might well be nowadays by the generality of people – even by those in their own localities or, for that matter, by those just vaguely interested in such military matters – but the Batteries were certainly not under-appreciated at the time – at least not by those in the know. Even now, those who really understand about such things will give them their place. General Sir Martin Farndale in his recent volume on the History of the Royal Regiment of Artillery entitled 'The Forgotten Fronts and the Home Base 1914-18'[9] writes, when talking of these final days of action on the Balkan front:-

'These gallant mountain gunners (The 4th (Highland) Mountain Brigade, Ross and Argyll Batteries) had been under great strain ... they had been engaged in the attack on Blaga Panina ... (and) had marched right across the front to Lake Arjan. They were present at Bogdanci and (then) in action all day with the 79th Infantry Brigade. In Kosturino they picked up the Bute Battery ... which had itself marched from east of Vardar. The next day they began to advance across the plain. This magnificent Brigade had covered over 80 miles across high mountain tracks in intense heat, in less than six days, without rest, and was yet to be in continuous action for a further four days. Once again these mountain gunners upheld and enhanced their great reputation in the service of the guns.'

And again, (read shortly):-

'To this day the Bulgarians remember Lake Dojran with respect and awe. It was here they fought the British so very hard. The Gunners were never out of the line and when others rested, they remained in their high, cold, wet mountain positions or in the

---

[9] At pages 169, 171 and 172

stinking, hot, malaria-ridden Struma Valley conducting attack after attack to keep the Bulgarians alert.'

And, later, right at the end of that section of his book:-

'The field gunners were everywhere, most of them Territorials, gallantly working with the infantry who learned true respect for them, for without the guns nothing was possible. Yet again it was the land of the mountain guns, so well designed for a theatre such as this – and so they were over-used. We owe so very much to these magnificent men with their mules and little guns, who knew no limit anywhere in the world and in Macedonia they proved it all again.' '

That I think is a quite sufficient series of quotations from *'The Last Warrior Band'* to be going on with. I won't have managed to read out much of that written above but if you care to you can, when you have time, go over the whole lot at your leisure.

The lads came home (those, that is, who came home) in April 1919, like millions of others with their stories, memories, wounds, disabilities and pensions. It all probably seems an awfully long time ago to younger members of our community – but it was my own father's war and really and truly not *all* that far away from us in the scheme of things. Some things should be remembered better and their salutary lessons acted upon.

The war finished and the RMB TF was disbanded with barely a sigh – though the survivors held annual reunions for Gallipoli Day every 25th April, or as near to it as was convenient, right up until 1968, when the dwindling band of ancient warriors felt that it was time to call it a day. They all felt somewhat aggrieved that even the UK media had by then started reporting such commemorations as 'Anzac' Days – as if the UK and French contributions at Gallipoli were not of such great consequence compared with that of the antipodeans – instead of being very much larger and much more significant. 'Anzac' day has, however, stuck and I doubt very much if anyone not closely connected with those from the UK who fought at Gallipoli would understand the slight irritation felt by them on such usage.

The whole volunteering scene was in any event changing again and the very name TF was changed to TA. A new Ross Battery was formed in 1920(?) as part of the 13th Highland Pack Brigade RGA TA, this time of the now famous 51st Division. In 1924 it was re-designated RA as opposed to RGA with 3.7 Howitzer weaponry and named the 51st Ross Battery. In 1927 the brigade was renamed the 13th Highland Light Brigade RA (TA).

Camps were of course still being attended annually, war memorials were being unveiled and the annual Battery Ball was still a signal event in the town's social calendar – but it is unfortunately true to say that by then the battery no longer held the local social pre-eminence it once had.

Nonetheless change followed change for little discernible reason. In 1936 the Brigade was reorganised as a mechanised army field brigade. The 51st (Ross) Light Battery became the 219 (Ross) Field Battery with 18pndr field guns. The local Ross Battery was that year the highest recruited unit in the highest recruited Division in the whole of the British TA. They won many cups at artillery contests and many plaudits. Al' 'Crae, our late friendly undertaker, beat all the regulars in a gunnery competition over and over again, getting possible after possible, much to the professionals' chagrin. He had a fantastically accurate eye, speedy reactions and a computer-like ability to calculate inclinations and declinations and whatever else a gunner required. He was not alone. The Ross Battery were then held to be the Best Detachment in their Brigade and one of the most efficient and well-trained units in the whole of the UK-wide TA. The following year (1937) they won *all* the Brigade trophies at camp. In 1939 the Ross Battery was yet again re-designated, this time to the 54th (West Highland) Army Field Regiment RA TA, and later the same year became the 203rd (Ross) Anti-Tank Battery of the 51st (West Highland) Anti-tank Regiment TA. If name changes could have improved their fighting capacity they surely could have won the impending war single-handed.

Once more the Ross Battery marched off to war, leaving for France in September 1939. This time their weaponry really was under-powered. Pea-shooters, they themselves called them. '*Would not go through the side of Mitchell's bus far less a tank,*' said another. They took up various positions near the Maginot

Line at the Belgian border. They never had a chance. They never even *saw* an enemy before they were ordered to lay down their anti-tank rifles at St Valerie en Caux. Some say they and the rest of the 51st Highland Division were sacrificed by Churchill in an attempt to appease the French, who were upset that the bulk of the British Expeditionary Force had been allowed to abandon the war at Dunkirk. That is another war story which controversy will trail for a long time, but suffice it to say that the islanders and their folk back home did feel that, as with Highlanders who had taken Quebec for the Empire all these years before, it still did not matter much to Whitehall if they fell in the process.

The Ross Battery, along with the rest of the 51st Highland Division was '*put in the bag*' – as was the expression at the time. The greater part of them spent the next five years in prison camps working for the Reich – largely in salt and coal mines and cement works. They did not get a chance to shine as had their counter-parts of twenty five years earlier. A few managed to escape and their colourful stories are worth hearing. Al' 'Crae had a lovely story about how he and an Aussie friend liberated an SS General's hoard of valuables once the Americans had arrived at their prison camp towards the end of the war. You'll find it in '*The Last Warrior Band*' if you're interested.

Of course that Ross Battery was still TA and basically volun-tary, but unlike the situation in WWI, the vast bulk of those who fought in WWII were conscripts – which perhaps puts a slightly different slant on things. In any event, Lewis again produced many more than its fair share of front line troops. The island, on the other hand and as I need hardly add, was once more well garrisoned with support and service units – almost all of whose personnel came from far away well beyond the Highland line – and almost none of them from home. As in the earlier conflict the islanders seem to have had little chance of a home posting.

After the end of WWII, the Ross Battery was stood down. A new Battery was, however, again reformed in 1947, known as the Ross Coast Defence Battery in 412 Coast Regiment RA (Highland) TA. After various vicissitudes and further changes of name the battery was amalgamated with the Lovat Scouts and emerged once more as an Anti-aircraft Battery 532 LAA Regiment.

As ever the Lewis lads proved their worth in all competitions. I recall stories of their gunnery competitions where the pilot towing a drone being used for target practice complained strenuously and bitterly, officially and to anyone who would listen, that 'Barney', I think it was, had actually shot the drone to pieces. Apparently the powers that were did not think that possible – they did not appreciate the ability of the islander to automatically make forward allowance when shooting either geese or drones.

Throughout all these changes the local Terriers had always managed – quite how I am not too sure – to retain *somewhere* amongst the layers of official nomenclature a reference to their being called 'The Ross Battery' – which is of course how they were still referred to at home. They were always highly regarded and in accolade received the Freedom of the Burgh in 1960 – no small honour – to mark 100 years since the formation of the original 1st Ross Volunteer Artillery Corps.

They did not have long to enjoy their status. All that came to an end when in 1966, the powers that be finally disbanded the Battery as an artillery unit and replaced it with an infantry platoon of Seaforths, later for a time in company strength. Not every soldier made the transition but most did.

Some years before the Ross Battery finally came to an end they had had their ordnance entitlement reduced to only one gun, to the great disappointment of the troops. It was some sort of centralised penny-pinching I suppose. Disbandment, however, led to panic in the QM's store (at least). That enterprising man had managed to acquire by fair or other means sufficient spare parts over the years to *build a second gun* – which obviously was not on strength! What was to be done? All stores now had to be returned and accounted for – and to have too many was as bad if not worse than having too few – especially, I suppose, anything as obvious as a full-sized anti-aircraft gun. There was thus, potentially a very serious crime in the army book just waiting to be uncovered. The Battery had in fact found it extremely useful for training purposes to have two guns but now what were they going to do? Simple. These enterprising lads took the unauthorised gun to the mainland along with their official gun and stores and, on passing one of larger remote reservoir lochs on the Ullapool/Inverness road, dropped off the extra gun at the deep-end, having earlier filed off any incriminating identifying numbers. No questions were asked about the rest of the equipment at handover.

Years and years later, there was a terrible drought one summer, the water was at an unprecedented low, and it was decided to repair the dam. To facilitate this, the water level was reduced still further. Workers so engaged were astonished to find a large and complete artillery gun revealed on the muddy bottom. No one could identify it, nor could anyone in the military establishment account for where on earth it had come from. Tremendous investigations were set in motion by the military, but to no avail. The culprits, who have now mostly gone the way of all flesh, are beyond earthly retribution but I was assured by one that the story is true – if probably quite incredible to those who believe that army records are infallible.

Once the transition to infantry was complete, again the local unit shone in competition with its peers – time after time after time – especially at range work. Dare one suggest that the occasional illegal stalk after deer improved upon their already inbuilt accuracy and remarkable eyesight?

The social eminence of the TA locally was coming to an end by then. For as long as there was a Company based in Stornoway, the occasional TA Ball was still much appreciated by the invited local dignitaries – but eventually that too petered out as everything became more mainland biased and based.

Nationally, every new Chief of Staff seemed to want to go for change – perpetual change it sometimes seemed. Perhaps that could be justified as the times themselves were again a-changing, but to an outsider it often seemed as if it were change for the sake of change. The TA itself was actually abolished and became briefly the TAVR, which was actually unpaid for a time (not as you can imagine a popular move with the men but a nucleus remained on strength all the same).

Despite all these knocks, the recruiting figures remained high until the unthinkable happened and the local and clan regiment of foot, the king-pin of local military consciousness, the Seaforths – one of the oldest, proudest and most decorated of British regiments – was itself done away with. This was devastating for The Ross Battery, which had long imagined itself as being the great regiment's supporting artillery. They never were, of course, but that is how they liked to think of their relationship.

This abolition had a dramatic knock on effect on all the traditional Highland and Island recruitment areas for the whole army, both TA and Regular – and dismayed a whole generation of the old and bold who would have supported and encouraged the next generation of recruits. Whitehall evidently thought that did not matter. I cannot think that the Top Brass were so traitorous as to *intend* to do what the enemy had never done and destroy the best recruiting ground in the north; but nevertheless they did. One can hear their excuses as they developed: after all, the Seaforths were just the same as the Camerons, with whom they were to be initially amalgamated (to form the Queen's Own Highlanders) and recruiting was (they said – though I don't believe it) to be barely affected. Then some decades later, when the QOH itself was joined with the Gordons to form The Highlanders (an artificial concept if ever there was one), it may have been reluctantly admitted that recruiting figures were decreasing a little bit more – but not to worry, things were going that way anyway, weren't they? How could they know, one wonders? Precious few recruits were coming out of the Highlands and Islands anyway, they said – one can hear their thought processes chuntering away – after all, they don't seem to need clans or such expensive tradition in the south of England, do they? Numbered units are often good enough there. Why should the Gael be any different? No, I suppose these tinkering reformers weren't really traitors, but merely awfully stupid like Hamilton's generals. *Anyone* in the Highlands and Islands could have told them (and no doubt many did) that what they were doing would be utterly disastrous for recruitment and so it largely proved. As a *grand finale*, they recently and effectively abolished all the proud regiments of Scotland, making them mere units of an entirely new Regiment of Scotland. Why? Because recruitment had fallen so low. And why was that? It is all a circularity, of course. Whitehall will never understand, alas.

Of course there are, I am sure, many other reasons for the parlous situation of modern recruitment, without even beginning to consider ill-advised military adventures in the Middle East (perhaps especially in this age of instant communication to a basically adverse or even hostile media) – but for the Army's leaders to have destroyed one of their traditional home support bases so wantonly should be seen to be the crime it really is.

All these machinations on the regular front *have* had their adverse effect on the volunteer scene. All the same, those who support our military need not despair – at least not totally. The blood is still strong and the heart is Highland (and Island). There will, one hopes, always be those who hanker after a military career and who understand its dangers and its advantages. Local TA lads and lasses have been to various hot spots and back on several tours of duty in recent times and have always acquitted themselves very well, as one would expect. We can be as sure as we can be that they will not let us or themselves down. New traditions will form (it's just such a pity that so many perfectly good older ones had to be jettisoned for little reason and to such little purpose or effect). New generations will, doubtless, always arise to fill any gaps which may appear when the need arises and the old warriors' genes from long ago will still drive young men's (and women's) ambitions – but the harvest may not be so prolific. There has to be a local mind-set to encourage potential soldiers and they must be trained to be effective – and if that essential mind-set has been allowed to wither if not exactly die (all through centralised ignorance and thoughtlessness) then we may all yet be in trouble.

We haven't got to that end stage yet and there are those working away to ensure that we never do. We *need* a defence force to ensure that both ourselves and our country's interests can be protected whenever necessary. There *are* weird people out there who would not hesitate to take advantage if they thought for one moment that we were totally defenceless. I don't know how the anti-army element in our society – present and articulate in every western nation – thinks we should deal with obvious potential problems. Many of us would really like to know their answers to the questions begged.

I personally believe we should do all we can to encourage young men especially to train *in the defence* of our country. I emphasise defence as I doubt that offensive campaigns ever generate anything other than sorrow for the initiator. Recruiting of any kind is more difficult now than it used to be. The recruiting teams are no longer allowed to visit schools to plant the seed. Furthermore, the Army does not necessarily help itself. Not so long ago, when the courts came across a young fellow (as they do from time to time) who could do with discipline and direction in life, but is not too far gone in criminality to be rescued, the Sheriff (or whoever) could suggest to the miscreant that if he really did want to join the Army (as is so often said in pleas in mitigation) he should go down to the recruiting office forthwith and, once the court is provided with proof that he has actually committed himself, then he may expect to escape most of whatever dire punishment he had otherwise earned. I would not classify them as '*excess vermin*' as did the recruiters of 1778, so we are told, – but they do need more than a hug. Nowadays the Army doesn't want to know these people, and who can blame them in a way, as some of them are truly awful, but it really was the making of some in the past.

Some of the very best were rescued at that stage of their careers. Those who could not be fitted into the Army and who refused to behave could, I would have thought, be dealt with suitably within the Army itself and then discharged. The Army does not, however, see itself nowadays (if it ever did) as a social work department rescuing the delinquent. Perhaps Human Rights legislation has simply made things too difficult along these lines.

As I said above I know next to nothing about the Royal Navy. I do not know a soul who ever opted for service in it – other than for war-time service, that is – or a very few who 'swung it' for National Service. Perhaps we recall the wise words of Samuel Johnston, that rent-a-quote Englishman, who remarked of the Navy of his time '*No one would go to sea who has contrivance enough to get put in jail.*'

The story of the merchant seamen from Lewis and Harris in WW2 has been recorded in a slim book by John and Annie Morrison. I am sure that they would not claim it to be totally exhaustive, excellent as it is, but I wonder if there is not a gap to filled for a similar book on the contribution from the rest of the Outer Isles and of course the Inner Hebrides as well.

The focus will ever, for many reasons, largely remain on the soldier – the person who must be able to occupy any objective without fear of being dislodged before any action can be said to have really been won. For us in the Hebrides, when we think on it (ever more infrequently it seems), it is the volunteer part-time soldier who occupies centre stage. The modern TA soldier is now trained to *exactly* the same standard as are regular troops and is an essential and integral part of the British Army. Not everyone wants to serve abroad and – just as it was in the days of the Fencibles in 1800, the TF in 1914 or the TA in 1939 – the basic commitment is home service only. Only those who actually volunteer for foreign service will be sent out of the country to fight. It is thought that there may be an idea circulating that foreign service is compulsory in today's TA, therefore making some potential recruits sheer away, but if so that is most unfortunate and I am assured that there is no such compulsion.

The local platoon is now called Stornoway Platoon, C Company, 51st Highland, 7th Battalion, The Royal Regiment of Scotland – a name no doubt its members will grow to love as they bond – one hopes so anyway. Perhaps it will remain like that long enough for the paint to dry on the noticeboards.

The Stornoway Platoon attends a two week annual camp and in that connection has been all over the UK in recent years and for training purposes does go further afield. They have been, for example, to Belgium, Romania and Cyprus recently. They are due to go to Poland later this year. Over the past decade members of the Platoon served with the 1st Bn. The Highlanders in Northern Ireland during 1999/00. In 2003 TA soldiers from Lewis served in Afghanistan, and in 2004, 2005, 2006 and 2007 up to ten members of the Stornoway Platoon served in Iraq, in Baghdad and Basra, and later this year another three will be deployed to Afghanistan again. Although there is only a platoon strength based in Stornoway now – just a shadow of former strengths – there is still a constant stream of volunteers, both for home and foreign service, seeking to do their bit for their country. Given our island's ageing and declining population these numbers are still sufficient to entitle us to hold our heads up in polite society!

There is a Gaelic proverb which says it all:-

> *'Am fear nach gleidh na h-airm 'nam na sìth*
> *Cha bhith iad aige 'n am a chogaidh.'*

('The man who keeps not his arms in time of peace will not have them in time of war').

THE FRIENDLY OCCUPATION OF THE FAROE ISLANDS

Erling Isholm

Soon after the start of the Second World War on the 3rd of September 1939, strange things began to happen in and around the Faroe Islands. Faroese fishing boats occasionally spotted warships in the waters around the islands and unknown airplanes began to fly very close by. Gunshots were also heard and soon people began to talk of the battle Britain was fighting in order to prevent big German warships from entering the Atlantic Ocean and disrupting the shipping between Britain and America. On the 29th of November 1939, a German military research aeroplane found itself in trouble over the most southerly island and it had to land in the sea not far from a village there. Local men immediately saw that the crew needed help and they saved the four German soldiers who were later shipped to Denmark (Arge 1985: 11-14).

Other events could be mentioned from these first few months of the war, but World War 2 didn't really affect the islands until the morning of the 9th of April 1940, when the news suddenly broke that German forces had occupied Denmark and parts of Norway. The administration of the Faroe Islands was carried out from Denmark through the Danish Governor, who was the chief administrator in the islands. Early on the morning of the 9th of April, he was on the phone to Denmark to try to receive some orders on how he was to act in this new situation, but he was cut off, and therefore he did not know what to do (Arge 1985: 18).

When the news of the occupation of Denmark arrived, the Faroese Parliament was gathered in the capital, Tórshavn, to try to resolve a dispute in the fishing industry, and together with the Danish Governor they tried to work out what to do. They didn't get much further than sending out a message to the people asking them to remain calm. This was necessary because there was both fear and confusion in a country that had never seen a real soldier on its soil before.

Everyone was anxious to know whether British or German forces were coming to occupy the islands. At 8:30 on the morning of the 10th of April, to the delight of the people in Tórshavn, a British aeroplane flew low over the town. We now know that this plane brought back to Britain the news that no signs of German occupation were to be seen. On that same day the BBC said in the news at 13:15: *'There are rumours in London, that Germany would land troops on the Faroe Islands, but these rumours were taken with amusement. They will never be allowed to take Faroe Islands'* (Arge 1985: 30).

The next morning yet another British plane flew over the capital, and then the BBC brought good news from the Houses of Parliament, where Sir Winston Churchill, then First Lord of the Admiralty, had presented Britain's response to the occupation of Denmark and Norway. When speaking of the Faroe Islands, Churchill was quoted as saying,

> 'We are also at this moment occupying the Faroe Islands, which belong to Denmark and which are a strategic point of high importance, and whose people showed every disposition to receive us with warm regard. We shall shield the Faroe Islands from all the severities of war and establish ourselves there conveniently by sea and air until the moment comes when they will be handed back to Denmark liberated from the foul thraldom into which they have been plunged by German aggression' (Arge 1985: 33).

That calmed everybody and as Churchill had promised to hand the Faroe Islands back to Denmark when the war was finished, it also resolved the main political issue of whether or not the Faroe Islands were now independent of Denmark.

Operation Valentine

The occupation Churchill mentioned in his speech was code named 'Operation Valentine' by the British military (Arge 1985: 45). Nothing could be seen of any occupying forces on the morning of the 12th of April, but soon after midday on that day two British destroyers, H 32 and H 57, named *Ardent* and *Acasta*,[1]

---

[1] At the conference Donald J. MacLeod kindly informed me, that Hebrideans frequently manned ships of this kind, because they were familiar with

approached the Swedish and Danish ships anchored in Tórshavn. Soon after, two officers came ashore and met with the three local British consuls. Later they all visited the Danish Governor. At this meeting, the British officers confirmed what Churchill had said the day before, and they ordered the authorities to prepare accomodation for 250 soldiers. Neither the Chairman of the Faroese Parliament nor the Governor could not see any other option but to accept the situation, so, with a force of only two officers, the Faroe Islands were officially occupied (Arge 1985: 41).

One order from the two British officers was to black out the whole town, so that possible German aeroplanes would have a hard time finding their target. It was therefore a dark night, but around noon on the next day, the 13th of April, the *Ardent* and the *Acasta* returned, together with two armed trawlers and the heavy cruiser *HMS Suffolk*. On board the *Suffolk* were Colonel Sandall, who was the first Commander of the military forces in the Faroes, and Frederick C. Mason, sent by Foreign Secretary Lord Halifax to be the British Consul in the Faroes. The two of them went straight to the Governor and repeated the message he had received the day before.

While Sandall and Mason were visiting the Governor, the two armed trawlers moored alongside the quay in Tórshavn and 250 Royal Marines disembarked. There were hundreds of local people there to greet them, grateful that they were British rather than German soldiers (Arge 1985: 55). The Royal Marines told local people that they thought they were on their way to Norway, so perhaps their plans were changed at the last minute, as happened in those critical days.

Mason makes the Faroese Flag Official

One of the first decisions Consul Mason had to take was the question of which flag Faroese ships were to fly, now that Denmark was occupied by Germany and while the Faroes were occupied by the British. The Admiralty made it clear that Faroese ships

sailing in the north Atlantic. He has also informed me, that *HMS Acasta* and *HMS Ardent* both sank on 8th June 1940, 400 miles west of Narvik, where they defended a convoy of British ships. One of the seamen lost onboard HMS Ardent was Seaman John MacLennan from North Tolsta on the Isle of Lewis.

sailing under the Danish flag would be taken in to harbour, while ships sailing under a Faroese flag were free to sail on. This decision was taken on the advice of a Faroese skipper, who happened to have a Faroese flag on board when he was taken to harbour (Arge 1985: 67).

The Danish Governor was not happy with this arrangement, because the Faroese flag was not official, and had been the subject of much dispute between the Faroese national movement and the Danish authorities since its inception in 1919. The Danish Governor therefore asked Mason about the matter. Mason already knew that he had to take a decision about which flag to choose as the official Faroese flag. He came up with a solution which he hoped would appease both parties; a green flag with a white cross. When people heard of this plan, they immediately protested, and in the end Mason changed his mind, declaring on the 25th of April 1940, that the existing Faroese flag was the official one, to be used on all Faroese ships, together with the word 'Faroes' in English, Faroese or Danish (Arge 1985: 77). This decision resulted in big celebrations on the streets of Tórshavn, and that night the 25th of April was declared National Flag Day, which it still is today. On this occasion Mason took a decision in favour of the national movement, but in accordance with the promise from Sir Winston Churchill, all other decisions of this kind were left for the Faroe islanders and the Danes to resolve after the war.

The Lovat Scouts Guard the Faroes

The outlying detachment of the Royal Marines did not stay long in the Faroe Islands, because the real occupying force in the first two years of the war was to be the famous Highland Regiment, the Lovat Scouts.

The Lovat Scouts received the order to mobilize at 19.05 hrs on the 1st of September 1939. The three squadrons assembled at Beauly; B squadron being from the Islands of North and South Uist, Benbecula and Skye (Leslie Melville 1981: 53). At first they thought that they were going to help the Finnish in their Winter War with the big Russian army. When that did not happen, the commanding officer tried to get the Regiment to France as front-line observers; a job the regiment had done so well in the First

World War. Soon after the German invasion of Denmark and
Norway, the regiment received the order to hand over all their
ponies, and so the Scouts thought that they were being shipped
to Norway to fight the German invaders, but all orders were
kept top secret.

One thing however was not top secret, and that was the joining instructions of the newly-arrived Dental Officer, Lieutenant
Young. He mentioned a mysterious sentence in his instructions
to some of the others. It read, '*There is a civilian dentist in Thor-
shavn.*' H.Q. Squadron Officers soon learned from a World Gazet-
teer that Tórshavn was the capital of the Faroe Islands (Leslie
Melville 1981: 65). On the 21st of May, 452 O.R.s and 28 officers embarked on the *Ulster Prince*, which sailed on the 23rd and
arrived in Tórshavn early on the misty morning of 25th of May.
The War Diary that day ended, '*As the ship came alongside the
pier with the pipers playing, crowds of people including hundreds
of children, came down from the town to look on and remained
there all day.*'(Leslie Melville 1981: 66)

It was vital for the Lovat Scouts to defend both the capital city
of Tórshavn, and Skálafjørð, which was thought to be one of the
best anchorages in the whole of the North Atlantic. One squadron
guarded Skálafjørð, and the two others remained in Tórshavn,
where one built defences and provided guards and fatigues, and
the other trained and carried out reconnaissance patrols to the
rest of Streymoy and neighboring islands. The squadrons were in
the same place for a month or two, and then they changed places
to prevent anyone from 'going native' or even mad in isolated
places, as Leslie Melville states in his story of the Lovat Scouts.

In autumn 1940, the Navy laid a long line of mines to try to
stop the Germans from entering the Atlantic. To the north of the
Faroes they mined an area going all the way up to Iceland (Arge
1985: 211), and a similar area was mined between the Faroes and
Scotland (Arge 1985: 223). In addition to this the Navy also mined
some of the firths between the islands. All this meant that skippers
had to get instructions before they could set sail. Unfortunately
many of the mines broke loose, and floated freely in the ocean.
It was possible that some of these mines might come ashore, and
that could lead to big disasters. Luckily most of the mines were
disarmed, but on a few occasions mines blew up near villages,

with horrifying results.

It was one of the duties of the Scouts to sink mines that came near the coast, and this gave them good target practice. By February 1941 the Scouts had already sunk 48 of these mines, but many more were to come.

In addition to the Lovat Scouts Regiment, the Fortress Commander Major Crowther had about 20 marines at his HQ in the fortress in Tórshavn. The Faroes were also defended by armed trawlers from Northern Patrol, with their fearless and unorthodox sailers. The armed trawlers in the Northern Patrol were usually named after English football teams. On the 20th of February two of them, *Leicester City* and *Lincoln City*, were in Tórshavn.[2] There were of course also Faroese ships in the harbour. At 15:00 hours the alarm was sounded, and two twin engined Heinkel 111 aeroplanes approached the town. First they flew west of the island and approached the city from that direction. When they were within range, the British guns started shooting and the German aeroplanes returned fire. No one was injured, but the aeroplanes were so badly hit that they had to change their plans. One of them dropped its bombs on the sea and fled eastwards, but no one present was in any doubt that it had been hit and had tried to lose weight in an effort to save itself (Arge 1986: 59).

The other German plane returned and dropped two 20 kg bombs intended for the oil supply tanks, but both of them missed their target. Then it dropped a third bomb, which looked like it was going to miss its target, however when it exploded a few seconds later, the *Lincoln City* was lifted up and broken into two pieces right in its middle, sinking immediately. Several Faroese boats rushed to the rescue. Donald McKay from the Lovat Scouts was in the Harbour Office, and he could not believe how quickly the Faroese were able to get their boats out to the sunken trawler and save the injured. In the end, eight of the 27 men on board

---

[2] At the conference Donald J. MacLeod kindly informed me that the fleet of the Northern Patrol, whose ships were named after English football teams, were trawlers that had belonged to a fishing company in Grimsby before the war. Most of them fished in Arctic and Icelandic waters pre-war, and many of the fishermen were conscripted into the Royal Navy, when war was declared and the Admiralty took the ships,. This being the case, it was not uncommon for Western Islanders to be part of the crew onboard these ships.

the *Lincoln City* were killed (Arge 1986: 60).

The German plane passed the fortress where a Royal Navy man, Frank Jordan, was in no doubt that he managed to hit it because it was only about 50 metres from him, and he could have hurled a rock at it (Arge 1986: 60). From Tórshavn the plane proceeded to Skálafjørð, where it received an even warmer welcome from the Hebrideans in B Squadron. After that barrage the plane tried to get away, dropping its remaining bombs out at sea, but soon it returned and made an emergency landing in the village of Syðrugøtu. In the village, Trooper J. Mackenzie from South Uist was on a routine motor-cycle patrol. The Germans rowed ashore in their rubber dinghy, and Mackenzie disarmed and arrested them. One of the villagers offered to give the Germans a cup of tea, receiving a pistol and a chronometer from them in return. The British took the pistol but the villager kept the chronometer in his house. Soon reinforcements came to pick up B squadron's well-deserved bag, and the *Aurora* took the aircrew to Scapa Flow. A few days later B squadron made a big effort to hoist the plane out of the water. The plane was sent to England, but the propeller remained, to adorn the Scouts' officers mess (Leslie Melville 1981: 74). It has been suggested that this huge effort to bring a shot down plane back to Britian could have had something to do with the Enigma-machine, or some other secrets they were hoping to find on the plane (Arge 1986: 68).

The pilot explained that they were hit over Tórshavn, but when they flew over Skálafjørð one of the engines was hit, and that was the end of their plane. Therefore the conclusion was that it was the Hebrideans from B Squadron on Skálafjørð who made the hit, and that is of no little importance, because this was the only definite hit the Lovat Scouts made in the Faroe Islands.

Before this attack, only a few German aircrafts were seen, but early in 1941 their attacks intensified, and the Lovat Scouts registered 164 sightings; in most cases of which bombs were dropped or there was random machine gun fire. Whenever possible the Scouts returned fire, and though they undoubtedly hit from time to time, there was only ever the one confirmed hit. Occasionally the German aeroplanes caused a lot of damage, but there was one incident which happily was avoided, as it could have had serious consequences indeed. A large Swedish tanker was allowed to sail straight into Tórshavn harbour, contrary to standing orders. While the Scouts' Adjutant tried to find out how this could have happened, a Heinkel attacked and narrowly missed the tanker with several bombs. On board the tanker were 20,000 tons of nitro-glycerine, destined for use in the Swedish iron-ore mines at Narvik. If the Heinkel had hit its target, two squadrons of the Lovat Scouts, together with most of the great city of Tórshavn, would have been annihilated (Leslie Melville 1981: 75).

Shooting at German airplanes was for many Scouts a welcome relief from all the training and marching that usually took up their spare time, which they had much of, being so far from the major warscene.

The Force is Increased

It was clear early on to both the Commander of the Lovat Scouts, Sir Leslie Melville, and Fortress Commander Crowther, that 470 Lovat Scouts armed with 12 Bren machine guns and 12 anti-tank rifles were too little to defend the islands properly (Arge 1987: 10). Leslie Melville came up with several proposals for which armaments were needed, but of course the Battle of Britain was at its height and all armaments were needed in more important places than the Faroes. The answer was therefore that no guns were available. The Admiral for Orkney and Shetland found a solution because one of his men knew of four old 5.5 inch guns from the aircraft carrier *Furious*, and without much ado, these guns were shipped to the Faroes. Two of them were mounted on the fortress in Tórshavn and the other two in Skálafjørður. Men from 663 Artisan Works Company, Royal Engineers, under Major Morgan, together with five officers from the Royal Artillery mounted the guns in Tórshavn . The first shots were fired on the 11th of August, but soon after, the Royal Engineers had to return to Britain, so six Lovat Scouts learned to operate the guns (Arge 1987: 14-16).

The Lovat Scouts operated the guns until the 13th of November 1940, when 350 men and 12 officers from the Royal Artillery took over. This new regiment was named '537 Coastal Regiment R.A.' and soon the Faroes were increasingly well armed and manned. On the 25th of March 1941, 57 men and two officers arrived to man two 12 pound guns in Strendur, on the western side of

Skálafjørð, therefore the Lovat Scouts could leave the village which they had defended for 11 months. Later on, another 270 men from the Royal Artillery came to Tórshavn and formed the 56th L.A.A. Battery, and 175 men manned the 285th L.A.A. troop in Skálafjørður (Arge 1987: 19).

When 1941 ended, the Lovat Scouts were not alone in the Faroes, and the Lovat Scouts Regiment itself had also increased from 470 to 747 men, with 30 officers. The increase in troop numbers meant that a new squadron could be formed, and with four squadrons it was now possible for the Scouts to have one of their squadrons stationed in Suðuroy (Leslie Melville 1981: 71).

The most tragic fatality during the occupation was not caused by bombs or mines but by the weather. On the 7th of December 1941, the French freighter *Sauternes* was on its way to Tórshavn with 1000 tons of cargo, a lot of mail and all the Christmas supplies the soldiers needed. When it reached Svínoy a gigantic gale sank it, and people on land could do nothing to save the few men that were spotted clinging to rafts. The next day, Faroese boats managed to find six corpses, but the 20 to 25 or so remaining crew and passengers were never found. They included several soldiers returning to duty in the Faroes (Arge 1987: 178-185).

On the lighter side, this shipwreck also meant that all the whisky and rum, which was to have given the soldiers a jolly happy Christmas, floated around Svínoy for days, and this was something that the brave Svínoymen were happy to fish for. Tales are told about how long some of them were drunk, and other accounts tell of them burying 'the catch' in the fields, where the treasure lasted for many many years. It may even still be possible to find a drink or two in Svínoy today which was originally intended for the British soldiers bravely defending the Faroes. In any case I have heard people say, and they meant it seriously, that this incident is the inspiration for the movie 'Whisky Galore!'

The Lovat Scouts stayed on the Faroes until June 1942, when they were relieved by the 12th Battalion of the Lowland Regiment, The Cameronians. The Cameronians advance party arrived on the 28th of May, and at 11.15 on the 10th of June, the *Lady of Mann*, escorted by *HMS Chiddingfold*, arrived in Tórshavn. The Cameronians disembarked and trans-shipped for seventeen different places, and the Scouts embarked immediately with all their stores. Late on this beautiful summer's evening, thousands of Faroese came to wave goodbye to their friends, and the pipers played 'Happy We Have Been Together', as the troopship backed out of the harbour and ended the story of the Lovat Scouts in the Faroe Islands (Leslie Melville 1981: 77).

Vágar – a British Island in the Faroes

In the spring of 1942, just before the Lovat Scouts left the islands, other parts of the British military were on their way to the Faroes, to fulfill the biggest project yet seen there by a long way. This was the building of an airfield, together with a dock in a lake, where aeroplanes could land. The R.A.F. had surveyed the islands from the beginning of the occupation and on the 2nd of March 1942, the decision was made to use the island of Vágar as an R.A.F. base. The Royal Engineers, together with a few soldiers, came to plan the big project.

Before this project, the total number of British soldiers had climbed to a total of about 1,700 all around the islands, but soon there were no fewer than 6,000 soldiers in Vágar alone (Arge 1989: 68). In addition to contingencies from the RAF, the Royal Engineers, the Royal Artillery and The Cameronians, there came a large number of Royal Pioneers. They were called the 30 Group Pioneer Corps, under the command of Lieutenant Colonel Jas. E. Adamson (Arge 1989: 51). It was their job to do the hard work of building the first, and to this day only, airfield in the Faroes.

In reality this huge number of British soldiers made the island more British than Faroese, and that feeling increased when new regulations came in which stated, not only that everyone had to have a passport to get on to the island, but also that it was now compulsory to drive on the left hand side of the road, contrary to the rest of the Faroes.

The 30 Group Pioneer Corps had been on the island for eighteen months when they left in autumn 1943. At around the same time, the Cameronians left as well, and the total number of soldiers in the Faroes fell back to a minimum. The reason was that the tide in the war had shifted, as by late 1943 the Allied forces were pushing the Germans back on all fronts. The Germans therefore had more than enough to do to defend themselves, instead of attacking small islands far out in the ocean. These changing fortunes also meant that the new airport was never used for the purpose for which it was intended. Only ten planes had landed on the airfield and around sixty-five on the lake, when the last RAF men left the island in autumn 1944.

On the other hand, the British forces left the Faroese with a new airfield, and with time it has been used more and more. It has been modernized several times since, but it is still a fact that when you visit the Faroes by plane, you land on an airfield originally built by the British military forces in World War 2.

References

Arge, Niels Juel, 1985: *Stríðsárini 1940-45. 1. bók. Hersettar oyggjar.* Forlagið Hvessingur, Tórshavn 1985.
Arge, Niels Juel, 1986: *Stríðsárini 1940-45. 2. bók. Sigla vandas-jógv.* Forlagið Hvessingur, Tórshavn 1986.
Arge, Niels Juel, 1987: *Stríðsárini 1940-45. 3. bók. Føroyar bumbaðar.* Forlagið Hvessingur, Tórshavn 1987.
Arge, Niels Juel, 1988: *Stríðsárini 1940-45. 4. bók. Millum minur og kavbátar.* Forlagið Hvessingur, Tórshavn 1988.
Arge, Niels Juel, 1989: *Stríðsárini 1940-45. 5. bók. Skansi í Atlantshavi.* Forlagið Hvessingur, Tórshavn 1989.
Arge, Niels Juel, 1990: *Stríðsárini 1940-45. 6. bók. Kríggið endar.* Forlagið Hvessingur, Tórshavn 1990.
Leslie Melville, Michael, 1981: *The Story of the Lovat Scouts 1900-1980.* The Saint Andrew Press. Edinburgh 1981.
Williamson, Kenneth, 1948: *The Atlantic Islands. A Study of the Faeroe Life and Scene.* Collins St. James's Place, London 1948.

THE ISLANDS BOOK TRUST
URRAS LEABHRAICHEAN NAN EILEAN